# Caldera®
# OpenLinux™ 2.2
## *fast&easy*™

## Rave reviews for PRIMA TECH's *fast & easy* series

"Excellent book! Easy to read, easy to comprehend, easy to implement!"
*Cheryl Johnson*
Reno, NV

"Fantastic! Remarkably to the point, yet not once does it neglect vital information."
*Joshua Loop*
Cincinnati, OH

"Excellent book. Easy to understand!"
*Cay Colberg*
Albuquerque, NM

"The best book I've found!"
*Bertha Podwys*
Iverness, FL

"Great for fast reference!"
*Janet White*
Orlando, FL

"Well presented, concise, and extremely helpful!"
*Julia Kogut*
Arlington, VA

"So well illustrated that one couldn't possibly fail to profit from its content."
*Charles Bendal*
Surrey, England

"Very thorough and easy to use."
*Cathy Mercer*
Clifton, TX

"This book dispels the myth that computing is complicated."
*Iain Clark*
Durham, England

## Send Us Your Comments

To comment on this book or any other PRIMA TECH title, visit our reader response page on the Web at **www.prima-tech.com/comments**.

## How to Order

For information on quantity discounts, contact the publisher: Prima Publishing, P.O. Box 1260BK, Rocklin, CA 95677-1260; (916) 632-4400. On your letterhead, include information concerning the intended use of the books and the number of books you wish to purchase. For individual orders, visit PRIMA TECH's Web site at **www.prima-tech.com**.

# Caldera® OpenLinux™ 2.2

## fast&easy™

Coletta Witherspoon

and

Craig Witherspoon

A DIVISION OF PRIMA PUBLISHING

A Division of Prima Publishing

Prima Publishing and colophon are registered trademarks of Prima Communications, Inc. PRIMA TECH and *Fast & Easy* are trademarks of Prima Communications, Inc., Rocklin, California 95677.

**Publisher:** Stacy L. Hiquet

**Associate Publisher:** Nancy Stevenson

**Marketing Manager:** Judi Taylor

**Managing Editor:** Dan J. Foster

**Senior Acquisitions Editor:** Deborah F. Abshier

**Acquisitions Editor:** Kim Spilker

**Project Editor:** Kevin W. Ferns

**Assistant Project Editor:** Brian J. Thomasson

**Copy Editor:** Sydney Jones

**Technical Editor:** Van Hendrickson

**Interior Layout:** Marian Hartsough

**Cover Design:** Prima Design Team

**Indexer:** Katherine Stimson

Microsoft and Windows are registered trademarks of Microsoft Corporation.

Caldera, the C-logo, OpenLinux, and DR-DOS are either registered trademarks or trademarks of Caldera, Inc.

Linux is a registered trademark of Linus Torvalds.

*Important:* If you have problems installing or running Caldera OpenLinux 2.2, go to Caldera's Web site at **www.calderasystems.com**. Prima Publishing cannot provide software support.

Prima Publishing and the authors have attempted throughout this book to distinguish proprietary trademarks from descriptive terms by following the capitalization style used by the manufacturer.

Information contained in this book has been obtained by Prima Publishing from sources believed to be reliable. However, because of the possibility of human or mechanical error by our sources, Prima Publishing, or others, the Publisher does not guarantee the accuracy, adequacy, or completeness of any information and is not responsible for any errors or omissions or the results obtained from the use of such information. Readers should be particularly aware of the fact that the Internet is an ever-changing entity. Some facts may have changed since this book went to press.

ISBN: 0-7615-2302-2
Library of Congress Catalog Card Number: 99-64501
Printed in the United States of America

99 00 01 02 03 DD 10 9 8 7 6 5 4 3 2 1

*To Percy V. Rentz*

# Acknowledgments

We'd like to thank everyone at Prima for their support. It is always a pleasure to work with such a talented and dedicated group of people.

# About the Authors

**COLETTA and CRAIG WITHERSPOON** have been involved in the growth of the computer revolution since the early 1970s. They began their writing careers producing procedure manuals, network disaster and recovery plans, and training manuals for multinational corporations. Coletta and Craig now have over a dozen published books, and they are the authors of several *Fast & Easy* series books from PRIMA TECH.

# Contents at a Glance

# Contents

# Introduction

This *Fast & Easy* series guide from PRIMA TECH will give you a well-organized and concise introduction to the Caldera OpenLinux operating system. With this guide you'll quickly get up to production speed with some of the professional applications included with OpenLinux. You'll also learn how to use KDE, the Caldera OpenLinux graphical user interface, to step through configuring your Linux computer and accessing the OpenLinux 2.2 features and programs. KDE's built-in desktop tools and applications work seamlessly within industry standard conventions and allow applications to cooperatively interact and remain consistent with each other. For those who prefer the familiar, the KDE environment can be easily configured to resemble the well-known interfaces of Microsoft Windows, Apple Macintosh OS, UNIX Motif, and others.

This book will quickly step you through the maze of tasks involved in learning a new operating system and help you to quickly become productive and comfortable with it.

## Who Should Read This Book?

As you thumb through this book, you'll find that it is filled with easy-to-follow directions and illustrations. As you progress through the directions, you'll see that the pictures on your screen are the same as those in the book. This is the perfect tool for those who are familiar with other computer operating systems and want to get up to speed with Caldera OpenLinux 2.2 and the KDE graphical user interface. You might want to read all the individual chapters in a particular section of the book to master the subject matter, or you might need to read only a certain chapter to fill in the gaps in your existing knowledge. Either way, this book is structured to support the method that suits you best.

This book also makes a great reference tool. As you continue working with Caldera OpenLinux and learning new things, you may need a quick refresher about how to perform a specific task or configure a new peripheral. You can easily refer to those tasks in this book and avoid wading through pages of technical material.

# Helpful Hints to Increase Your Skills

The use of step-by-step instructions and detailed illustrations will help you to learn quickly. Explanations are kept to a minimum to help speed your progress. Included in this book are additional elements that will provide you with more information on how to work with Caldera OpenLinux 2.2 and the KDE user interface without encumbering your progress:

- Tips offer shortcuts for various OpenLinux and KDE features, which make your job a little easier.

- Notes offer additional information about a feature or advice on how to use the feature.

Also, the appendixes show you how to install Caldera OpenLinux 2.2 on your computer, as well as any other software you may have purchased or downloaded from the Web.

Have fun with this *Fast & Easy* guide. It's the quickest and simplest way to get started with the Caldera OpenLinux 2.2 operating system.

# PART I

# Getting Started with Caldera OpenLinux and KDE

# 1

# Exploring OpenLinux

Congratulations! You've made a good choice selecting this easy way to introduce yourself to Linux. Caldera OpenLinux is a good option if you are familiar with the Microsoft Windows or Macintosh operating systems. Caldera OpenLinux uses KDE to provide a graphical user interface with familiar icon and menu elements to open applications, perform tasks, and navigate around the screen. Before you begin looking around, however, take the time to create the user accounts that you'll need for everyone who will be using the computer. After you do that, you can switch to your own user account and safely explore OpenLinux and KDE. In this chapter, you'll learn how to:

- Start the OpenLinux operating system and KDE
- Create a user account for your daily Linux activities
- Use the different KDE screen elements
- Find additional help using Linux and KDE
- Exit KDE and Linux

# Starting OpenLinux for the First Time

When you installed OpenLinux on your computer, the installation program set up your computer so that anyone with the installation password can log on using root as the user ID and access the entire operating system. This could be dangerous, especially if there are multiple users on the system. The person in charge of the computer (the administrator for your system) should set up a user account for each person using the system. Every user can then use OpenLinux according to their personal preferences or job requirements.

## Logging on as Root

When you start Caldera OpenLinux 2.2 after your computer boots up, you have an opportunity to choose how you want to log on. You will initially be given two choices for logging on; you can log on as root if you intend to do some system administration work, or you can log on as the regular user that you created during the OpenLinux installation.

If you set up your computer to run two operating systems, when you turn on your computer, BootMagic will appear.

**1.** In the BootMagic screen, **click** on **Linux**. The Linux operating system will load and a graphical login screen will appear.

**2. Click** on the **Root button**. The root account will be selected and the cursor will be in the Password text box.

**3. Type** the root **password**. The password will appear in the text box, but will be displayed as a series of asterisks to protect others from reading your password over your shoulder as you type.

**4. Click** on the **Go! button**. KDE will open and you'll be in the root account.

**CAUTION**

Be careful when you are logged on to the system as root. The root user account has access to the entire Linux operating system and no built-in safeguards.

## Creating New User Accounts

If others will be using the computer, create a user account for each person. This is a job for the system administrator. You will want to use the root account only for performing system administration and maintenance duties.

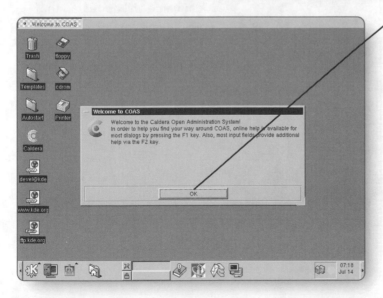

**1. Click** on the **Caldera Open Administration System button**. A menu will appear.

**2. Move** the **mouse pointer** to **System**. The System menu will appear.

**3. Click** on **Accounts**. The Welcome to COAS dialog box will open.

**4. Click** on **OK**. The User Accounts window will open.

**5. Click** on **Actions** on the menu bar. The Actions menu will appear.

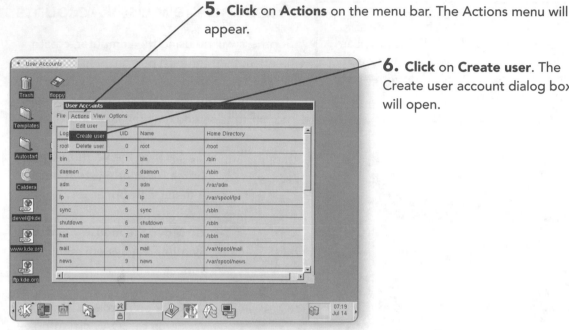

**6. Click** on **Create user**. The Create user account dialog box will open.

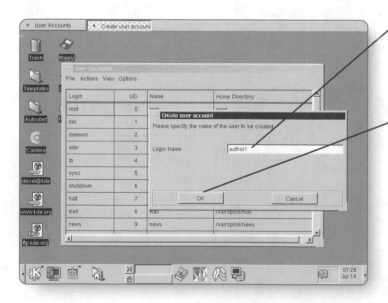

**7. Type** the **Login Name** of the user you want to create. The login name will appear in the Login Name text box.

**8. Click** on **OK**. The Edit User dialog box for the user you named will open.

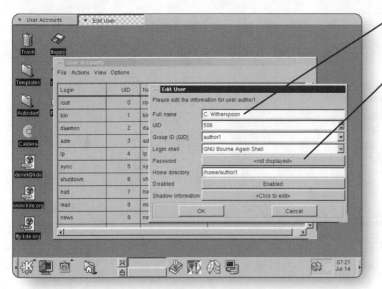

**9. Type** the **Full name** of the user.

**10. Click** on the **Password button**. The Change Password dialog box will open.

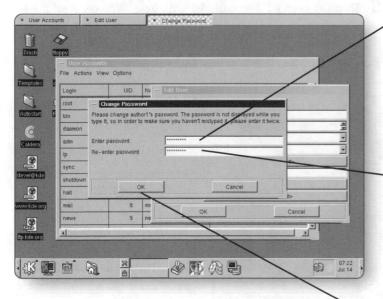

**11. Type** a **password** for the new user in the Enter password text box. A series of asterisks will appear in place of the password you typed. This is to prevent others from finding out the password.

**12. Click** in the **Re-enter password text box** and **type** the same **password** a second time to confirm that it is correct. The same series of asterisks will appear in place of the password that was typed.

**13. Click** on **OK**. You will be returned to the Edit User dialog box.

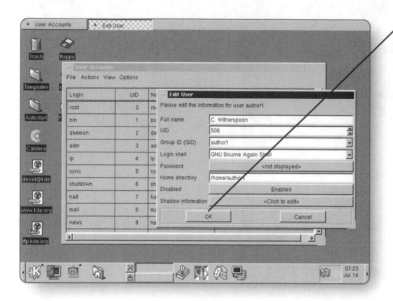

**14. Click** on **OK**. You will be returned to the User Accounts window.

**15. Repeat steps 5 through 14** until you have created a user account for everyone who will be using the computer.

**16. Click** on **File**. The File menu will appear.

**17. Click** on **Exit**. The User Accounts window will close.

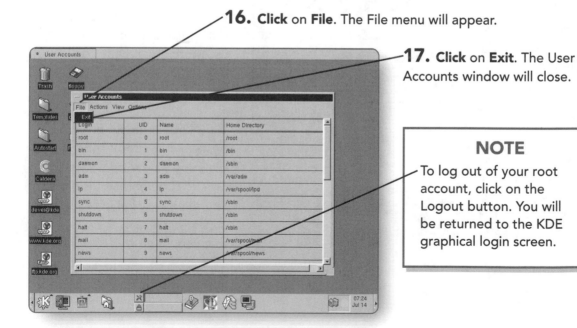

## NOTE

To log out of your root account, click on the Logout button. You will be returned to the KDE graphical login screen.

# Exploring KDE

When KDE appears on your screen, you'll see some familiar sights. Many of the icons and window decorations are similar to the ones in the Microsoft Windows and Apple Macintosh graphical user interfaces. Here's a brief explanation of the elements that you'll find at first glance.

## Understanding Desktop Elements

- The taskbar contains icons for each of the applications you have open and any other windows that may be in a minimized, maximized, or iconified state. Click on a taskbar icon to display the window on the top of your desktop. You'll learn how to open programs in Chapter 2.

- Desktop icons open applications, files, or directories quickly. You can place icons on your desktop for the programs and files you use frequently. Learn more about this in Chapter 4, "Customizing the Screen Display."

- Windows are framed areas that contain buttons, scroll bars, and menus. Applications and files appear inside windows. You'll find out how to resize a window in Chapter 2, "Working with Windows." Find out how to work with several windows at one time in Chapter 3, "Navigating Your Desktop."

- The desktop is the background for all of the elements you see on your screen. You'll learn how to change the desktop background in Chapter 4, "Customizing the Screen Display."

The KDE Panel resides at the bottom of the screen. The Panel contains the Application Starter, the KDE Control Center button, Virtual Desktop buttons, and icons for other applications that can be started from the Panel. Hold the mouse pointer over a button to see a Tooltip that tells you what you can do if you click on the button.

- The Application Starter opens a menu of applications, utilities, and actions you can perform with OpenLinux and KDE. To display the menu, click on the K button on the left end of the Panel. To close the menu, click on an empty area of the desktop.

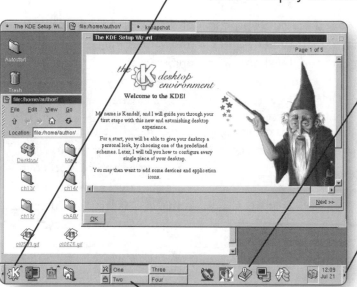

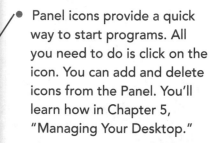

- Panel icons provide a quick way to start programs. All you need to do is click on the icon. You can add and delete icons from the Panel. You'll learn how in Chapter 5, "Managing Your Desktop."

- At each end of the Panel is a small arrow. These arrows hide and display the Panel. Click on the arrow to watch the Panel slide out of sight.

- The Virtual Desktop icons show you which desktops are being used and provide you with a quick way to move between them. There's also some handy shortcut buttons. You'll learn more about KDE's Virtual Desktops in Chapter 3, "Navigating your Desktop."

## Starting Programs from the Application Starter

Now it's time to take a look at some of the software applications that are installed along with OpenLinux. Here's a quick overview of how to use the common window interface elements. The next few sections will show you how to use the basic elements of an OpenLinux application by opening KOrganizer; the calendar and organization program that comes with KDE.

**1. Click** on the **Application Starter**. The main menu will appear.

**2. Move** the **mouse pointer** to the Applications menu item. The Applications menu will appear.

### TIP

As you move the pointer up the menu, each item you move over will become highlighted. Menu choices with a small arrow to the right include a submenu. When you highlight those menu choices, their extended menus will appear.

**3. Click** on **Organizer**. The application window for the KOrganizer will appear on your screen, and an icon and title for it will appear on the taskbar across the top of your screen.

## Using Buttons, Menus, and Dialog Boxes

You've successfully opened a Linux application, and now you're ready to see how it works. Program windows contain menus, command buttons, resize buttons, and a host of other elements. Take some time to explore the different menus in the application window to see what is available. This section will show you how to use buttons and menus to execute commands.

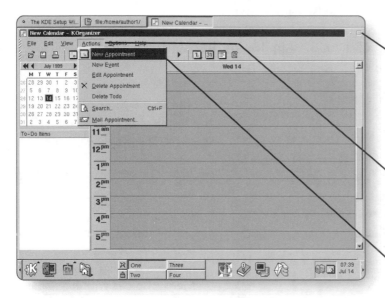

**TIP**

If you want the KOrganizer window to fill the entire screen, click on the Maximize button.

**1. Click** on a **menu item** on the menu bar. A drop-down menu will appear with a list of menu commands.

**2. Click** on a **command**. The command will be executed automatically or a dialog box will open enabling you to make choices about the command you want to execute.

**TIP**

Holding the mouse pointer over a button on the toolbar will cause a Tooltip to appear telling you what function the button performs.

Dialog boxes contain elements such as tabs that group several dialog boxes into one, buttons that display secondary dialog boxes, toolbars with buttons that enable you to control dialog box actions, and drop-down lists that enable you to select from predetermined options.

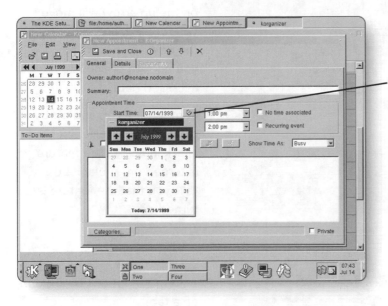

- Applets can help you perform a task or make a selection. Open the applet by clicking on its icon. Then click on applet elements to make your choice. The choices you make in the applets will appear in the text box next to the applet icon.

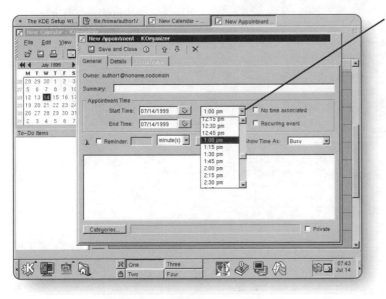

- Open drop-down lists by clicking on the down arrow to display a list of options; then click on the option you want. The choice you make will appear in the text box next to the down arrow.

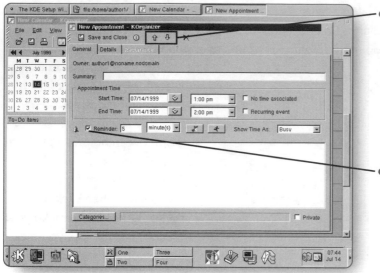

- Move back and forth through data files by clicking on the up and down arrows. Clicking on the up arrow will move you forward, and clicking on the down arrow will move you back to previously accessed data.

- Turn features on and off by clicking on a check box. A check indicates the feature is turned on. A blank box tells you that the feature is turned off.

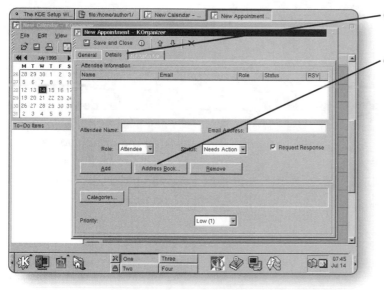

- Find more options by clicking on a tab.

- Access a secondary dialog box by clicking on a button.

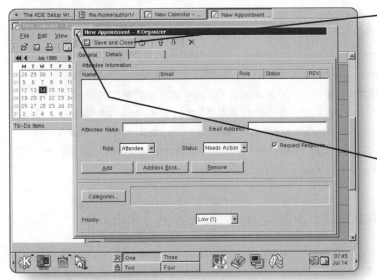

**3. Click** on **Save and Close**. The dialog box will close; the options will be applied, and you will be returned to the program window.

## TIP

Click on the window menu and select Close if you don't want to apply any of the changes you made to the dialog box or decide that you no longer want to execute the command.

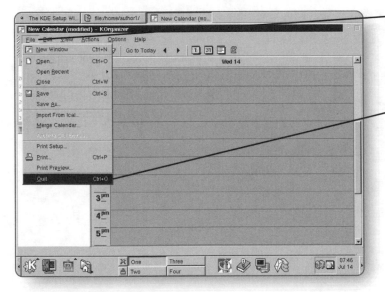

**4. Click** on **File** when you are finished working with the application. The File menu will appear.

**5. Click** on **Quit**. The application will close, and you will be returned to the desktop.

# Getting Help

After reading this book, you'll feel comfortable using OpenLinux with the KDE interface. But this is just the beginning of your journey. As you get more involved in the Linux operating system, you'll find new uses for some of the features you've learned about so far, and you'll discover new features that you'll want to explore. Here are a few places where you can turn for help.

## Using the Mouse to Get Help

When you're looking for a quick answer to what function a button performs or how to work with a window, place the mouse pointer over the element and see whether a Tooltip appears.

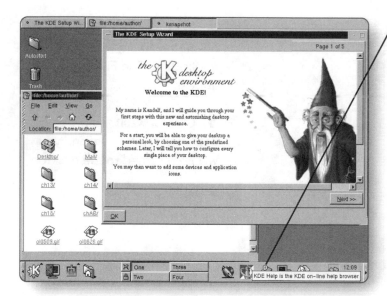

**1.** **Hold** the **mouse pointer** over a screen or window element. A Tooltip will appear and provide you with information about the function that the element performs.

# Browsing the Help Files

The KDE Help browser is your one-stop place for all the OpenLinux and KDE Help files, including a list of online resources. The Help system contains a Search feature. You can use it to search through the contents of the online manuals, the KDE information, and support files. Clicking on the KDE Help icon will open the Help browser. The browser opens with an introduction and information to guide you through accessing and using the KDE Help browser.

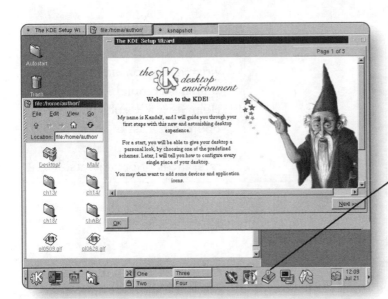

**1. Click** on the **KDE Help** icon. The KDE Help browser will open.

## NOTE

Read through the list of topics until you find the one that is the closest match to the information you need.

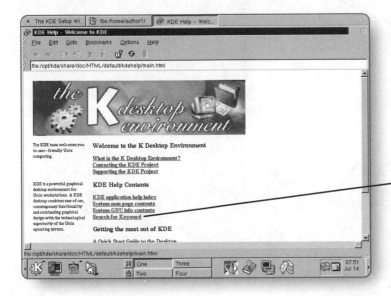

**2. Click** on the **Search for Keyword link**. The KDE Help Search page will appear.

**3.** **Type** in a **keyword**.

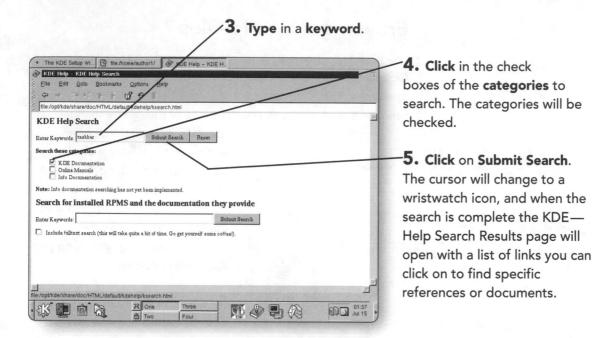

**4.** **Click** in the check boxes of the **categories** to search. The categories will be checked.

**5.** **Click** on **Submit Search**. The cursor will change to a wristwatch icon, and when the search is complete the KDE— Help Search Results page will open with a list of links you can click on to find specific references or documents.

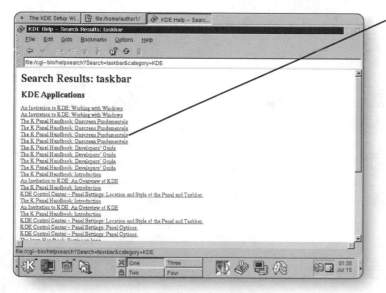

**6.** **Click** on any **link**. You will be taken to that page and subheading in the Help system.

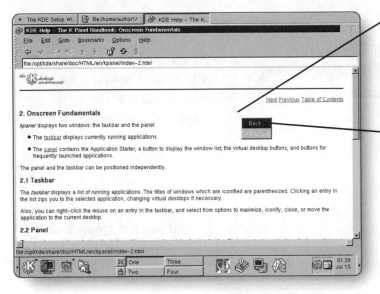

**7.** After you read the information on the page, **right-click** on the screen to return to the Search Results page. A menu will appear.

**8. Click** on **Back** in the menu. The previous page will appear in the browser.

## Setting Bookmarks

When you find a page that contains useful information that you'll need again, you can set a bookmark to make it easy to find the information. If you're reading the User's Guide from one end to another and want to remember where you left off, you can mark the spot with a bookmark.

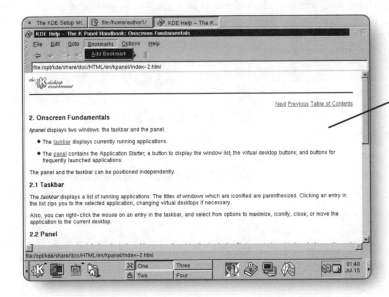

**1. Open** the **page** to which you want to set a bookmark in the Browser window. The page will appear in the browser.

**2. Click** on **Bookmarks**. The Bookmarks menu will appear.

**3. Click** on **Add Bookmark**. A bookmark will be created for the page and added to the Bookmark drop-down list.

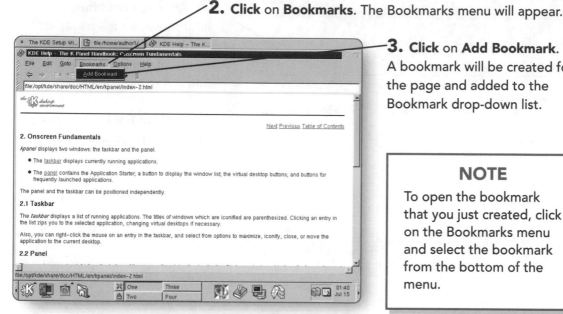

### NOTE

To open the bookmark that you just created, click on the Bookmarks menu and select the bookmark from the bottom of the menu.

## Finding Help Files in Applications

You can find help that is specific to an application or window in which you are working right in the application. If the application does not have a Help button or menu item, you can still find help from the KDE Help system.

**1. Click** on **Goto**. The Goto menu will appear.

**2. Click** on **Contents**. The Welcome to KDE Help page will appear.

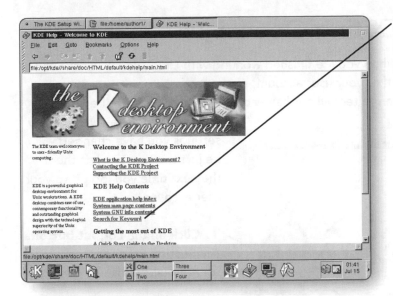

**3. Click** on **Search for Keyword**. The KDE Help Search page will appear.

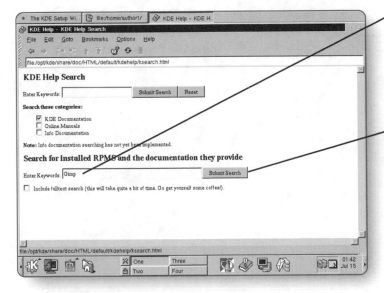

**4. Type** the **name** of your application or other **keywords** in the Enter Keywords text box. The application name will appear in the text box.

**5. Click** on the **Submit Search button**. The Caldera Query RPMs search page will open. Your query will be answered with links to the pertinent documentation.

# Exiting OpenLinux

When you are finished working with Linux, you'll want to log off of your user account, so that others using the same computer will not have access to your files and directories.

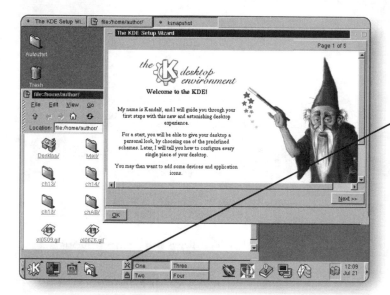

You can also make sure that any settings you have changed will be just the way you left them the next time you log on to your user account.

**1. Click** on the **Logout button**. The Session Prepared for Logout dialog box will open.

**2. Click** on **Logout**. The Caldera OpenLinux graphical Login screen will appear. The computer is now ready for the next user to log on.

# 2

# Working with Windows

The screen element that you'll see most is the program window. A program window is a boxed area on your screen where you can work with an application, view your computer's filing system, and perform computer maintenance tasks. In addition, there are ways to customize the appearance of a window. In this chapter, you'll learn how to:

- Open and resize windows
- Move and hide windows on your screen
- Alter the appearance and behavior of windows

# Opening Program Windows

When you start an application, a window appears on the desktop containing the application and a number of elements that control the window's size and position. Take some time to learn how to manipulate a single window. These skills will help when you begin working with multiple windows. It only takes a few mouse clicks to open a window. In this section, you'll learn to work with windows by opening the KLyX word-processor application.

**1. Click** on the **Application Starter**. The main menu will appear.

**2. Move** the **mouse pointer** to Applications. The Applications menu will appear.

**3. Click** on **KLyx**. The Question dialog box will open. This dialog box will create a directory in which to store your KLyX configuration.

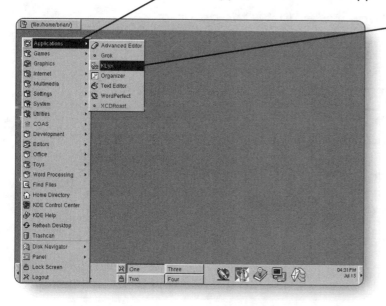

**4. Click** on **Yes**. The KLyX text editor will open.

Most windows share a number of common elements that make it easy for you to move and resize a window.

• The window menu contains all the commands that control the actions you can perform on an individual window.

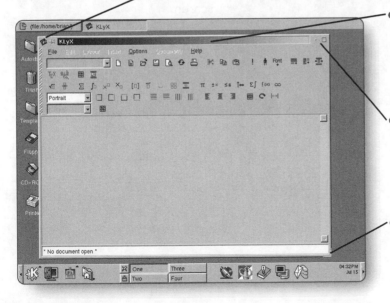

• The title bar tells you which application you are working in and also provides the easiest way to move a window around on your screen.

• The Minimize and Maximize buttons reduce a window into an icon on the taskbar and change the size of the window.

• The window border is the frame around the outside edge of the window that you can use to resize the window.

# Resizing a Window

When a window opens on your screen, it might fill the entire screen, or it might take up only a small space. This default size can be changed. You can enlarge a window to fill the whole screen area to make it easier to work with. Or, you can shrink it to fit more windows onto the desktop for drag and drop operations. You can resize KDE's program windows in several ways.

## Using the Maximize Button

The easiest place to change the size of a window is with the Maximize button. Use the Maximize button to resize the window to fill the screen. When you click on the Maximize button a second time, the window reverts to its original, smaller size.

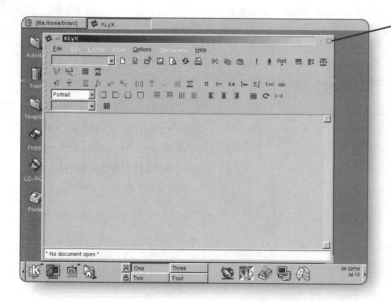

**1.** **Click** on the **Maximize button** on a window that is smaller than the screen area. The window will fill the entire screen.

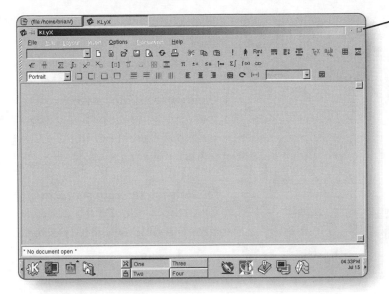

**2. Click** on the **Maximize button** on a window that fills the entire screen. The window will revert to its smaller, default size.

## Using the Mouse

If you want more control over the size of a window, use the mouse. By dragging the window borders, you can create a window that is any size you need.

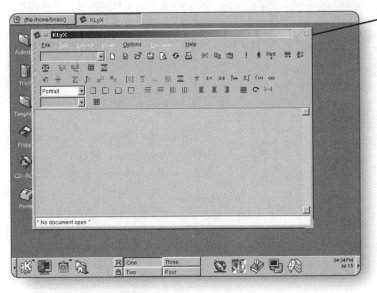

**1. Click** and **drag** either the **left** or **right window border**. Move the mouse pointer toward the window to make the window narrower. Move the mouse pointer away from the window to make the window wider. An outline of the window will appear.

**2. Release** the **mouse button** when the window is the desired size. The window will be resized.

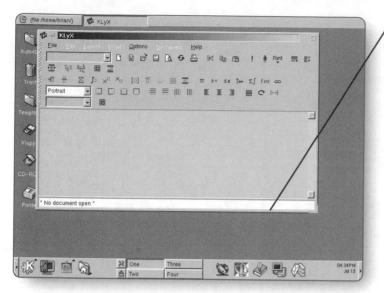

**3. Click** and **drag** the **bottom border**. Move the mouse pointer toward the window to make the window shorter. Move the mouse pointer away from the window to make the window longer. An outline of the window will appear.

**4. Release** the **mouse button** when the window is the desired size. The window will be resized.

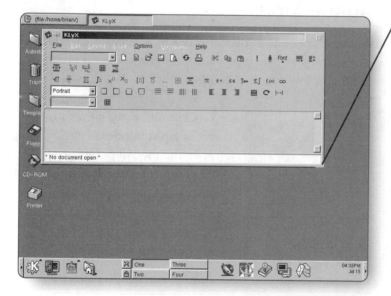

**5. Click** and **drag** the **bottom right** or **bottom left corner** of the window. Move the mouse pointer away from the window to make it wider and longer at the same time. Move the mouse pointer toward the window to make it shorter and narrower at the same time. An outline of the window will appear.

**6. Release** the **mouse button** when the window is the desired size. The window will be resized.

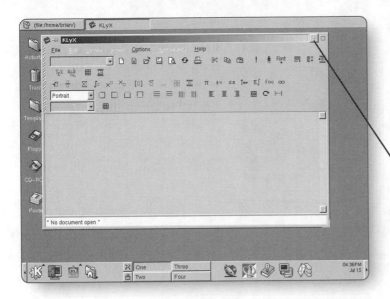

## Shading and Hiding Windows

You can hide a window on the screen without closing the program or the window.

**1.** **Click** on the **Minimize button** at the right of the drag bar. The window will become an icon on the taskbar.

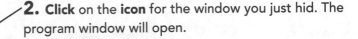

**2.** **Click** on the **icon** for the window you just hid. The program window will open.

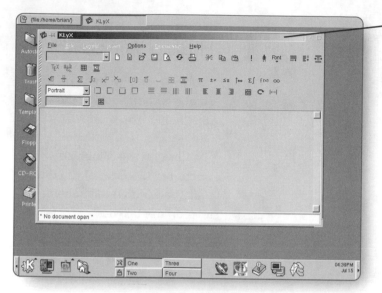

**3.** **Double-click** on the **title bar** located at the top of the program window. The program window will disappear (or shade) so that only the title bar displays.

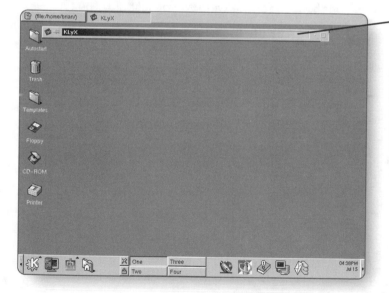

**4.** **Double-click** on the **title bar**. The window will unshade.

### NOTE

You can click and drag the shaded title bar to any location on your screen.

**5. Click** on the **window menu** located on the left of the title bar. A menu of window functions will appear.

**6. Click** on **Iconify**. The program window will become an icon on the taskbar.

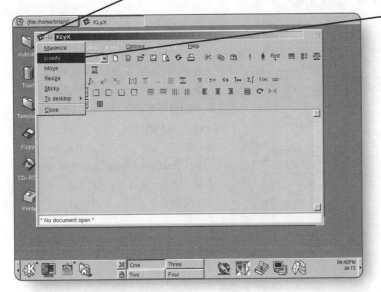

**7. Click** on the **program icon** on the taskbar. The program window will appear on your screen.

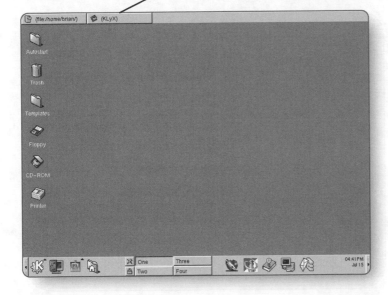

# Moving a Window Around the Screen

You may want to move a window around on your screen to make room for another program window. Or you may want to move it out of the way, so that you can see something (such as a program or shortcut icon) on your desktop.

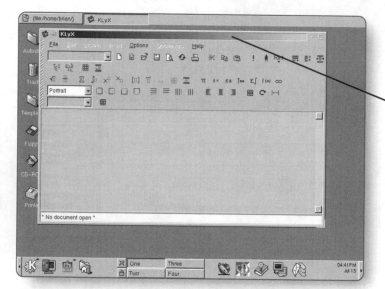

**1. Click and hold** on the **title bar**. The window will be selected.

**2. Drag** the **window** to the desired position. The window will follow the mouse pointer.

**3. Release** the **mouse button** when the window is in the desired position. The window will be moved.

# Closing a Program Window

By default, the windows you see on your screen don't have a convenient Close button. You'll need to go to the KDE Control Center to add one, and you'll learn about that later in this chapter. There's a Close command hidden in the Window menu. If you've been working in the program, you'll first need to save your work. You'll learn more about this in Chapter 10, "Working with Files."

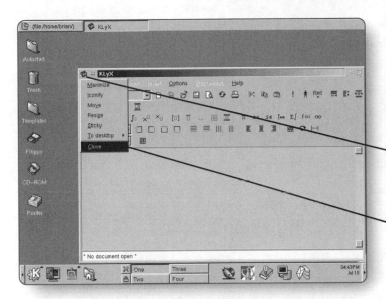

**1. Click** on the **window menu** located at the far left of the title bar. A menu will appear.

**2. Click** on **Close**. The window will close.

# Altering the Look and Behavior of Windows

Now that you understand the basics of working with windows, it's time to take more control over how windows work for you. Let's go to the KDE Control Center and adjust some of the window settings to fit your personal preferences.

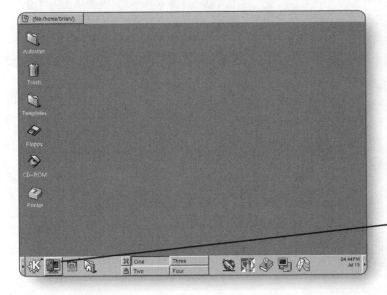

**1. Click** on the **KDE Control Center icon** on the panel. The KDE Control Center will open.

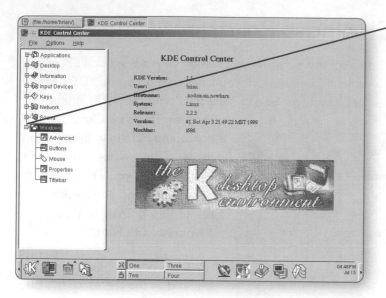

**2. Click** on the **plus sign** next to the Windows category. The Windows category will expand. The Windows controls make it easy for you to change how windows respond when you move the mouse pointer around the screen. You can also change the control buttons that appear in the title bar.

## Determining Focus Policy

If you want to make it easier to change the window with which you are working, change its focus policy. The focus policy lets you use the mouse pointer to make a window active. The default is to make a window active only if you click inside a window. You can change this, so that all you have to do is move the mouse pointer inside the window area to make it active.

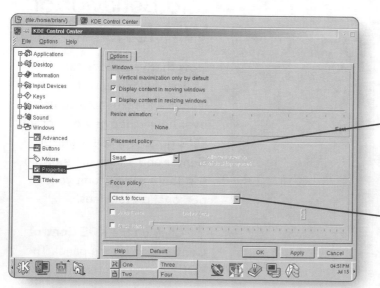

**1. Click** on the **Properties subcategory**. The Options tab will appear in the Control Center.

**2. Click** on the **down arrow** in the Focus policy section. A list of focus options will appear.

**3. Click** on a **focus policy**. The focus policy will appear in the list box.

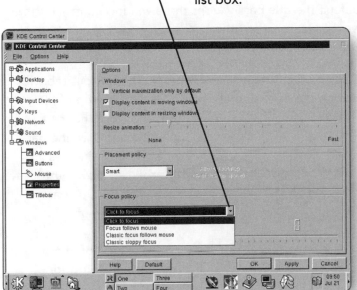

- **Click to focus** means that you must click inside a window to make the window active.

- **Focus follows mouse** keeps one window active at all times. When the mouse is placed over a window, the window is active until the mouse is placed over another window. If the mouse is placed over a desktop area, the last active window stays active.

- **Classic focus follows mouse** keeps a window active only if the mouse is placed over the window. If the mouse pointer is on the desktop, there is no active window.

**4. Click** on **OK**. Your changes will be applied.

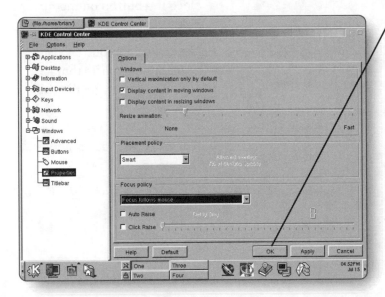

## Changing Title Bar Buttons

By default the title bar includes three window control buttons. However, you can add others. You can also change where a button is located on the title bar.

**1. Click** on the **Buttons subcategory**. The Buttons tab will appear on the right side of the window. At the top of the Buttons tab, you'll notice a sample title bar. This title bar shows how your windows are set up. You can move buttons to either side of the title bar, or you can turn them off.

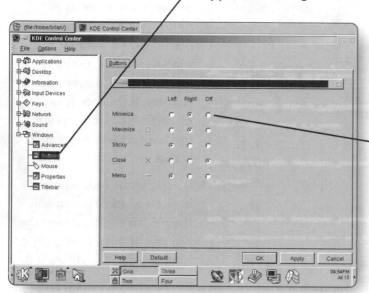

**2.** For each type of title bar button, **click** on an **option button**.

* The Left option button will place the button to the left of the window title.

* The Right option button will place the button on the far right end of the title bar.

* The Off option button will turn off a button so that it does not display on the title bar.

**3. Click** on **OK**. Your changes will be made.

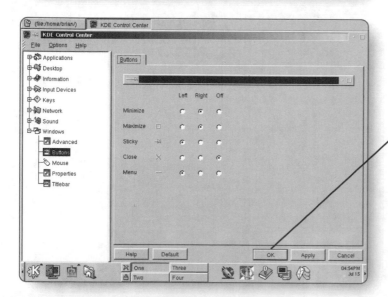

## Placing Windows on the Desktop

You can change how new windows appear on the desktop. You have several options to explore. You may want to see how each option works for you and pick the one you like best.

**1. Click** on the **Properties subcategory**. The Options tab will appear in the Control Center.

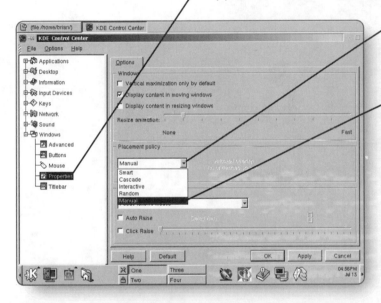

**2. Click** on the **down arrow** in the Placement policy section. A list of options will appear.

**3. Click** on an **option**. The option will appear in the list box.

- Smart will make the window placement decision for you and will try to place windows so that as much window area is visible as possible.

- Cascade will place each window so that the new window covers up the previous window, except for the title bar. The windows will look stair-stepped.

- Manual will enable you to decide where you want the new window placed. The new window will follow the mouse pointer until you click on the desktop.

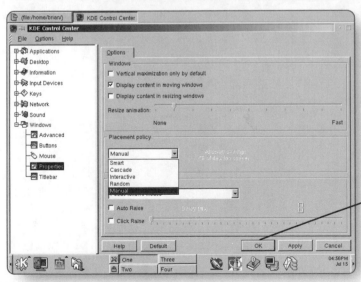

**4. Click** on **OK**. Your changes will be applied.

**5.** When you are finished with the Control Center, **click** on **File**. The File menu will appear.

**6. Click** on **Exit**. The Control Center will close.

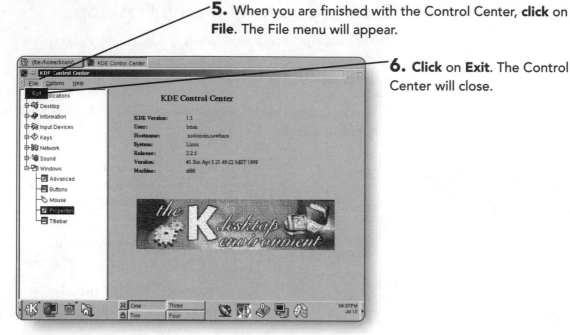

# 3

# Navigating Your Desktop

In Chapter 2, "Working with Windows," you learned a few tricks for working with individual windows. It's easy to resize a window and move it around a desktop when you're only working with a single window. Let's make things more complex by working with multiple windows on the desktop. With Linux, it is easy to work with multiple applications, multiple windows, and even multiple desktops. In this chapter, you'll learn how to:

- Arrange multiple windows on a single desktop
- Move windows between Virtual Desktops
- Use a single window on all desktops
- Change the quantity of Virtual Desktops

# Working with Multiple Windows

If you find that you use several applications at one time to do a job, Linux is a good choice. Its multitasking capabilities make it easy for you to get a job done efficiently. You can simultaneously write a manuscript, draw pictures to illustrate the manuscript, and watch a calendar to make sure you get the job done on time, all without taxing your computer's resources. But with all these windows open, it can be hard to keep your place.

## Finding a Few Applications to Open

Not only can you work with multiple applications at one time, but you can also group them on different desktop areas. Open a few windows on your desktop and experiment with the examples in this chapter.

**1. Click** on the **Application Starter icon**. The main menu will appear.

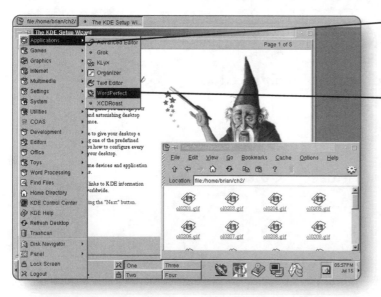

**2. Move** the **mouse pointer** to Applications. The Applications menu will appear.

**3. Click** on an **application**. The default program window for the application will open on your desktop area.

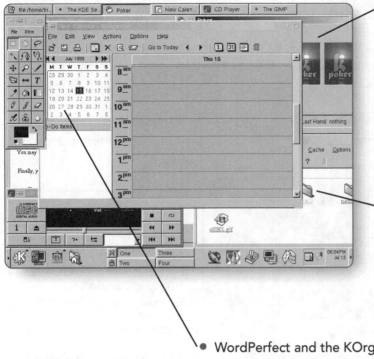

**4. Open** more **applications and utilities** until you have a half dozen open windows on your desktop area. The desktop will probably look cluttered and disorganized.

In this example, it may be hard to see, but there are seven open windows.

- By default, when you start KDE, the File Manager will open showing the Home directory for your user account and Kandalf will appear to help make setting up your desktop easier.

- WordPerfect and the KOrganizer can be found in the Applications menu. These are just a few of the productivity tools that you may find useful.

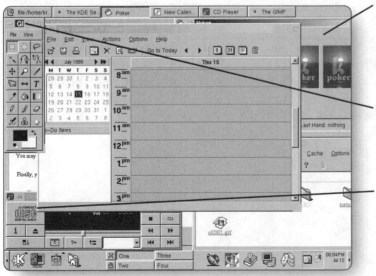

- The Games menu contains a bunch of fun games to help you waste a little time (and practice your mouse skills, of course).

- If you feel artistic or want to enhance scanned images, look in the Graphics menu for The GIMP.

- When only tunes will get you through times of hard work, plug in the CD Player and listen to the music. You'll find the CD Player in the Multimedia menu.

## Cleaning Up Your Desktop

KDE can organize the open windows on your desktop. It will try to place open windows so that a portion of each window is visible on your screen.

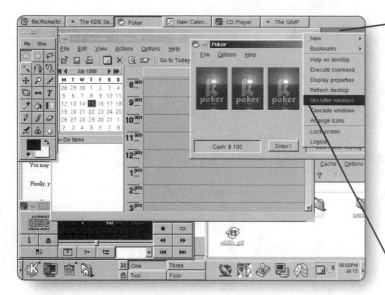

**1. Right-click** on an **empty area** of the desktop. A menu will appear.

### NOTE

You may have to move one of the windows out of the way to find an empty space on the desktop background.

**2. Click** on either **Unclutter windows** or **Cascade windows**. The desktop area will be reorganized.

- Unclutter windows will try to organize the windows so that some portion of each window can be seen on the desktop.

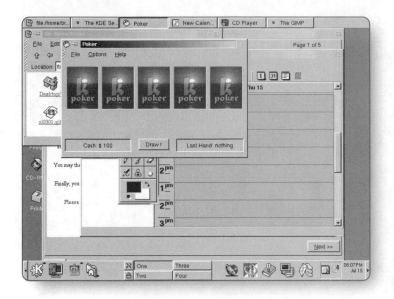

- Cascade windows will rearrange the windows so that you can see the title bar for each open window. The title bars will appear in a stacked formation.

## Shading and Organizing Windows

The automatic window arrangement may be less user-friendly than you'd like. You still have too many application windows to manage them efficiently or to quickly find the one you want. Furthermore, your desk is still cluttered. Here's another trick for working with multiple applications and files at one time.

**1. Double-click** on the **title bar** of one of the application windows. The window will become shaded by rolling up inside the title bar.

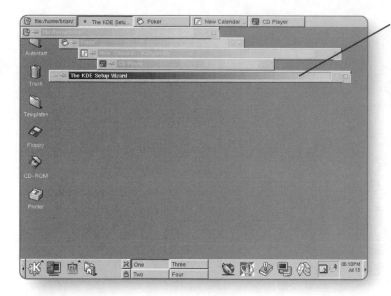

**2. Double-click** on the **title bars** of the other open windows on your desktop until all of the windows are shaded. Only the titles of the applications running in the window will show on the title bar of each window.

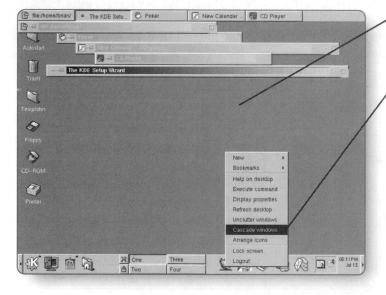

**3. Right-click** on an **empty area** of the **desktop**. A menu will appear.

**4. Click** on either **Unclutter windows** or **Cascade windows**. The shaded application windows will be organized into a list.

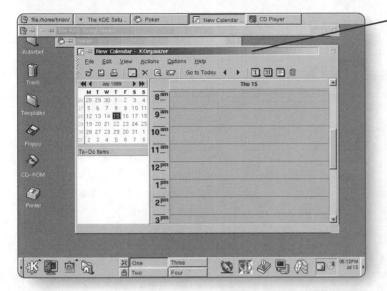

**5. Double-click** on the **title bar** of the application with which you want to work. The application window will open.

> **NOTE**
>
> This can be a useful way to store windows temporarily when you need space on the desktop to work, but the real solution is to get more desktop areas.

# Working with Virtual Desktops

You may have noticed the four buttons on the KDE Panel labeled One, Two, Three, and Four. These icons represent the four different desktop areas, or Virtual Desktops, that are available to you. This is like having four different monitors at your disposal. If you work with several applications at one time, you may want to place different applications on different Virtual Desktops.

# Moving Windows Between Desktops

Some people deal with cluttered desks by moving piles of paper from their desk to some other flat surface. If you have a cluttered screen, one alternative is to minimize the windows that you are not using. KDE offers another alternative: you can add more desktops to your screen. By default, you have four different Virtual Desktops with which to work. Here's how you can move windows to a different desktop.

**1. Click** on the **Window menu** of an open window on your desktop. A menu will appear.

**2. Move** the **mouse pointer** to **To desktop**. A second menu will appear.

**3. Click** on the **desktop number** to which you want to move the window. The window will be moved.

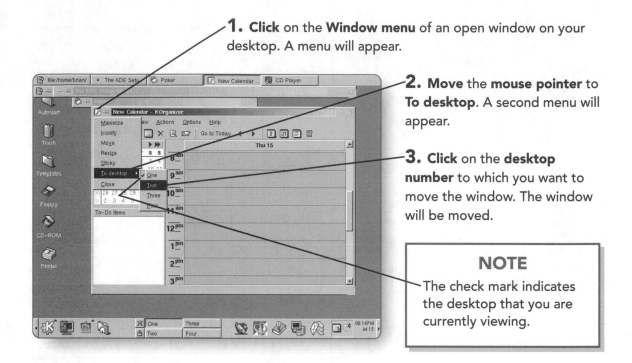

### NOTE

The check mark indicates the desktop that you are currently viewing.

**4. Click** on the **icon** on the panel that corresponds to the Virtual Desktop to which you moved the window. Another desktop area will appear, and you'll see the window that you moved off the original desktop area.

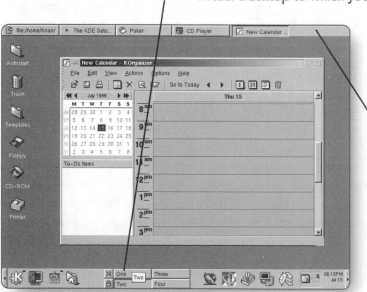

### TIP

If you want to work with an application, but you forgot which Virtual Desktop you stored the program on, click on the application icon on the taskbar.

# Renaming Desktop Buttons

One way to make it easier to remember on which desktop you stored a window is to rename the Virtual Desktop icons. Give each icon a descriptive name that will help you remember how your Virtual Desktop is organized.

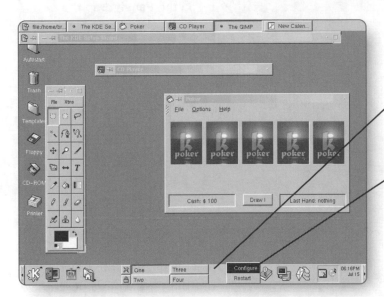

**1. Right-click** on an **empty area** of the **Panel**. A menu will appear.

**2. Click** on **Configure**. The KPanel Configuration dialog box will open and the Panel tab should be at the top of the stack.

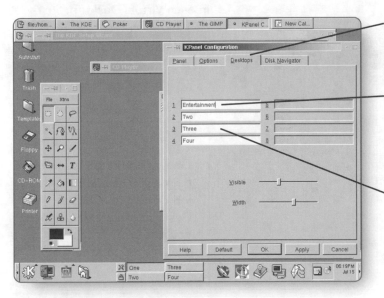

**3. Click** on the **Desktops tab**. The Desktops tab will come to the top of the stack.

**4. Double-click** on the **text** in the 1 text box and **type** a different **title** for the first Virtual Desktop icon.

**5. Change** the **text** for the other desktop areas.

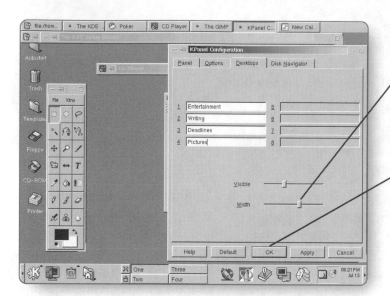

**TIP**

To change the width of the Virtual Desktop icon on the Panel, drag the Width slider.

**6. Click** on **OK**. The Virtual Desktop icons will change.

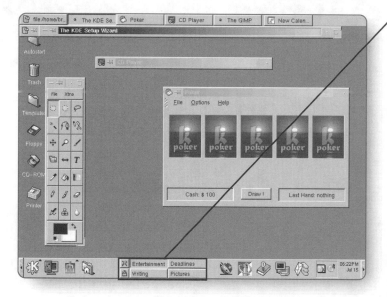

Now that your Virtual Desktop buttons have a more descriptive name, you can easily see which application windows are placed in each Virtual Desktop. Just click on an icon to see the associated desktop.

**TIP**

One way to organize your desktop is to assign each job or task to a Virtual Desktop of its own. Then you just click on the Virtual Desktop that you want.

# Sticking Windows to Desktops

There may be some windows that you want to appear on all your Virtual Desktops. If you have an Internet connection, you may want to see the status of your connection at all times. Or maybe you want to keep a game going. There's no need to open a new application window for each Virtual Desktop; you can make a window sticky so that it follows you wherever you go.

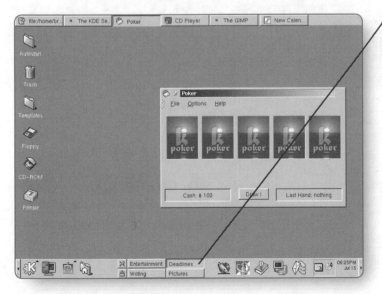

**1. Click** on the **Window menu**. A menu will appear.

**2. Click** on **Sticky**. The window will appear on every Virtual Desktop.

**3. Click** on a **Virtual Desktop icon**. You'll see the sticky window on the Virtual Desktop.

---

### NOTE

The window will be located in the same position on each Virtual Desktop. If you move the window, it will move in all of the Virtual Desktops.

---

# Changing the Number of Virtual Desktops

Now you have a feel for dancing through the four desktop areas that KDE provides by default. You've also spent some time moving application windows between desktop areas, so now it's time to learn how to create more desktop areas, or fewer if you want a simpler desktop.

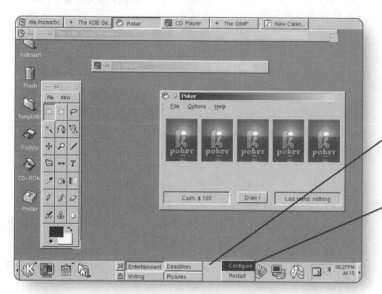

**1. Right-click** on an **empty area** of the Panel. A menu will appear.

**2. Click** on **Configure**. The KPanel Configuration dialog box will open and the Panel tab should be at the top of the stack.

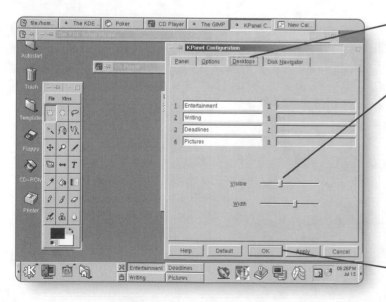

**3. Click** on the **Desktops tab**. The Desktops tab will come to the top of the stack.

**4a. Click and drag** the **Visible slider** to the **right**. More Virtual Desktops will be created.

**OR**

**4b. Click and drag** the **Visible slider** to the **left**. Some of the Virtual Desktops will disappear.

**5. Click** on **OK**. Your changes will be made.

# 4

# Customizing the Screen Display

If you want to change the look of your desktop to make it more functional or attractive, there are some cosmetic changes that you can make. To add a little variety, you can change the picture or pattern that you use for a desktop background. To keep your screen from staying in one place for too long when you're not working, use a screen saver. You can choose from several screen savers, and you can change the settings if you need to slow down the motion. You can also change the appearance of window borders, mouse pointers, and dialog boxes. In this chapter, you'll learn how to:

- Create stylish desktop backgrounds
- Find some fun screen savers
- Use themes to change the look of window borders, mouse pointers, and dialog boxes.

# Changing the Desktop Background

Whenever you're not looking at an application window, you'll probably see part of your desktop. You can have some fun here, or you can opt for a background that makes it easier for you to see other screen elements, such as windows and desktop icons.

## Using a Solid Color Background

The easiest background to create and the one easiest on your eyes is the solid color.

**1. Click** on the **KDE Control Center icon** on the Panel. The KDE Control Center will appear.

**2. Click** on the **Plus sign** to the left of Desktop. The Desktop category will expand

**3. Click** on the **Background option**. The desktop Background configuration tab will appear on the right side of the KDE Control Center.

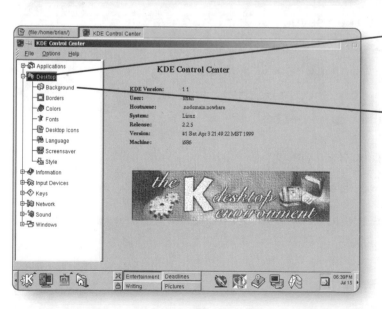

The Background configuration tab has options for you to
choose a background for each of the four Virtual Desktops
configured on your machine or a common background for all.
You can select from a huge list of backgrounds and display
options.

> ### NOTE
> If you didn't change the names of the Virtual
> Desktops (see Chapter 3 to learn how to do this),
> the Virtual Desktops will be named "One," "Two,"
> "Three," and "Four."

**4a. Click** on the **desktop** to which you want to apply the
desktop background. The desktop will be selected.

**OR**

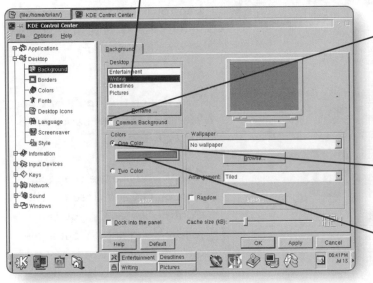

**4b. Click** on the **Common
Background check box** if you
want one background to be
applied to all of your Virtual
Desktops. A check will appear in
the box.

**5. Click** on the **One Color
option button**. The option will
be selected.

**6. Click** on the **One Color bar**.
The Select Color dialog box will
open.

**7. Click** on a **Color box** in the System Colors palette. The color in the sample box will change to the color you selected.

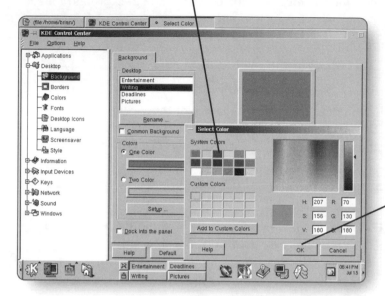

## TIP

You can select a custom color. Click on a color in the color gradient panel. You can then drag the tone gradient slider to adjust the color.

**8. Click** on **OK**. You will be returned to the KDE Control Center. The color you selected will appear on the One Color bar. You'll also see the new color in the preview area (it looks like a computer monitor).

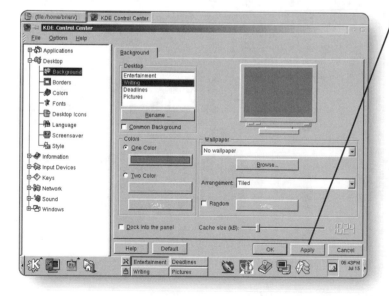

**9. Click** on the **Apply button**. You'll see the new background on your desktop.

**10.** If you like the changes, **click** on **OK** and close the KDE Control Center. Or, you can follow along and try out some different backgrounds.

## Creating a Gradient Background

A gradient is a combination of two colors. One color goes from darker to lighter and then blends with the second color that also changes in brightness. If you're looking for a slightly psychedelic look that's also easy on the eyes, experiment with this background effect.

**1. Open** the **KDE Control Center** and **select** the **Background option** in the Desktop category. The Background tab will appear.

**2a. Click** on the **Desktop** to which you want to apply the desktop background. The desktop will be selected.

**OR**

**2b. Click** on the **Common Background check box** if you want one background to be applied to all of your Virtual Desktops. A check will appear in the box.

**3. Click** on the **One Color option button**. The option will be selected.

**4. Click** on the **One Color bar**. The Select Color dialog box will open.

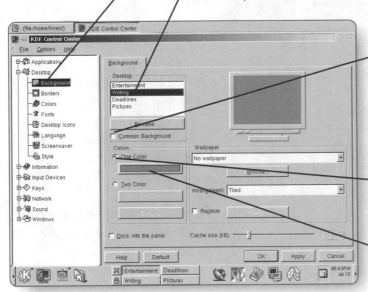

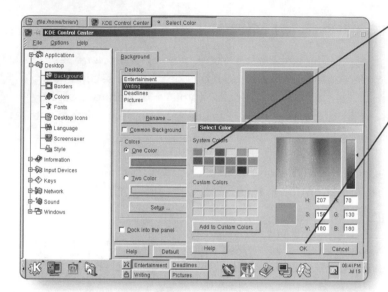

**5. Click** on a **color box** in the System Colors palette. The color in the sample box will change to the color you selected.

**6. Click** on **OK**. You will be returned to the KDE Control Center. The color you selected will appear in the One Color bar.

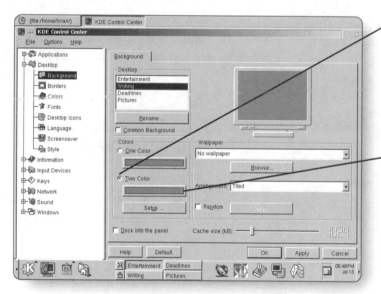

**7. Click** on the **Two Color option button** on the Background tab. The option will be selected. You'll also notice that the Setup button will be highlighted.

**8. Click** on the **Two Color bar**. The Select Color dialog box will open.

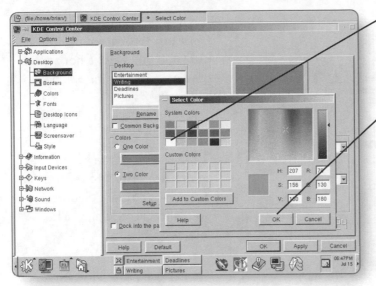

**9. Click** on a **color** to be the second color in the gradient. The color will appear in the sample color box.

**10. Click** on **OK**. You'll be returned to the KDE Control Center, and the color you selected will appear on the Two Color bar.

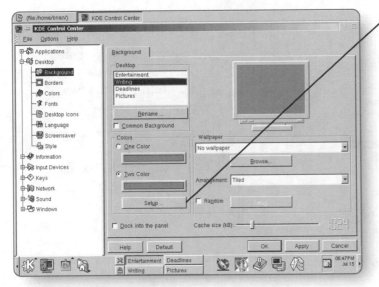

**11. Click** on the **Setup button**. The Two color backgrounds dialog box will appear.

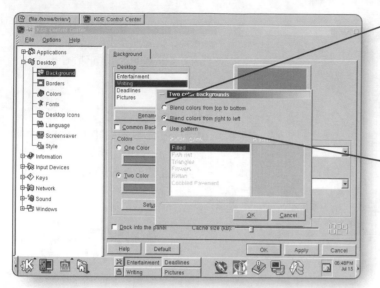

**12a.** **Click** on the **Blend colors from top to bottom option button** if you want a horizontal gradient. The option will be selected.

**OR**

**12b.** **Click** on the **Blend colors from right to left option button** if you want a vertical gradient. The option will be selected.

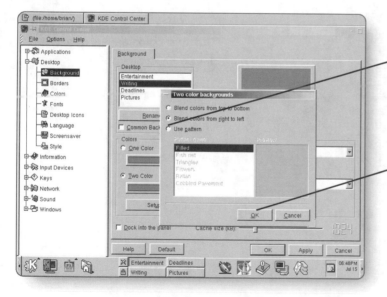

### TIP

You can add more detail to your background by using a pattern with the two colors that you select.

**13.** **Click** on **OK**. You'll be returned to the KDE Control Center.

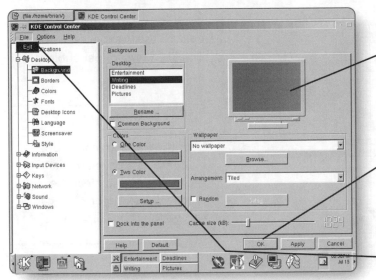

**NOTE**

Notice that the new background that you created displays in the preview monitor.

**14.** **Click** on **OK** when you are satisfied with your desktop background. Your changes will be made.

**15.** If you're done using the KDE Control Center, close the Control Center window by selecting Exit from the File menu.

## Selecting Wallpaper

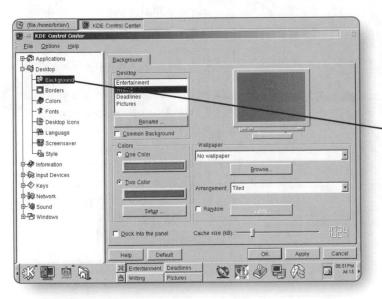

Caldera OpenLinux is loaded with lots of patterns and images that you can arrange in various ways to create wallpaper for your desktops.

**1.** **Open** the **KDE Control Center** and **select** the **Background option** in the Desktop category. The Background tab will appear.

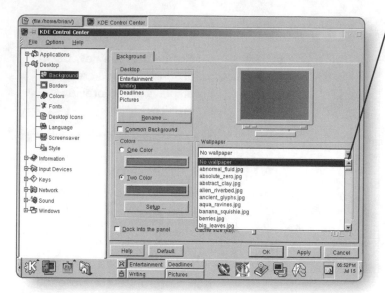

**2. Click** on the **down arrow** next to the Wallpaper list box. The list of wallpaper choices will appear.

### TIP

If the Random check box contains a check mark, you'll need to clear the check box before you can change the wallpaper.

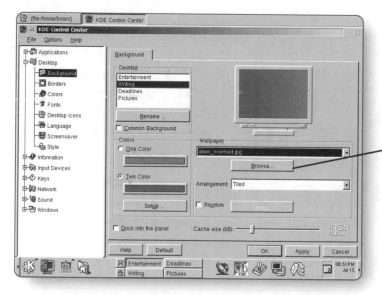

**3. Click** on a **wallpaper name.** The wallpaper you select will appear in the preview monitor.

### TIP

If you have a picture you want to use as wallpaper, click on the Browse button and navigate to the directory where the picture is stored. You can create your own wallpaper using a graphics program such as The GIMP.

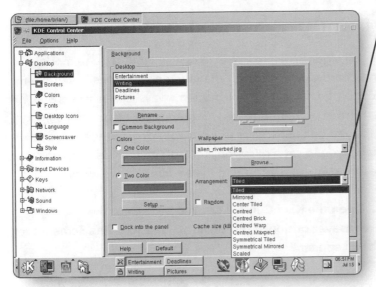

**4. Click** on the **down arrow** next to the Arrangement list box and **click** on an **arrangement option**. The option will appear in the list box. You can try any of the Arrangement choices and see the effect in the preview monitor.

- *Tiled* places multiple copies of the image in rows and columns across the screen.

- *Mirrored* places mirrored copies of the image on the screen.

- *Centered* places one copy of the image in the center of the desktop. Any areas that are not used by the image will display the background color(s) in use.

- *Scaled* fills the entire desktop with the image. The image might appear distorted.

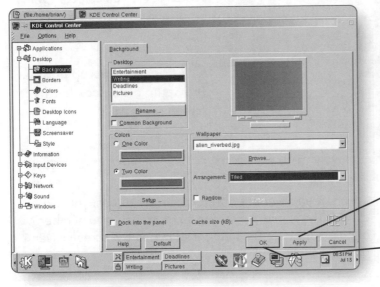

**NOTE**

If you are not happy with the way the background looks in the preview monitor, try different combinations of colors, wallpapers, and arrangements until you have one you like.

**5. Click** on the **Apply button**. Your choices will be applied.

**6. Click** on **OK**. The Background tab will close, and you will be returned to the KDE Control Center.

# Finding a Screen Saver

It's still a good idea to use a screen saver. Although modern video hardware and power management options have taken most of the risk of monitor burn-in away, screen savers still perform important functions. Screen savers change the image displayed on the monitor at a set speed. Screen savers also enable you to set a password to protect your desktop and files from intrusion or prying eyes while you are away.

**1. Open** the **KDE Control Center** and **select** the **Screensaver option** in the Desktop category. The Screensaver tab will appear.

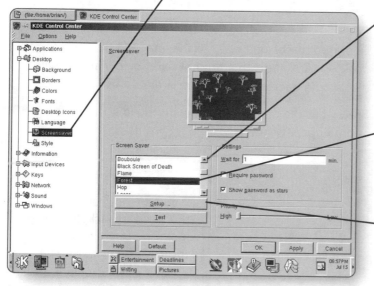

**2. Click** on the **up and down arrows** to scroll up and down the list of screen savers. You will view the list of available screen savers.

**3. Click** on a **screen saver**. The screen saver you selected will be displayed in the preview monitor.

**4. Click** on the **Setup button**. The Setup dialog box for the screen saver will open.

---

## NOTE

Each screen saver has different setup options. You can change the speed the screen saver travels, the number of colors used, or the number of cycles the screen saver goes through.

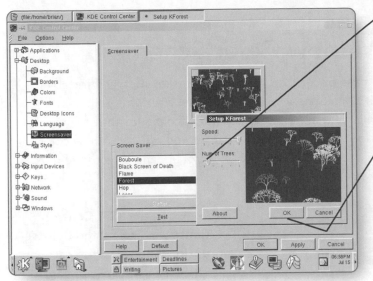

**5. Click and drag** the **slider**. The setup options will change. Dragging the slider to the right increases the setting. Dragging the slider to the left reduces the setting.

**6. Click** on **OK**. You will be returned to the Screensaver tab.

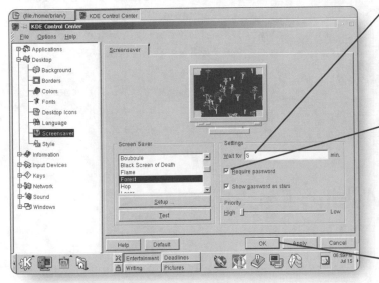

**7. Clear** the **entry** in the Wait for text box and **type** the **number of minutes** you want your computer to sit idle before the screen saver starts.

**8. Click** in the **Require password check box** if you want to type a password to clear the screen saver so you can use your computer. A check will appear in the box.

**9. Click** on **OK**. Your changes will be made, and you can close the KDE Control Center if you are finished making changes. Or, leave the Control Center open and follow along for more desktop fun.

## NOTE

The screen saver will use your user password to control access to the screen.

# Selecting a Window Color Scheme

The use of color on the desktop makes for a comfortable working atmosphere. There are several color schemes available that use complementary colors for the various widgets that make up a window. You can give a new color to the title bar, the window background, and selected text, to name a few.

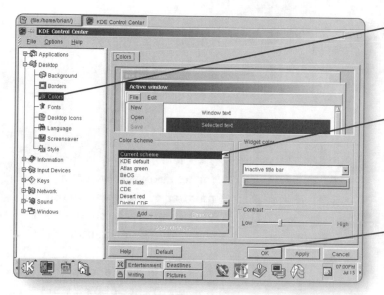

**1. Open** the **KDE Control Center** and **select** the **Colors option** in the Desktop category. The Colors tab will appear.

**2. Scroll** through the **Color Scheme list** and **click** on a **color scheme**. The preview pane will show how the window colors will be displayed.

**3. Click** on **OK**. Your changes will be applied to all of your window widgets.

# Making Desktop Icons Transparent

You may have noticed that the descriptive text below the icons on your desktop is enclosed in a filled box. You can change the look of the icon text so that the filled box cannot be seen. Instead, you'll only see the text on top of the desktop background. You can also change the color of this text.

**1. Open** the **KDE Control Center** and **select** the **Desktop Icons option** in the Desktop category. The Desktop Icons tab will appear.

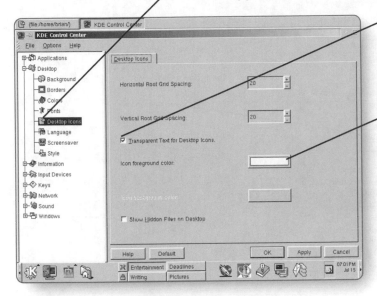

**2. Click** in the **Transparent Text for Desktop Icons check box**. A check will appear in the box.

**3. Click** on the **Icon foreground color bar** if you want to change the color of the text that appears below the icon. The Select Color dialog box will open.

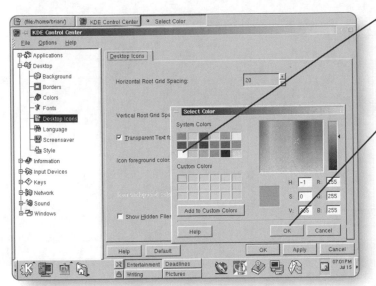

**4. Click** on the **color box** from the System Colors palette to select a different color for the text. The color will appear in the sample color box.

**5. Click** on **OK**. You'll be returned to the KDE Control Center, and the color you selected will be shown on the Icon foreground color bar.

---

### TIP

To make it easier to read the icon text, choose a color that contrasts with the desktop background.

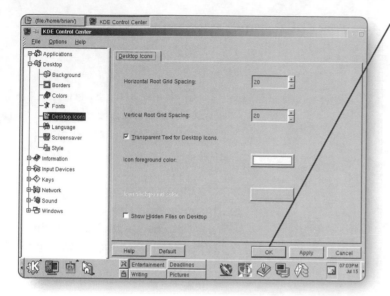

**6. Click** on **OK**. Your changes will be made, and you can close the KDE Control Center.

# 5

# Managing Your Desktop

Buttons on the Panel make it easy for you to work with OpenLinux through the KDE interface. These buttons make it a one-click job for you to open menus, switch back and forth between desktops, launch applications, get Help, lock your screen with a password, open the KDE Control Center, log out, and more. You can change the button icons and the Tooltips associated with them. You can add new buttons to the Panel and configure them to fit your needs. In this chapter, you'll learn how to:

- Configure and position the Panel
- Set Tooltips for buttons
- Add and remove buttons on the Panel
- Work with the Personal menu

# Creating Application Launch Buttons

KDE has several options for buttons that you can add to the Panel. You can add an application launch button to the Panel for a favorite application, or you might want to add a menu button to the Panel with a menu tailored to your particular applications or tools.

## Adding a Button to the Panel

**1. Click** on the **Application Starter** on the Panel. The KDE Main menu will appear.

**2. Move** the **mouse pointer** to **Panel**. The Panel menu will appear.

**3. Move** the **mouse pointer** to **Add Application**. The Add Applications menu will appear.

**4. Move** the **mouse pointer** to a **category** of programs. The list of applications will appear.

**5. Click** on an **application**. The application launch button will appear on the Panel.

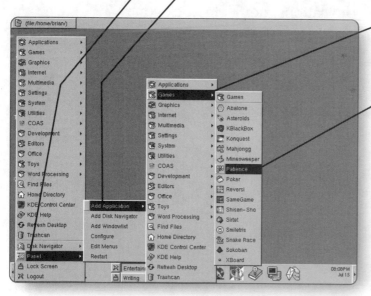

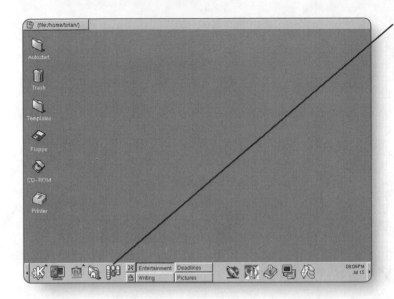

**6. Click** on the **application launch button** on the Panel. The application will open.

## Setting Tooltips for Application Launch Buttons

After you've added buttons here and there for all your favorite tools and games you may find that your memory is a little hazy about which icon button you assigned to which application. Obviously an easy way to find out the real identity behind the sunflower icon you configured last week is needed. Tooltips are the perfect solution.

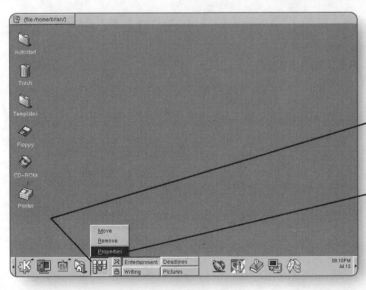

**1. Right-click** on an **application launch button**. The button menu will appear.

**2. Click** on **Properties**. The kfm dialog box will open.

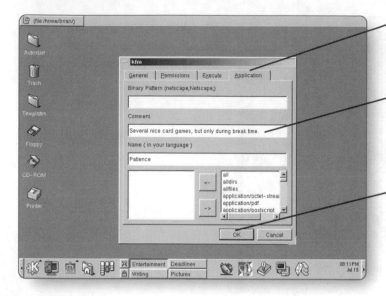

**3. Click** on the **Application tab**. The Application tab will come to the top of the stack.

**4. Select** the **text** in the Comment text box and **type** the **Tooltip** text for the button. The text will appear in the text box.

**5. Click** on **OK**. The Tooltip text will appear when you hold the mouse pointer over the button.

### TIP

If you don't see the new Tooltip, you may need to restart the Panel. You'll learn about restarting the Panel later in this chapter.

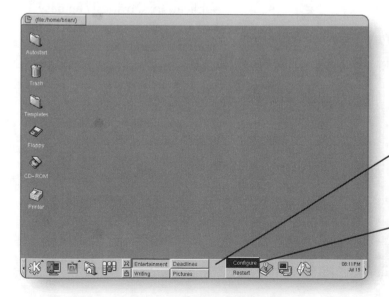

## Turning Off Tooltips

If you don't want to see the Tooltips when you hold the mouse pointer over buttons, you can turn them off.

**1. Right-click** on an **empty area** of the Panel. A menu will appear.

**2. Click** on **Configure**. The KPanel Configuration dialog box will open.

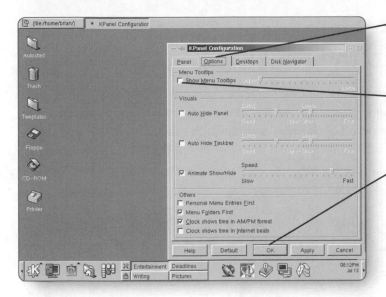

**3. Click** on the **Options tab**. The Options tab will come to the top of the stack.

**4. Click** in the **Show Menu Tooltips check box**. The check mark will be cleared.

**5. Click** on **OK**. Your changes will be applied, and you'll no longer see the Tooltips.

## Restarting the Panel

It might be necessary to restart the Panel for any changes that you made to the Tooltips to take effect.

**1. Click** on the **Application Starter**. The Main menu will appear.

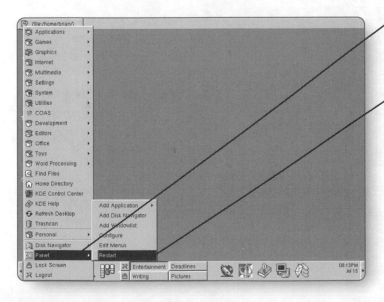

**2. Move** the **mouse pointer** to **Panel**. The Panel menu will appear.

**3. Click** on **Restart**. The Panel and the taskbar will disappear for a few seconds and then return.

# Adding Menu Buttons to the Panel

Here is another way that you can use a Panel button to speed things up and make it easier to work with OpenLinux. If you are tired of drilling down through the KDE menus to get to one of the buried submenus, take a shortcut and add the whole menu to the Panel.

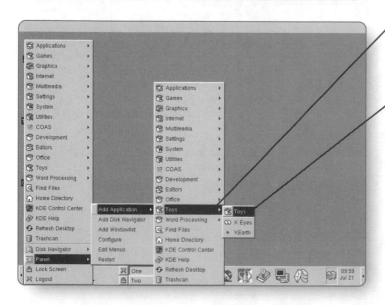

**1.** **Click** on the **Application Starter.** The KDE main menu will appear.

**2.** **Move** the **mouse pointer** to **Panel**. The Panel menu will appear.

**3.** **Move** the **mouse pointer** to **Add Application**. The Add Application menu will appear.

**4.** **Move** the **mouse pointer** to a category of programs. The list of applications will appear.

**5.** **Click** on the **first choice** in the menu (the menu name). An icon for the menu category will appear on the Panel.

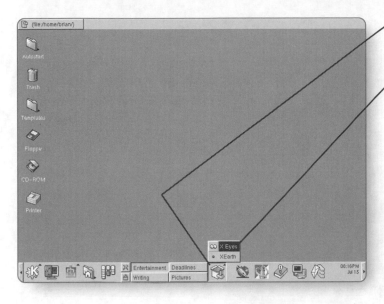

**6. Click** on the **menu button**. The menu will appear.

**7. Click** on an **application**. The application will open.

# Working with Buttons on the Panel

You may have buttons on the panel that you are no longer using, or perhaps things are getting too crowded and you have to move something or remove something to make room. KDE can't help you choose which buttons to move or remove, but it sure makes it easy to move or remove them.

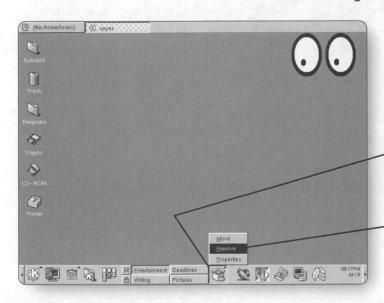

## Deleting a Button

**1. Right-click** on the **button** you want to remove. A menu will appear.

**2. Click** on **Remove**. The button will disappear from the Panel.

# Moving Buttons Around

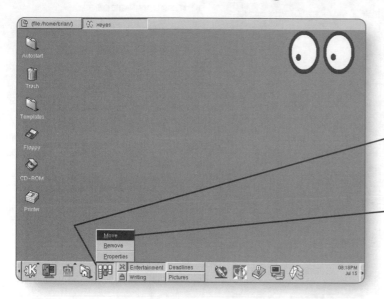

Now that you have some extra space on the Panel, you can make use of the Move function to move some of the other buttons around.

**1. Right-click** on a **button** that you would like to move. A menu will appear.

**2. Click** on **Move**. The button will be highlighted.

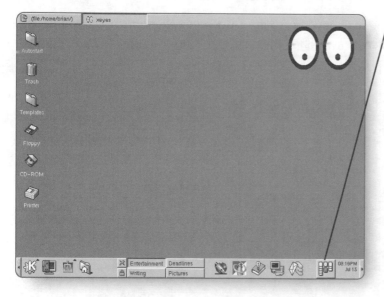

**3. Drag** the **mouse pointer** to the **place** where you want to move the button. The button will follow the mouse pointer.

**4. Click** the **mouse button** to place the button on the spot you want. The button will be repositioned on the Panel.

# Changing the Panel Position and Behavior

You have lots of options in KDE to tailor the Panel's position and behavior to your taste or needs.

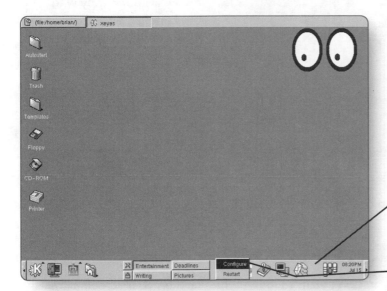

## Moving the Panel

The Panel is normally located at the bottom of your screen. If you would rather try out a different location, give it a shot. You might like working with the Panel better if it ran along the right side of your screen.

**1. Right-click** on an empty area of the **Panel**. A menu will appear.

**2. Click** on **Configure**. The KPanel Configuration dialog box will open and the Panel tab should be at the top of the stack.

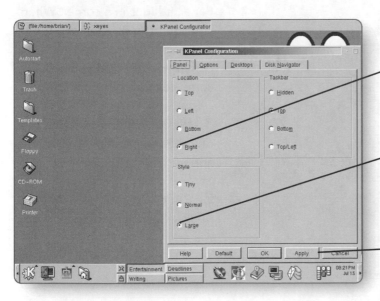

**3. Click** on a **Location option button** to change where on the screen the Panel resides. The option will be selected.

**4. Click** on a **Style option button** to change the size of the buttons that appear on the Panel. The option will be selected.

**5. Click** on **Apply**. Your changes will be made.

The Panel will appear in the new position and the button size will change.

**6. Click** on **OK** when you are satisfied with your changes. The dialog box will close.

## Hiding the Panel

If you don't want to look at the Panel on your screen all the time, use the Auto Hide feature. When you don't need the

Panel, it hides in a corner. When you need the Panel, move the mouse pointer to the Panel's corner and watch the Panel come out to do its next job.

**1. Right-click** on an empty area of the **Panel**. A menu will appear.

**2. Click** on **Configure**. The KPanel Configuration dialog box will open.

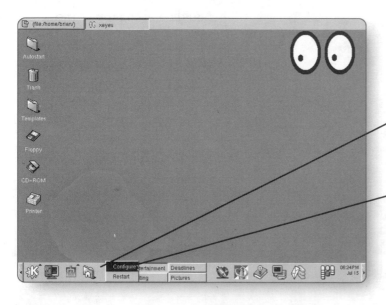

**3. Click** on the **Options tab**. The Options tab will come to the top of the stack.

**4. Click** on the **Auto Hide Panel check box**. The controls that control the Delay before hiding and showing, and the speed at which the Panel shows and hides, will be displayed.

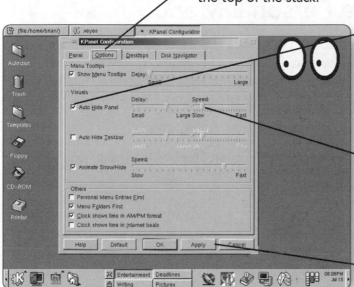

**5. Click and drag** the **sliders** to set the delay before the Panel hides itself and the speed at which it hides. The delay and speed will be adjusted.

**6. Click** on **Apply**. The Panel will automatically hide itself after the delay time set in the dialog box has passed.

**7. Move** the **mouse pointer** over the **area** where the Panel was displayed. The Panel will reappear.

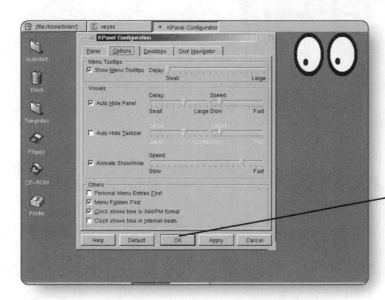

**8. Move** the **mouse pointer** off of the Panel. After the delay, the Panel will disappear (hide).

**9. Click** on **OK** in the KPanel Configuration dialog box when you are satisfied with the result. Your new changes will be put into effect.

# Working with the Personal Menu

It is possible to customize the Personal menu section of the Application Starter menu. KMenuedit is the program you use to add and make changes to the Personal menu that appears in the KDE Main menu. KMenuedit makes changing this menu simple.

**1. Click** on the **Application Starter**. The main menu will appear.

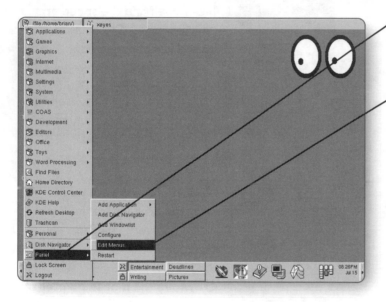

**2. Move** the **mouse pointer** to **Panel**. The Panel menu will appear.

**3. Click** on **Edit Menus**. The KMenuedit Handbook page from the kdehelp browser will appear on your screen.

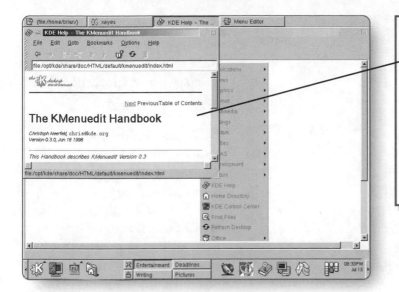

**NOTE**

When you're finished reading the KMenuedit Handbook, you can either close the window or minimize it. The KMenuedit Handbook will close when you close the Menu Editor.

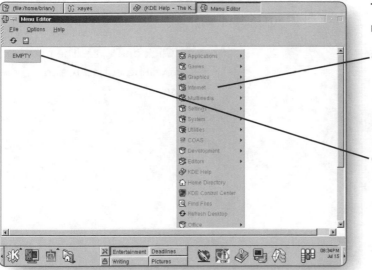

The Menu Editor contains two menus.

- The menu on the right is the system menu. You will select the items that you want to add to your Personal menu from here.

- The button on the left is the beginning of your Personal menu. It probably says EMPTY if you are just starting and haven't added anything to your Personal menu yet.

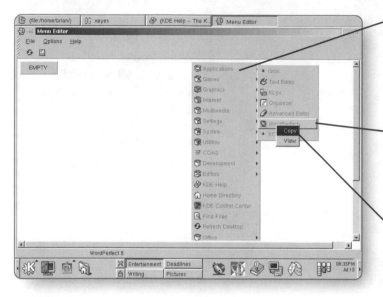

**4. Click** on the **menu item** that contains the application that you want to add to your Personal menu. A list of applications will appear.

**5. Right-click** on the **application** that you want to add to your Personal menu. A menu will appear.

**6. Click** on **Copy**. The menu item will be selected so that it can be added to your Personal menu.

**7. Right-click** on the **EMPTY button** on the left menu. A menu will appear.

**8. Click** on **Paste**. The menu item will be added to the Personal menu.

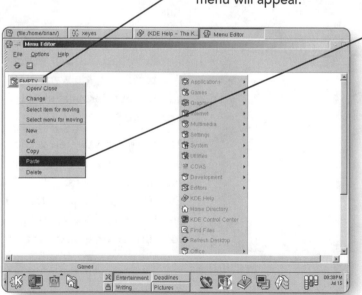

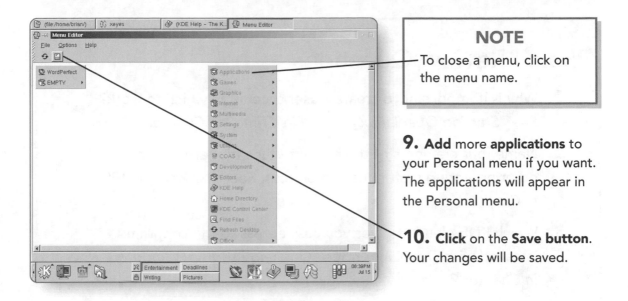

**NOTE**

To close a menu, click on the menu name.

**9.** **Add** more **applications** to your Personal menu if you want. The applications will appear in the Personal menu.

**10.** **Click** on the **Save button**. Your changes will be saved.

**11.** **Click** on **File**. The File menu will appear.

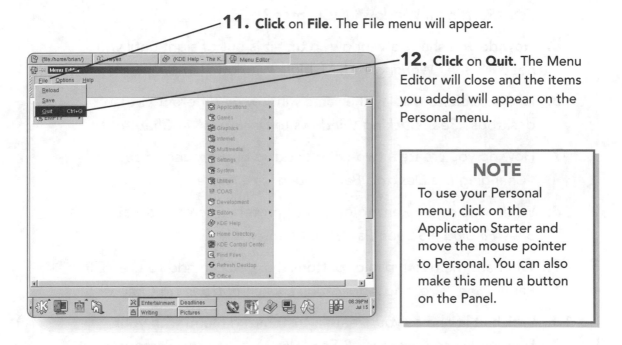

**12.** **Click** on **Quit**. The Menu Editor will close and the items you added will appear on the Personal menu.

**NOTE**

To use your Personal menu, click on the Application Starter and move the mouse pointer to Personal. You can also make this menu a button on the Panel.

# Part I Review Questions

**1.** Why is it important to create a user account in which to work? *See "Starting OpenLinux for the First Time" in Chapter 1*

**2.** Name four elements of the KDE interface that are common to other operating system user interfaces. *See "Exploring KDE" in Chapter 1*

**3.** Which KDE element gives you easy access to the programs installed with OpenLinux? *See "Opening Program Windows" in Chapter 2*

**4.** What are the different ways in which you can resize a window? *See "Resizing a Window" in Chapter 2*

**5.** How do you shade a window so that it is out of sight until you need it? *See "Working with Multiple Windows" in Chapter 3*

**6.** Is it possible to display the same window on different virtual desktops? *See "Sticking Windows to Desktops" in Chapter 3*

**7.** How do you create a two-color desktop background? *See "Changing the Desktop Background" in Chapter 4*

**8.** When would you want to password protect a screen saver? *See "Finding a Screen Saver" in Chapter 4*

**9.** What are the two types of buttons that you can add to the KDE Panel? *See "Creating Application Launch Buttons" in Chapter 5*

**10.** Which utility helps you create a customized menu with your frequently used programs? *See "Working with the Personal Menu" in Chapter 5*

# PART II

# Using the File System

# 6

# Exploring the KDE File Manager

The KDE File Manager is integrated tightly into the KDE interface and one just seems to pop up magically every time a need arises. Whenever you mount a new file system, such as a floppy disk or a CD-ROM, you will get a new File Manager window with the contents of the file system displayed in the directory window. Using drag-and-drop, you can add new files, move files, launch and update applications, use tools and utilities, perform file system maintenance, and many other file system functions. You'll find that the OpenLinux filing system is different than the filing systems you may have experienced with other operating systems. In this chapter, you'll learn how to:

- Identify the basic parts of the File Manager
- Understand the Linux file system
- Navigate the directory structure
- Select files in the directory structure
- Search through your file list

# Opening the File System

Take a little time to get familiar with the KDE File Manager before you start working with applications and creating files. The File Manager's easy-to-use graphical interface is where you'll perform most of your file maintenance tasks.

**1.** **Click** on the **Application Starter**. The main menu will appear.

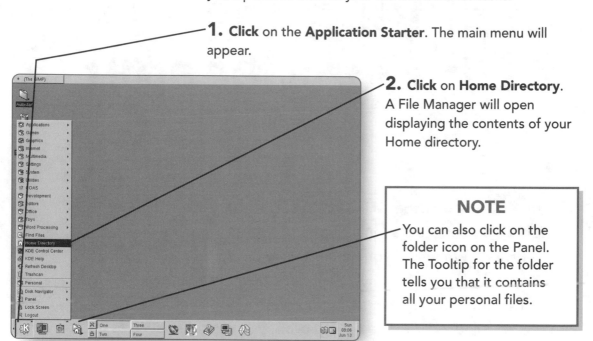

**2.** **Click** on **Home Directory**. A File Manager will open displaying the contents of your Home directory.

### NOTE
You can also click on the folder icon on the Panel. The Tooltip for the folder tells you that it contains all your personal files.

Before you can learn about the Linux file system, you'll need to change the File Manager display to the tree option, so that you can see the Linux directory structure.

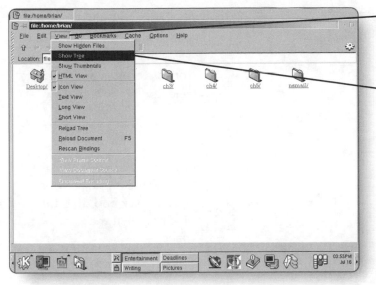

**3. Click** on **View** in the File Manager menu bar. The View menu will appear.

**4. Click** on **Show Tree**. The File Manager display will change to a two-panel display with icons and file names to show the contents of the currently open directory displayed on the right and a tree-style directory shown on the left with the icon for Desktop showing an open folder.

• The menus contain all the commands you can perform with the File Manager. You can create directories, delete files, sort files, and view directories.

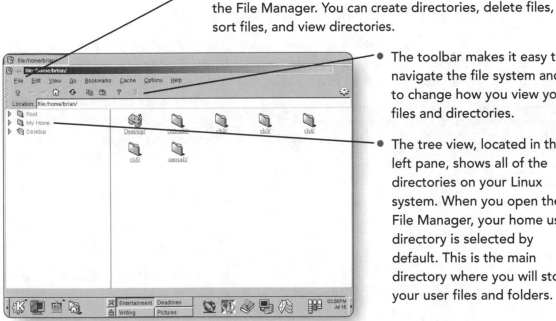

• The toolbar makes it easy to navigate the file system and to change how you view your files and directories.

• The tree view, located in the left pane, shows all of the directories on your Linux system. When you open the File Manager, your home user directory is selected by default. This is the main directory where you will store your user files and folders.

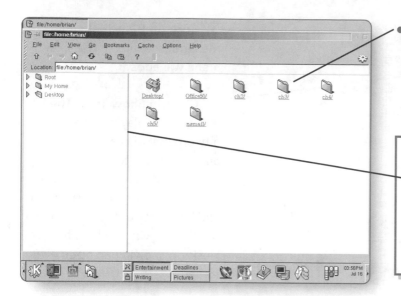

- The directory view is located in the right pane and shows all of the files and subdirectories stored in a directory selected in the tree view.

### TIP

You can change the size of the tree and directory views. Click and drag the line between the two panes.

# Understanding the Linux File System

Before you dive into the Linux file system, you need to understand the contents of the directory structure that was set up when you installed OpenLinux. Some of these directories contain information that you'll find useful. Other directories are best left alone, unless you are a Linux expert.

**1. Click** on the **right-pointing arrow** next to the Root directory. The directories contained under Root will appear.

- The / or Root directory is the base of the OpenLinux file system. All of the files and directories for the system are contained in this directory. Do not store any of your files in the Root directory!

The /bin directory contains the binary files for the basic OpenLinux programs and commands. You probably won't need to use this directory. The KDE interface accesses many of these programs and commands for you.

The /dev directory is where all the device files (drivers) for the hardware components (floppy drive, hard drive, CD-ROM, and so on) on your computer are stored.

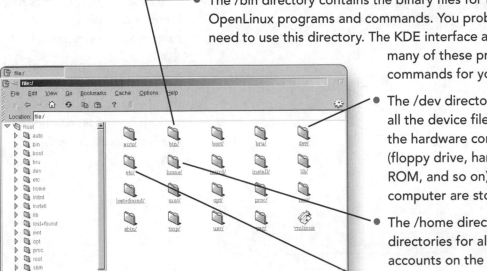

The /home directory contains directories for all the user accounts on the system.

The /etc directory contains system configuration files and initialization scripts.

Each user has their own home directory in which to store personal files. You cannot access another user's files from your user account.

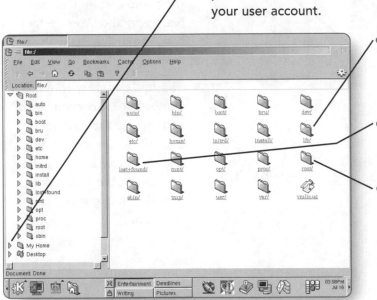

The /lib directory is where the library files for the C and other programming languages are stored.

If Linux has lost a file, it might be found in the /lost+found directory.

The home directory for the root account is /root.

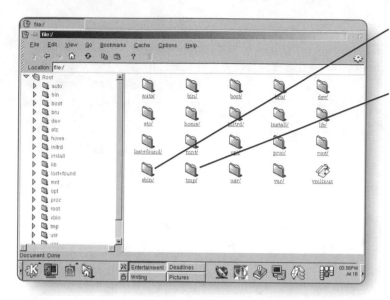

- The /sbin directory contains a number of tools used for system administration.

- The /tmp directory is a place where all users can store files on a temporary basis. If the system is rebooted, all files in the /tmp directory will be lost.

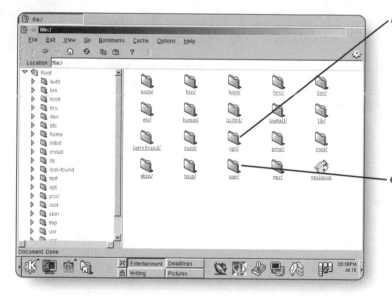

- The /opt directory contains files for the tools and applications shared by all users, such as the KDE files, the audio system files, the Netscape and WordPerfect files, the online manuals, and others.

- The /usr directory contains a number of Linux commands and utilities that are not a part of the Linux operating system, documentation files and some utility programs, and the Linux game collection.

# Browsing the File System

The graphical interface used by the File Manager makes it easy to move around and view the contents of directories and files. Because you probably don't have many directories created in your user account, a good place to look around in the file system is the /usr directory.

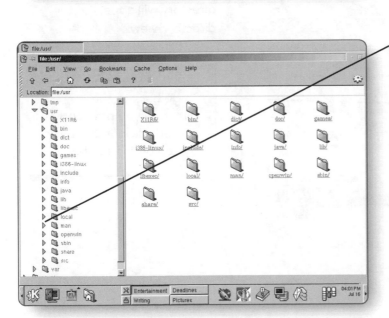

**1. Click** on the **usr folder icon** in the tree view. The list of subdirectories and files contained in the /usr directory will appear in the directory view as icons.

**2. Click** on the **arrow** next to the usr folder icon. The list of subdirectories will appear under the usr folder icon in the tree view.

**3. Click** on the **arrow** next to the man folder icon. The directory in the tree view will expand and the list of directories and files contained in the /usr/man directory will appear in the directory view.

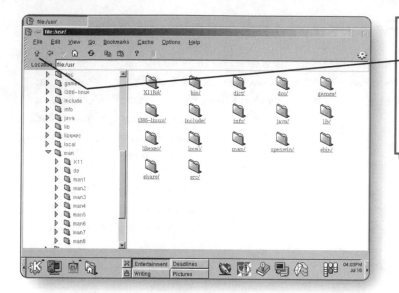

**NOTE**

To move to the directory one level up from the selected directory, click on the Up arrow on the toolbar.

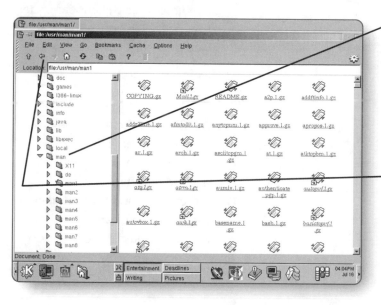

**4. Click** on a **folder icon** listed under the /usr/man directory. The list of files contained in the directory will appear in the directory view.

**NOTE**

To go back to the directory you previously viewed, click on the Back button on the toolbar.

**5. Click** on **View**. A drop-down menu will appear. Items that you have selected, such as Show Tree, will have a check mark beside them. You can view the contents of a directory in several ways in the File Manager.

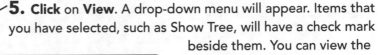

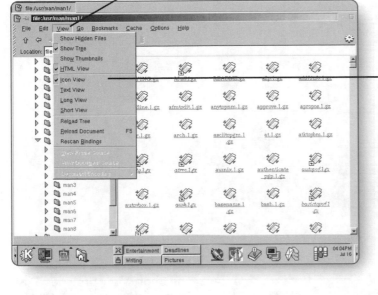

- The Icon View shows a picture that represents the file type and the name of the file underneath. This is useful if you're looking for a quick way to determine file types.

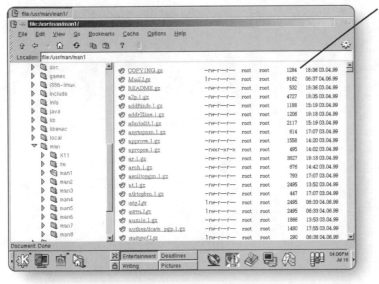

- The Text View provides a simple text list of the files stored in the directory and some information about ownership and permissions.

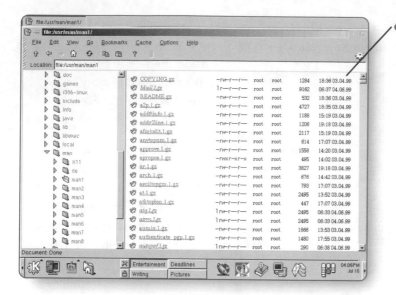

The Long View provides the largest amount of information about the files.

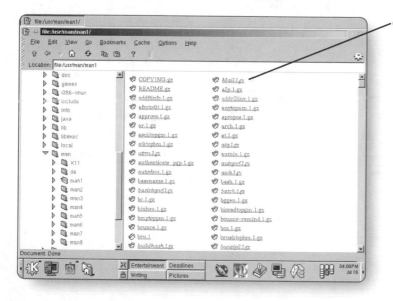

The Short View provides a list of the small icons and the file and folder names with no other information shown.

# Selecting Files

Before you can perform any work on a file (such as copy or rename), you'll have to select the file in the File Manager. You have the choice of selecting files yourself by clicking on the files with the mouse. You can also tell the File Manager the types of files you want to select and it will search the directory and select those files for you.

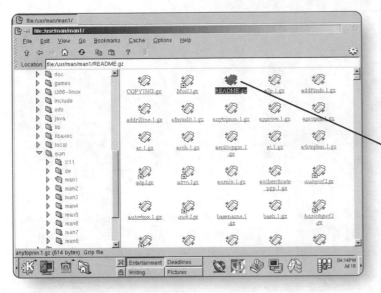

## Using the Mouse to Select Files

● To select a single file, click on the file.

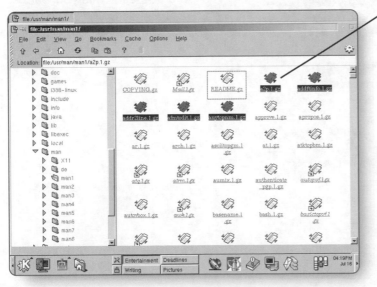

● To select several contiguous files, click on the first file that you want to select, then press the Shift key and click on the last file you want to select.

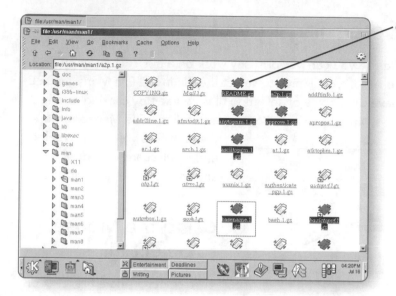

- To select files that are not located next to each other, press and hold the Ctrl key while you click on each file that you want to select.

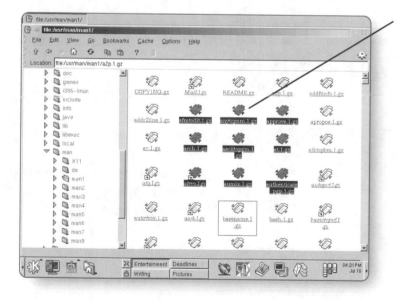

- To select several contiguous files in the Icons View, click and hold the mouse button at the beginning of one file; then drag the mouse to the end of the last file you want to select.

# Using Selection Criteria

Maybe you don't want to search through a directory and select files yourself. If the files all contain a common element, such as the same file extension or mime type, or perhaps all of the files begin with the same combination of letters, you can use the find selections in the Edit menu to search for you.

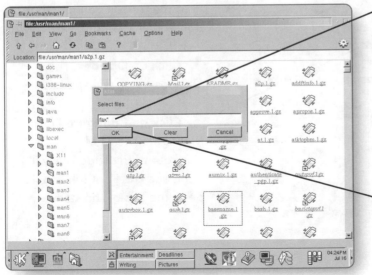

**1. Click** on **Edit**. The Edit menu will appear.

**2. Click** on **Select**. The kfm dialog box will open.

**3. Type** the **criteria** for the files you want to select. For example, if you know the name of the application or file you want or if you want to find files of a certain type, type *.pcx. If you want to select files starting with a specific letter combination, type LX*.

**4. Click** on **OK**. The File Manager will search for those files that match the criteria you typed.

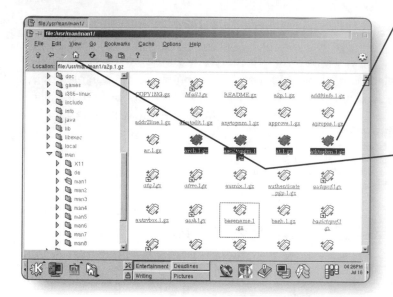

All the files that match the criteria will be displayed in the File Manager in the directory view.

### TIP

When you are finished looking through the /usr directory and want to go back to your user account directory, click on the Home button on the toolbar.

# Changing the Look of the K File Manager

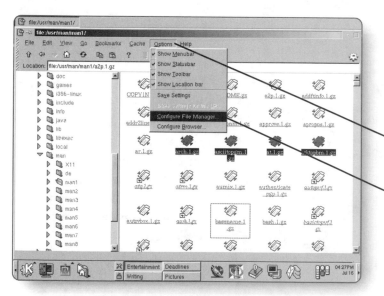

You have several options for changing the look of the File Manager to something other than the default configuration that you are working with now.

**1. Click** on **Options**. The Options menu will appear.

**2. Click** on **Configure File Manager**. The KFM Configuration dialog box will open and the Font tab should be at the top of the stack.

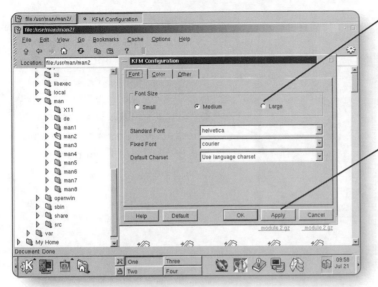

**3.** **Click** on the **Medium or Large option button** if you want to increase the font size that displays in the File Manager window. The option will be selected.

**4.** **Click** on **Apply**. You will see the effect of your changes.

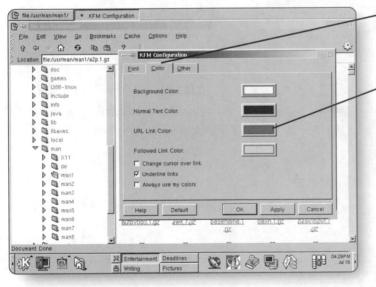

**5.** **Click** on the **Color tab**. The Color tab will come to the top of the stack.

**6.** **Click** on the **color bar** to change the color of an item. The Select Color dialog box will open.

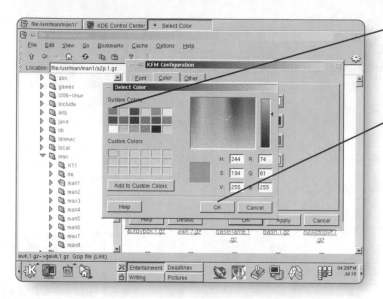

**7.** **Click** on a **color box** in the System Colors area. The color will be selected and will appear in the preview area.

**8.** **Click** on **OK**. The color you selected will appear in the color bar of the KFM Configuration dialog box.

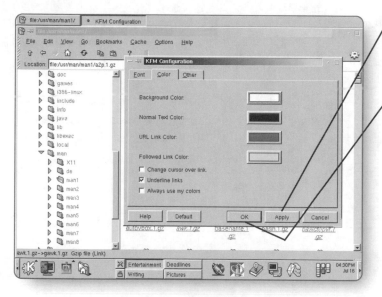

**9.** **Click** on the **Apply** button. The changes you made will be applied.

**10.** **Click** on **OK**. The KFM Configuration dialog box will close.

# 7

# Organizing the Filing System

When you first open the File Manager, the Home directory for your user account is already selected. This is one of the few places on the Linux system where you have permission to store your files. You'll notice that there is just a single directory. To make it easier to store files, you'll want to create a directory structure within your Home directory. After you build a personal filing system, you can begin to move your files around. When you have enough files stored in your user directory, you may need some help trying to find a file. There's a search function to help you do this. A few other tricks can also help you manage your filing system. In this chapter, you'll learn how to:

- Create directories and subdirectories
- Copy and move files and directories
- Search for misplaced files in your Home directory
- Move frequently used files to your desktop
- Use thumbnails to preview files

# Creating Directories

When you create a file in an application, you'll most likely save it to your Home directory. You could place all your files here, but things would get cluttered in due time. To help you keep your filing system organized, you need to create a few directories in which to categorize your work. For example, create a folder for each type of document you create—word processing, spreadsheet, graphics. If you run a small business, set up a separate folder for each client or project.

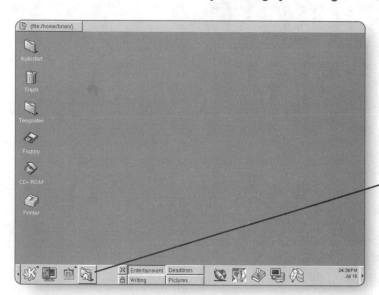

**1.** **Click** on the **Home Directory icon** on the Panel. The /home/*useraccount* directory for your user account will appear in the File Manager window.

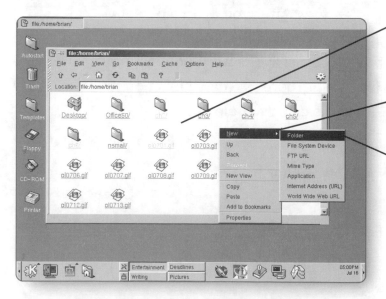

**2.** **Right-click** on an **empty area** of the directory view. A menu will appear.

**3.** **Click** on **New**. A second menu will appear.

**4.** **Click** on **Folder**. The kfm dialog box will open.

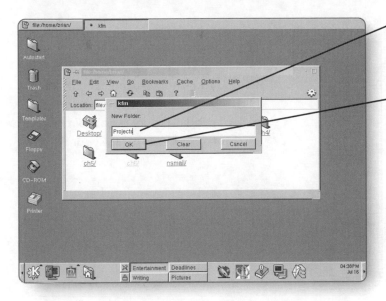

**5. Type** a **name** for the directory in the New Folder text box.

**6. Click** on **OK**. The new directory will appear in the directory view.

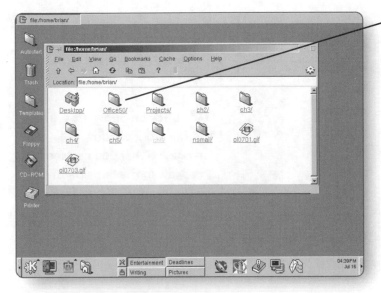

**7. Click** on the **directory** you just created in the directory view. The folder will be added to your user account.

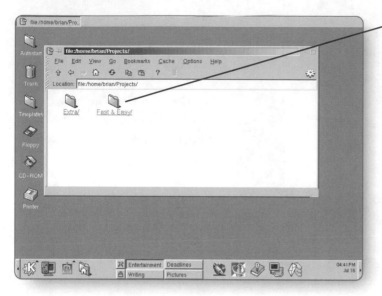

**8. Create** other **directories** that you might need. You can make more directories under your /home/*useraccount* directory, or make subdirectories within directories to further organize your files.

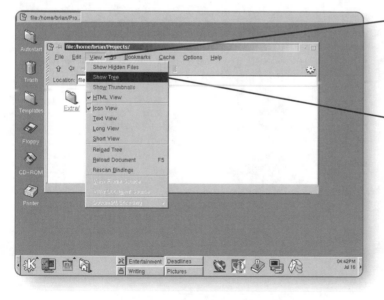

**9.** To make it easier to see your entire directory structure, **click** on **View**. The View menu will appear.

**10. Click** on **Show Tree**. The File Manager window will change, so that you can see the tree view in the left side of the window and the list of files in the right side of the window.

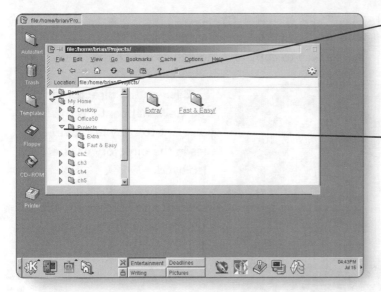

**11. Click** on the **arrow** next to the My Home folder icon. The tree view will expand and you will see the directory structure you just created.

**12. Click** on the **arrow** next to a folder icon in your user account in the /home directory. The tree view will expand and you will see the subdirectories within the selected directory.

## Copying and Moving Files

If you've used any Linux applications and created a file, the default location where the file was saved was your user account in the /home directory. You can copy or move these files into directories that you've created in your user account. This will make it easier to keep your filing system organized. You'll learn how to create files in Chapter 10, "Working with Files."

# Using Drag and Drop

The easiest way to copy and move files is with the mouse.

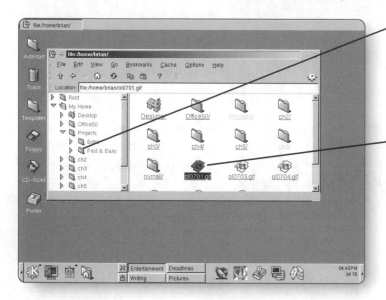

**1. Click** on the **directory** in the tree view that contains the file you want to copy or move. The files in the directory will be displayed.

**2. Click** and **hold** on the **file** that you want to copy. The file will be selected.

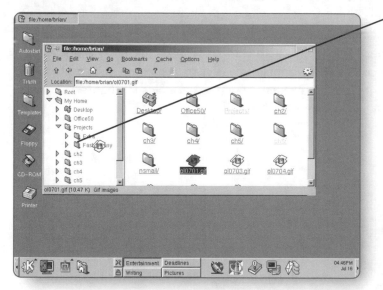

**3. Drag** the **mouse pointer** to the directory where you want to copy the file. The directory will be selected.

**4. Release** the **mouse button**. A menu will appear.

---

### TIP

You can copy or move multiple files. Select all the files that you want to copy or move, and then click and drag one of the files in the group to the destination directory. All of the files will move.

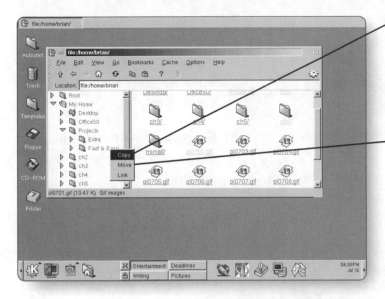

**5a.** **Click** on **Copy** if you want to make a copy of the file to place in the directory. The file will be copied.

**OR**

**5b.** **Click** on **Move** if you want to move the file to the selected directory. The file will be moved from one directory to another directory.

## Using a Right-Click

If you just can't get the hang of drag-and-drop, you can also copy files using a menu.

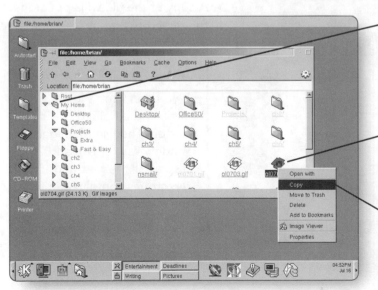

**1.** **Open** the **directory** that contains the file you want to copy. The list of files contained in the directory will appear in the directory view.

**2.** **Right-click** on the **file** that you want to copy. A menu will appear.

**3.** **Click** on **Copy** if you want to make a copy of the file to place in another directory. The file will be copied.

**4. Navigate** to the **directory** in which you want to make a copy of the file. The directory will appear in the tree view and the list of files already contained in the directory will appear in the directory list.

**5. Click** on the **Paste button**. The file will be copied to the directory.

### NOTE

Files can only be copied in this manner. You cannot move files this way.

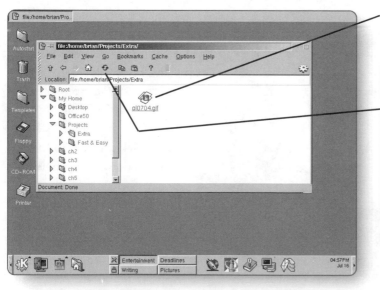

A copy of the file will appear in the directory list.

### NOTE

If you don't see the file, click on the Reload button. The File Manager window will refresh and display all the files and directories contained in the directory.

# Renaming Files

You may need to rename a file or a folder. Maybe you need a file name that is easier to remember. Or, if you copied a file to a new directory, you'll need to rename the file to fit its new purpose. You can easily change the name.

**1. Right-click** on the **file** that you want to rename. A menu will appear.

**2. Click** on **Properties**. The kfm dialog box for the file will open and the General tab should be at the top of the stack.

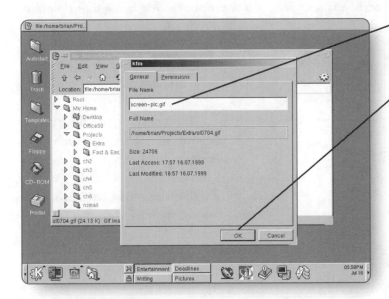

**3. Click** in the **File Name text box** and **type** a new **name** for the file.

**4. Click** on **OK**. The file will be renamed.

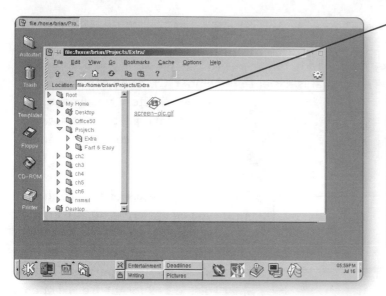

The new file name will appear in the directory view.

**TIP**

You can change a directory name. Display the directory in the directory view, right-click on the directory, and then select Properties from the menu that appears.

# Removing Files and Directories

You may decide to delete some files and directories in your user account in the /home directory. Before you can delete a directory, you'll first need to delete all the files from the directory. Linux gives you two options: you can either delete a file or you can move it to the Trash Bin. Use the Trash Bin and then remember to empty the trash on occasion.

**1. Right-click** on the **file** you want to delete. A menu will appear.

**2. Click** on **Move to Trash**. The file will be moved to the Trash icon on the desktop. Think of the Trash Bin as temporary storage. Place unneeded files in the Trash Bin.

### TIP

If you discover you need the file, you can look through the Trash Bin and retrieve it. Right-click on the Trash Bin icon and select the Open command. This opens a File Manager window from which you can copy files back into your filing system.

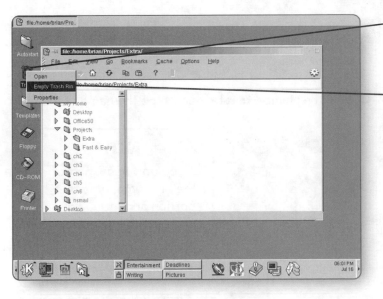

**3. Right-click** on the **Trash icon** on the desktop. A menu will appear.

**4. Click** on **Empty Trash Bin**. The files and directories in the Trash Bin will be permanently deleted.

# Finding Files

After moving and copying files in your filing system, you may have some trouble trying to find a specific file. There's no need to go looking through each of the directories. The File Manager can perform this search for you.

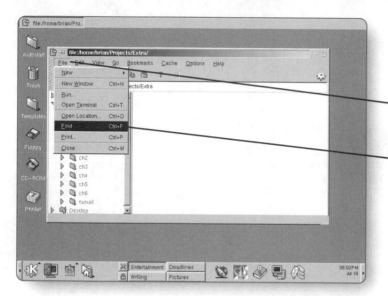

**1. Click** on **File**. The File menu will appear.

**2. Click** on **Find**. The kfind dialog box will open.

**3. Click** in the **Named text box** and **type** the **name** of the file.

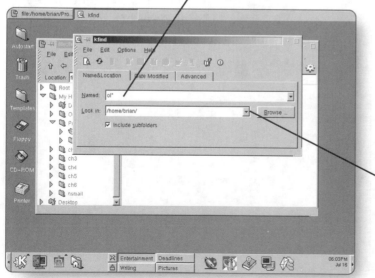

## NOTE

If you only know part of the file name, type that portion and include a wildcard character, such as an asterisk (*).

**4. Click** on the **down arrow** next to the Look in list box, and **click** on the **directory** where you want to begin the search. The directory will appear in the list box.

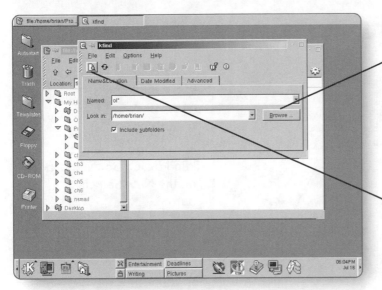

**TIP**

If you don't see the directory in the list, click on the Browse button and select the directory from the dialog box that appears.

**5. Click** on the **Start Search button**. The kfind dialog box will expand and display the directory in which the file can be found or the directories where closely matching files can be found.

**6. Click** on the **directory** that contains the file you want. The directory will be selected.

**7. Click** on the **Open Containing Folder button**. The selected directory will open in a new File Manager window.

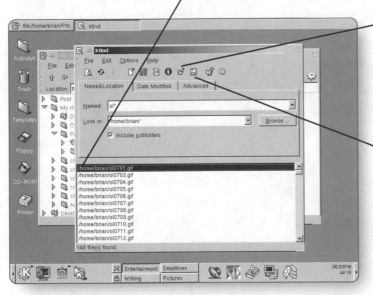

**TIP**

If you think you may need these search results in the future, click on the Save Search Results button.

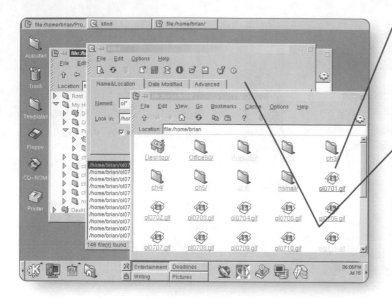

You'll see the file you were searching for in the directory view.

**NOTE**

If this is not the file you wanted, go back to the kfind dialog box and click on the New Search button.

# Placing Files and Folders on the Desktop

If you have a file that you use frequently and want to have it at your fingertips, move it onto your desktop. You can also move entire directories onto the desktop using this same drag-and-drop method. Once a file or folder is on the desktop, all you need to do is click on the desktop icon to open it.

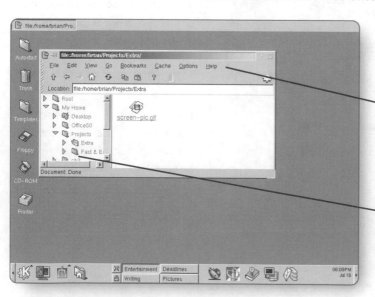

**1. Resize** the **File Manager window**, so that the desktop area can be seen behind the window. The File Manager window will be resized.

**2. Open** the **directory** that contains the file or folder that you want to place on your desktop. The file or folder will appear in the directory list.

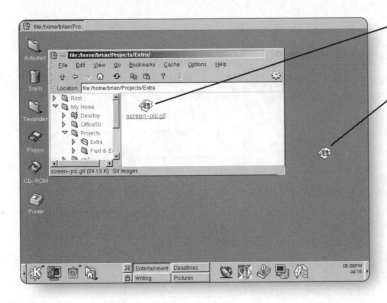

**3.** **Click** and **hold** the **mouse pointer** on the file or folder. The file or folder will be selected.

**4.** **Drag** the **file or folder** to an empty area on the desktop.

**5.** **Release** the **mouse button**. A menu will appear.

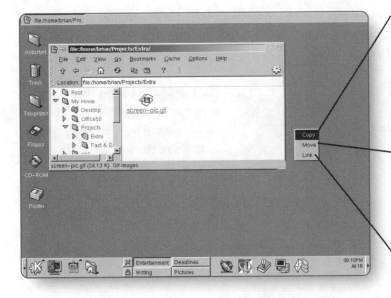

**6a.** **Click** on **Copy**. A copy of the file will be placed on the desktop, and the original file can still be found in the File Manager.

**OR**

**6b.** **Click** on **Move**. The file will be moved from the File Manager and onto the desktop.

**OR**

**6c.** **Click** on **Link**. A link will be created on the desktop pointing to the file in the File Manager.

**TIP**

To move the icon to a different place on your desktop, click and drag the icon to the new position.

# Working with Thumbnails

If you'd like to see a preview of the file contained in a directory, just ask the File Manager to show you a miniature picture of the file.

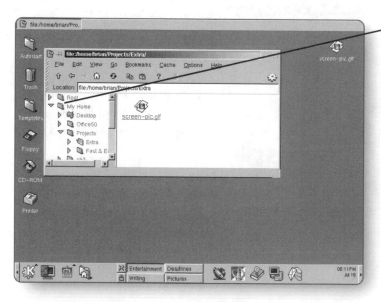

**1. Navigate** to the **directory** that contains the file you want to preview. The file will appear in the directory list.

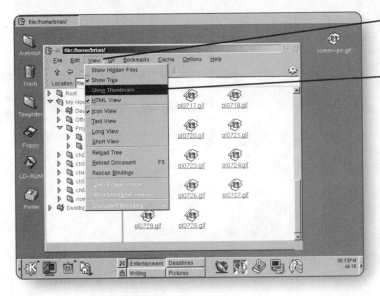

**2. Click** on **View**. The View menu will appear.

**3. Click** on **Show Thumbnails**. The directory list will change.

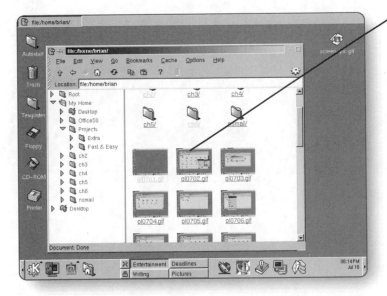

Thumbnails will only appear for those files that are in a format recognized by the File Manager.

**NOTE**

To turn off the thumbnails, open the View menu and click on Show Thumbnails.

# 8

# Managing Disk Drives

Floppy disks and CD-ROMs are common media used to store information. If you come from a Microsoft Windows or Apple Macintosh background, you'll need to change the way you use the devices that process the information on these storage media. Before you can use a disk drive in Linux, you'll need to mount the drive. Linux needs to be informed of this new file system that you are introducing into the system. Then, before you can remove the floppy or CD, you need to unmount the drive so that Linux can release the file system to your control. In this chapter, you'll learn how to:

- Mount floppy drives to be used by Linux
- Copy files onto a floppy disk
- Format floppy disks
- Access your CD-ROM drive

# Working with Floppy Disk Drives

It is very important that you mount a floppy drive after you put the disk into the drive. You also need to remember to unmount the drive before you take the floppy disk out of the drive. If you don't do this, Linux will not be able to read the contents of the next floppy that you put into the drive. But before you can work with a floppy disk drive, you'll need to let Linux know that your system has a floppy drive.

## Letting Kandalf Create a Floppy Drive

The easiest way to get your floppy disk drive working is to let the KDE Configuration Wizard do it for you. Kandalf knows all the magic tricks that can get your system up and running with a wave of his wand.

**1. Click** on the **Application Starter**. The main menu will appear.

**2. Move** the **mouse pointer** to **Utilities**. The Utilities menu will appear.

**3. Click** on **KDE Configuration Wizard**. The KDE Setup Wizard window will open.

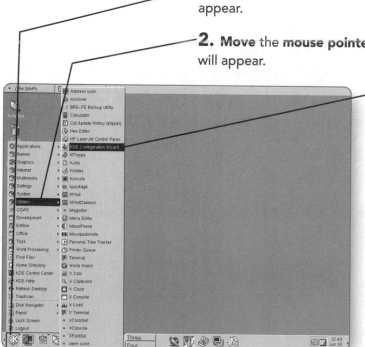

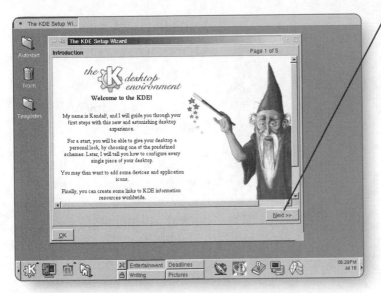

**4. Click** on the **Next button** until you come to the Drive configuration screen. The Drive configuration screen will appear.

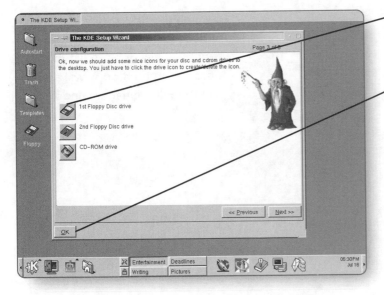

**5. Click** on the **1st Floppy Disk drive icon**. A floppy drive icon will appear on your desktop.

**6. Click** on the **OK button**. The KDE Setup Wizard will close.

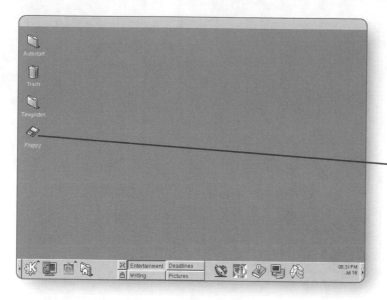

# Mounting and Unmounting the Floppy

**1. Place** the **floppy disk** in the floppy disk drive.

**2. Click** on the **floppy disk icon** on your desktop. The floppy will be recognized by the system and mounted.

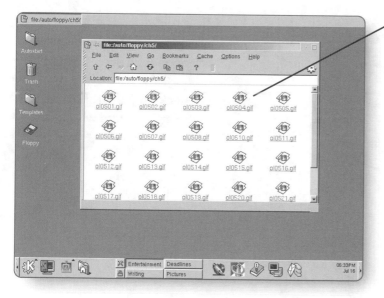

When the floppy disk is mounted, the File Manager window will open. A list of files stored on the floppy will appear in the File Manager window.

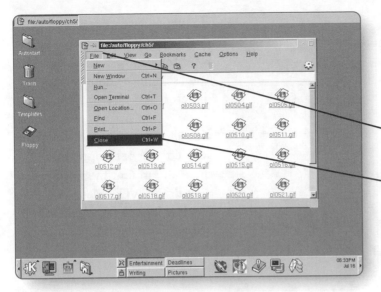

When you are finished working with the floppy disk, you'll need to unmount the drive before you can take the disk out of the drive.

**3. Click** on **File**. The File menu will appear.

**4. Click** on **Close**. The File Manager window will close and the drive will be unmounted.

## Copying Files to a Floppy Disk

You can easily copy files from the File Manager onto a floppy disk. Mount the drive, and practice those drag-and-drop dance steps.

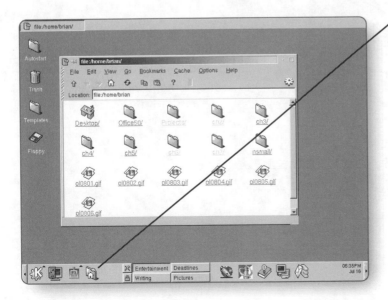

**1. Click** on the **Home directory icon** on the Panel. The File Manager will open, and the contents of your user account in the /home directory will be displayed.

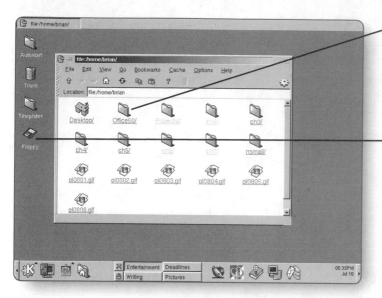

**2. Navigate** to the **directory** that contains the files that you want to copy to the floppy disk. The list of files contained in the directory will be displayed.

**3. Place** the **floppy disk** into your computer's floppy disk drive and **mount** the **floppy disk drive**. A File Manager window for the floppy drive will open. This tells you that the floppy drive is mounted.

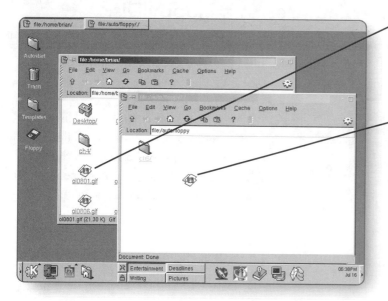

**4. Click and hold** on the **file** that you want to copy to the floppy disk. The file will be selected.

**5. Drag** the **file** until it is over the floppy drive File Manager window, and then release the file. A menu will appear.

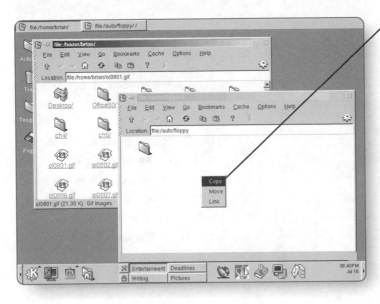

**6. Click** on **Copy**. The file will be copied to the floppy disk.

**7.** When you are ready to remove the floppy disk from the drive, **unmount** the **floppy drive**. The File Manager window will close, indicating that the floppy drive is unmounted.

**8. Remove** the **floppy disk** from the floppy disk drive.

---

> ### NOTE
>
> You can also copy files from the floppy disk into the Linux file system.

## Formatting a Floppy Disk

Not only do disks need to be mounted before Linux can read them, but they also need to be formatted. Linux can format a floppy in one of two file systems. If you'll be using floppy disks between Linux and DOS computers, format using the DOS file system. If the floppies will only be used on Linux machines, format using the ext2 file system.

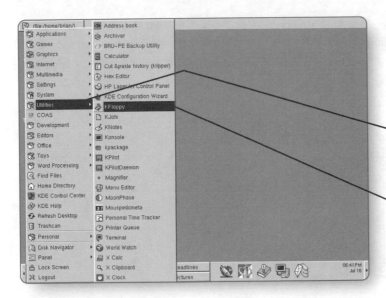

**1. Click** on the **Application Starter**. The main menu will appear.

**2. Move** the **mouse pointer** to Utilities. The Utilities menu will appear.

**3. Click** on **KFloppy**. The KDE Floppy Formatter dialog box will open.

**CAUTION**

You cannot format a mounted drive.

**4. Place** the **floppy disk** that you want to format into the floppy disk drive.

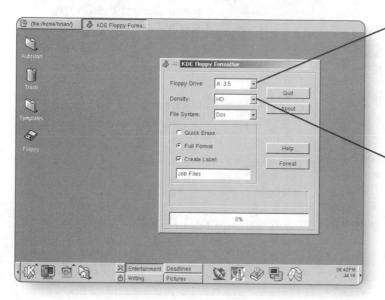

**5. Click** on the **down arrow** next to the Floppy Drive list box, and **click** on the **drive and floppy disk size** that you want to format. The option will appear in the list box.

**6. Click** on the **down arrow** next to the Density list box, and **click** on the **density** of the floppy disk. The option will appear in the list box.

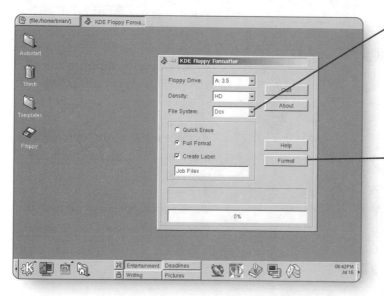

**7. Click** on the **down arrow** next to the File System list box, and **click** on the type of **file system** you want to use on the floppy disk. The option will appear in the list box.

**8. Click** on the **Format button**. The format process will begin.

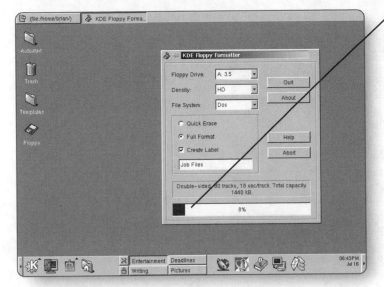

The status bar at the bottom of the dialog box will display information about the disk being formatted.

When the disk is formatted, Linux will begin verifying the disk. When the process is complete, a confirmation dialog box will open.

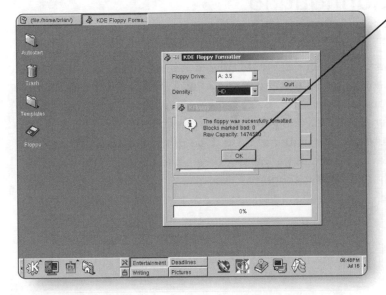

**9. Click** on **OK**. You will be returned to the KDE Floppy Formatter dialog box.

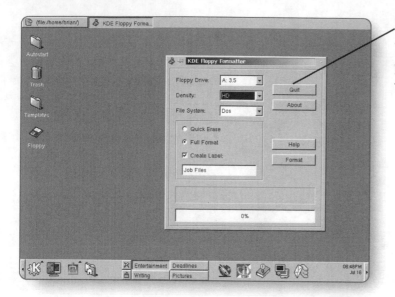

**10. Click** on the **Quit button**. The dialog box will close, and you will be able to use the newly formatted floppy disk.

# Configuring the CD-ROM Drive

Setting up your CD-ROM drive can be a simple task if you ask Kandalf for help. Kandalf knows all the tricks of the trade, but you can learn a few of its secrets. The secrets are stored in the Templates icon on your desktop. Templates help you automate a number of tasks. One of them is to set up devices, such as floppy disk drives and CD-ROM drives, so that Linux will recognize them.

## Creating the CD-ROM Desktop Icon

Before you can work with CDs, you need to tell Linux that you will be using the CD-ROM drive. Use the Device template to automate this task.

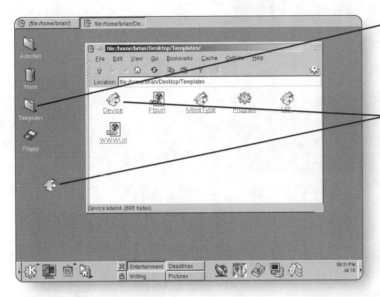

**1. Click** on the **Templates icon** on your desktop. The templates directory of your user account in the File Manager will appear.

**2. Click and hold** on the **Device icon**, and **drag** the **icon** to the desktop. An outline of the icon will be attached to the mouse pointer.

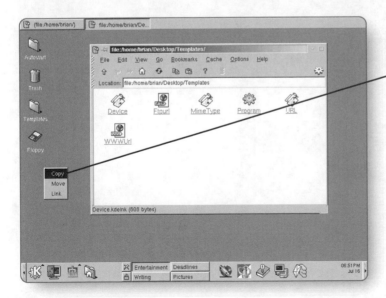

**3. Drop** the **icon** on the desktop. A menu will appear.

**4. Click** on **Copy**. A device icon will appear on the desktop.

### NOTE

You can close the File Manager window if you want. Or, if you want to learn more about templates, open the Help menu and click on Contents. This takes you to the KFM Handbook.

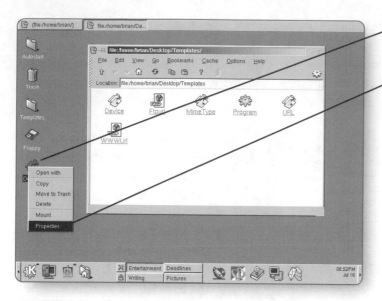

**5. Right-click** on the **device icon**. A menu will appear.

**6. Click** on **Properties**. The kfm dialog box will open.

**7. Clear** the **text** in the File Name text box, and **type cdrom.kdelnk**.

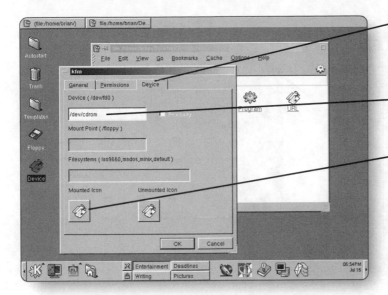

**8. Click** on the **Device tab**. The Device tab will come to the top of the stack.

**9. Click** in the **Device text box,** and **type /dev/cdrom**.

**10. Click** on the **Mounted Icon button**. The Select Icon dialog box will open.

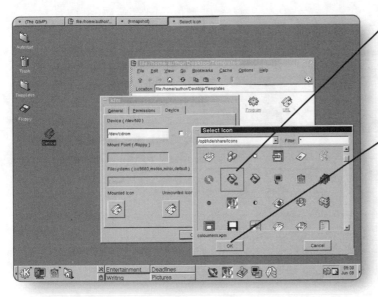

**11. Click** on a **CD-ROM icon** that has a green light next to it. The name of the icon is cdrom_mount.xpm. The icon will be selected.

**12. Click** on **OK**. You will be returned to the kfm dialog box.

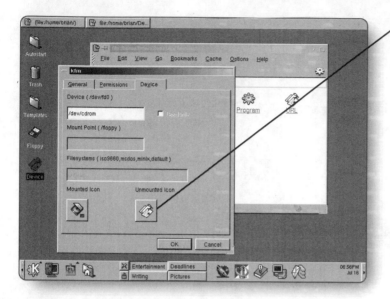

**13. Click** on the **Unmounted Icon button**. The Select Icon dialog box will open.

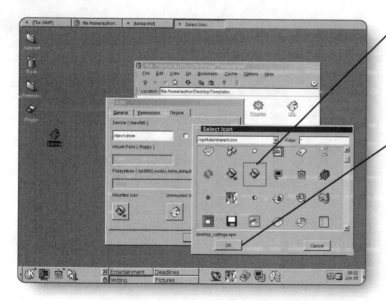

**14. Click** on a **CD-ROM icon** that does not have the green light. The name of the icon is cdrom_unmount.xpm. The icon will be selected.

**15. Click** on **OK**. You will be returned to the kfm dialog box.

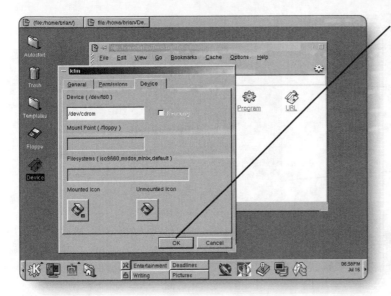

**16. Click** on **OK**. The CD-ROM icon will appear on your desktop.

## Mounting the CD

The drive icons that Kandalf creates are easy to mount and unmount. You just click on the icon. The drive icons that you create using the device template give you a visual clue as to whether or not the floppy drive or CD-ROM drive are mounted.

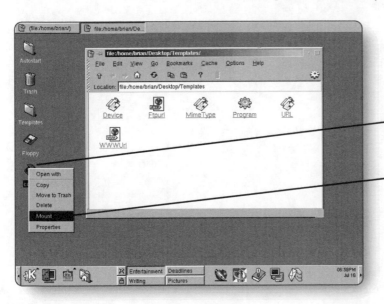

**1. Place** the **CD** in your computer's CD-ROM drive.

**2. Right-click** on the **CD-ROM icon**. A menu will appear.

**3. Click** on **Mount**. The CD will be mounted.

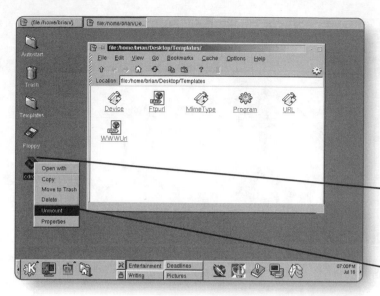

## TIP

If you want to view the contents of the CD, open the File Manager and navigate to the /mnt/cdrom directory.

**4.** Before you remove the CD, **right-click** on the **CD-ROM icon**. A menu will appear.

**5.** **Click** on **Unmount**. The CD-ROM drive will be unmounted and you can safely take the CD out of the drive.

# 9

# Maintaining Your OpenLinux

Whenever you upgrade hardware on your computer or install certain types of software, you need to know information about your computer system. OpenLinux has a handy little place for you to find all the information you may need. Another part of keeping your computer maintained is to keep the clock current. Chances are you may never have to do this, but if you move, your time zone won't move with you. And, when it's time to back up all those files stored on your hard drive, you'll want to compress them and place them in an archive that you can store until you need the files in the archive. In this chapter, you'll learn how to:

- Find information about your computer system
- Change the time on your computer clock
- Archive your files

# Finding System Information

If you need information about the devices running on your computer, there's an easy way to find it. You can find out lots of information about your computer, the CPU, the OpenLinux distribution you're running, and which kernel version you have installed on your system.

**1.** **Click** on the **KDE Control Center button** on the Panel. The KDE Control Center will open.

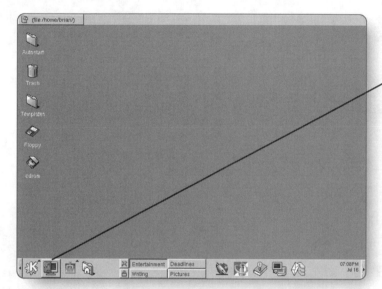

**2.** **Click** on the **plus sign** beside Information. The menu will expand.

**3.** **Click** on **Devices**. The System Information Devices panel will open and display your computer system's device information.

System devices are divided into three categories:

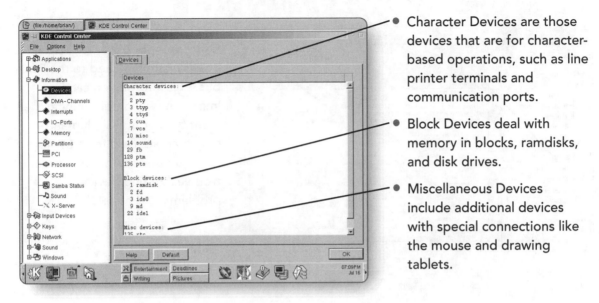

- Character Devices are those devices that are for character-based operations, such as line printer terminals and communication ports.

- Block Devices deal with memory in blocks, ramdisks, and disk drives.

- Miscellaneous Devices include additional devices with special connections like the mouse and drawing tablets.

**4. Click** on **X Server**. The System Information X-Server panel will open.

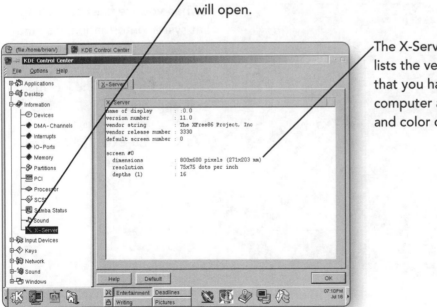

The X-Server information panel lists the version of X Windows that you have installed on your computer and the resolution and color depth of the display.

**5. Click** on the **PCI icon**. The PCI-Bus information will display.

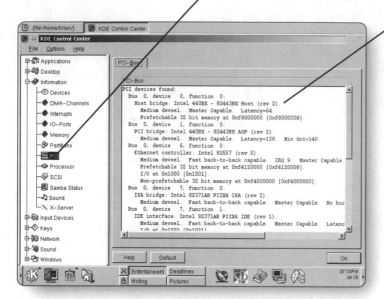

The information in the right panel describes the devices on your system attached to the PCI bus. This information can be important when determining the identity of your PCI plug-and-play graphics card for X Server configuration information or for troubleshooting device problems.

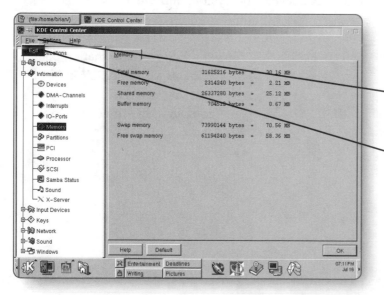

When you are finished looking at system information, it's time to close the Control Center.

**6. Click** on **File**. The File menu will appear.

**7. Click** on **Exit**. The Control Center will close.

# Resetting the Clock

If you are taking OpenLinux on a laptop on a trip or perhaps on the computer you are taking back to school after summer break, you might need to reset the clock to a new time or time zone. KDE has a simple way to access the settings for the system clock.

## Changing the Time

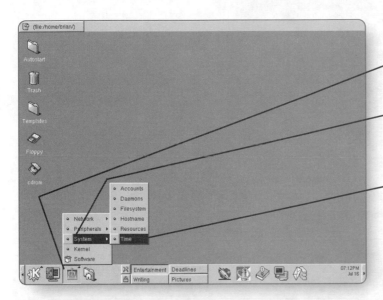

**1. Click** on the **COAS button**. The COAS menu will appear.

**2. Move** the **mouse pointer** to System. The System menu will appear.

**3. Click** on **Time**. If you are logged in as root, the Welcome to COAS panel will appear. If you are not logged in as root, the COAS su wrapper will appear and ask you for the root password.

### NOTE

If you do not have root privileges, you won't be able to change the clock settings.

**4. Type** the root **password**. The password will appear in the text box as asterisks(*).

**5. Click** on **OK**. The Welcome to COAS dialog box will open.

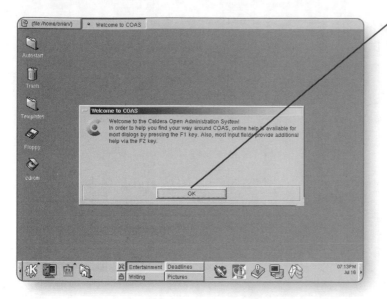

**6. Click** on **OK**. The System Time dialog box will open.

You'll notice three different things about the System Time dialog box:

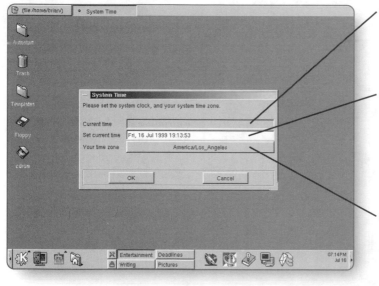

- The Current time shows the currently set system time as grayed out; you cannot change this information.

- The Set current time is where you can type in changes to the system time. You may only need to update the clock a few minutes to catch up to real time.

- The Your time zone shows the time zone which is set, which should be the zone in which you live.

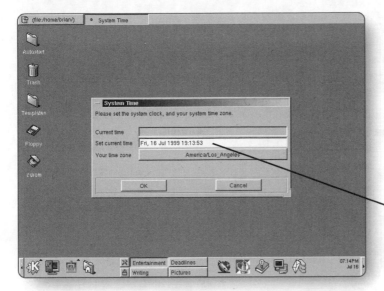

If you need to change the time display on the Panel, follow these steps.

**7. Click and drag** the **mouse pointer** over the information that you want to change. The time information will be highlighted.

**8. Type** the correct **information** for the day, date, and hour. The new time will appear.

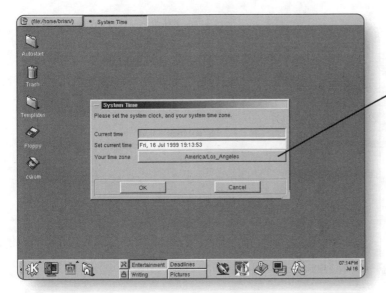

If the time zone shown on the Your time zone button does not match yours, follow these steps.

**9. Click** on the **Your time zone button**. The Continent dialog box will open.

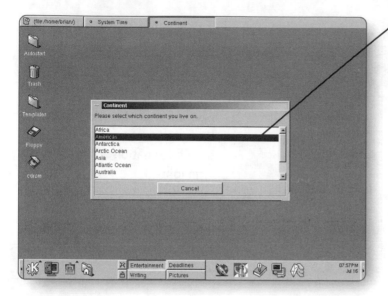

**10.** **Click** on the **name of the continent** on which you live. The continent name will be selected and the Country dialog box will open.

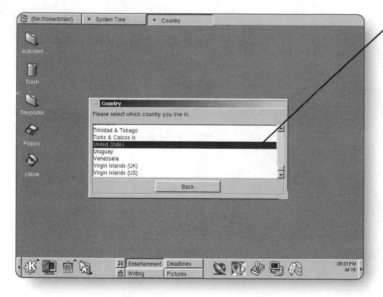

**11.** **Click** on the **country** in which you live. The Region dialog box will open.

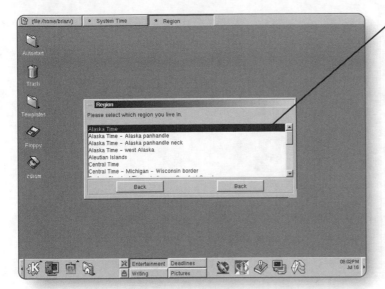

**12. Click** on the **region** of the selected country in which you live. The region will be selected and you'll be returned to the System Time dialog box.

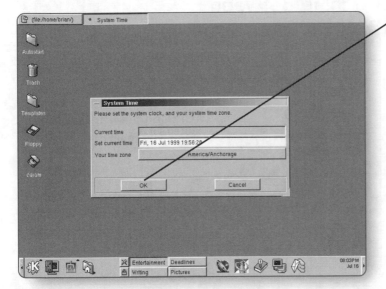

**13. Click** on **OK** to accept the changes. The Commit dialog box will open.

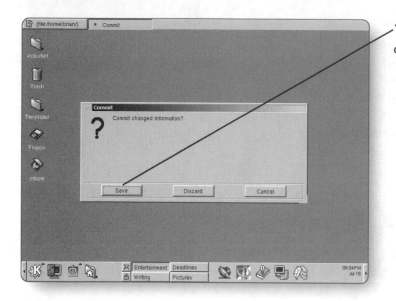

**14.** Click on **Save**. Your changes will be made.

## Switching Between 12 and 24 Hour Time

If the time is shown in 24-hour military time, and you really prefer the AM/PM version, there's a quick fix.

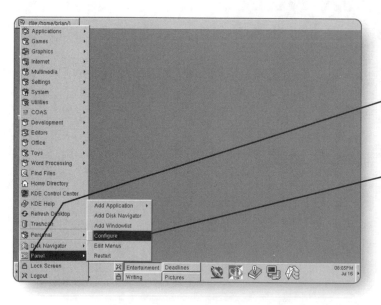

**1.** Click on the **Application Starter**. The main menu will appear.

**2.** Move the **mouse pointer** to **Panel**. The Panel menu will appear.

**3.** Click on **Configure**. The KPanel Configuration dialog box will open.

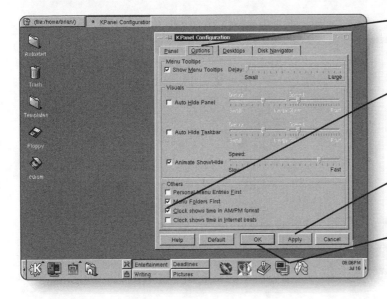

**4. Click** on the **Options tab**. The Options tab will come to the top of the stack.

**5. Click** in the **Clock shows time in AM/PM format check box**. A check will appear in the box.

**6. Click** on **Apply**. The change will be made to the clock.

**7. Click** on **OK**. The KPanel Configuration dialog box will close.

# Archiving Your Files

The Caldera OpenLinux installation on your machine includes an archive utility called Archiver. You can use this utility to store files that you are not currently using. You can also use Archiver to save some space on your hard drive.

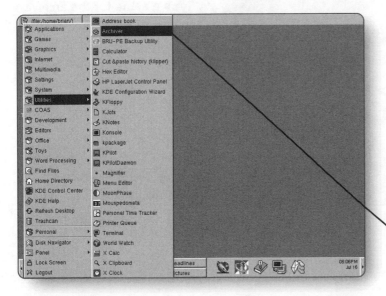

## Creating the Archive File

**1. Click** on the **Application Starter**. The main menu will appear.

**2. Move** the **mouse pointer** to **Utilities**. The Utilities menu will appear.

**3. Click** on the **Archiver**. The Archiver window will open.

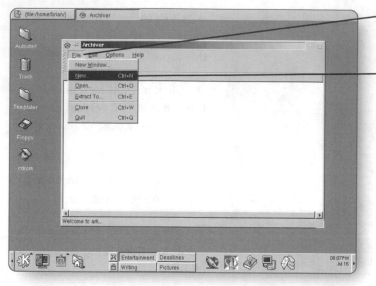

**4. Click** on **File**. The File menu will appear.

**5. Click** on **New**. The Save As dialog box will open.

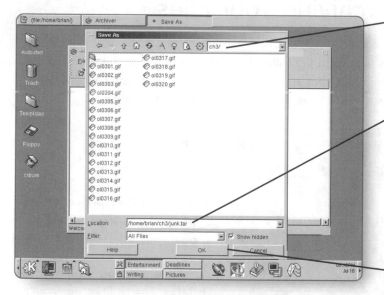

**6. Navigate** to the **directory** in which you want to store the archive. The list of files contained in the directory will appear.

**7. Type** a **name** for the archive in the Location text box. Be sure to add an extension to specify the type of compression. Linux uses GNU Tar, which are .tar files (also called tar balls). You can also use .zip files.

**8. Click** on **OK**. The archive will be created and the Archiver window will be displayed. You can now begin moving the files to be archived.

**9. Open** the **File Manager** and **navigate** to the **directory** where the files you want to archive are stored. The files in the directory will appear in the directory list.

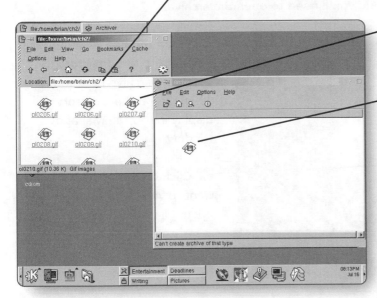

**10. Click and drag** on a **file** in the File Manager window. The file will be selected.

**11. Drag** the **file** to the Archiver window and release the mouse button. The file will be added to the archive.

### TIP

You can also drag multiple files. Just select the files first.

When you have placed all of the files in the archive, you can close the archive.

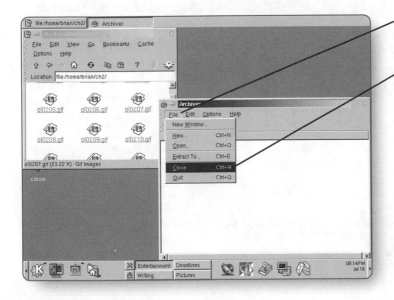

**12. Click** on **File**. The File menu will appear.

**13. Click** on **Close**. The Archiver will close.

### TIP

Not only can you archive your files this way, but it also compresses the files so that the archive can be copied to a floppy disk, a tape backup, or e-mailed to friends and colleagues.

# Opening an Archive

When you have files in an archive with which you want to work, you'll need to open the archive.

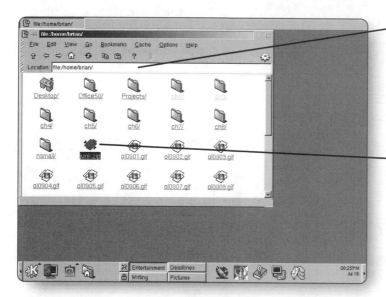

**1. Open** the **File Manager** and **navigate** to the **directory** in which the archive is stored. The list of files in the directory will display in the File Manager window.

**2. Click** on the **archive** that you want to view. The Archiver will open.

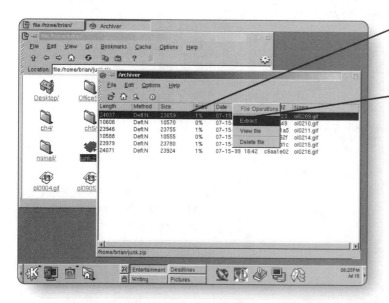

**3. Right-click** on the **file** that you want to remove from the archive. A menu will appear.

**4. Click** on **Extract**. The Extract dialog box will open.

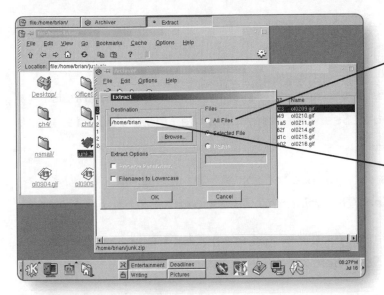

**TIP**

You can extract all of the files in the archive by clicking on the All Files option button.

**5. Click** in the **Destination text box** and **type** the **directory** in which you want to place the extracted file.

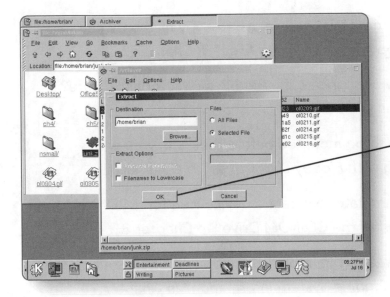

**NOTE**

You can also use the Browse button to find the directory you need.

**6. Click** on **OK**. The file will be copied to the selected directory. Open the File Manager to find it.

# Part II Review Questions

1. Which two directories in the Linux file system contain user manuals or help documentation? *See "Understanding the Linux File System" in Chapter 6*

2. What different views can you use to look at files in the File Manager window? *See "Browsing the File System" in Chapter 6*

3. How do you select a group of files that are not located next to each other in the file list? *See "Selecting Files" in Chapter 6*

4. Under which directory do you create your user account files? *See "Creating Directories" in Chapter 7*

5. Name two different methods you can use to copy files between directories. *See "Copying and Moving Files" in Chapter 7*

6. What is the easiest way to locate files within a directory structure? *See "Finding Files" in Chapter 7*

7. Why do drives need to be mounted before they will work with Linux? *See "Working with Floppy Disk Drives" in Chapter 8*

8. How do you use a template to create a device icon for a CD-ROM drive? *See "Configuring the CD-ROM Drive" in Chapter 8*

9. Which Panel icon contains the information about your computer's configuration? *See "Finding System Information" in Chapter 9*

10. What different compression formats can Linux use to compress and archive files? *See "Archiving Your Files" in Chapter 9*

# PART III

# Making OpenLinux Work for You

# 10

# Working with Files

Earlier in this book, you were introduced to the Linux file system. You also learned how to create directories in which to store files. Now it's time to use an application to see how the Linux applications interact with the file system. All applications create files and save files to the computer's hard drive. Try your hand at some of the applications that were installed with OpenLinux, and create a file or two to store in those directories you created. In this chapter, you'll learn how to:

- Open KlyX and create a new file
- Select and edit text
- Save a file
- Close and reopen a file

# Creating a New File

Your first step is to open an OpenLinux application and create a new file. Some applications will open with a blank page, whereas other applications make you create your own blank page. You'll learn how to use the KLyX application to perform basic file tasks in OpenLinux. KLyX is much more than a word processor. It is the WYSIWYG (What You See Is What You Get) interface for the TeX typesetting language. You can use KLyX to create complex documents or simple letterheads.

**1. Click** on the **Application Starter**. The main menu will appear.

**2. Move** the **mouse pointer** to **Applications**. The Applications menu will appear.

**3. Click** on **KLyx**. The KLyX word processor will open.

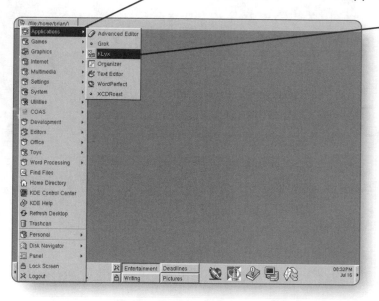

Some OpenLinux applications do not display a blank page. If this is the case, you'll need to open a new document.

**4. Click** on **File**. The File menu will appear.

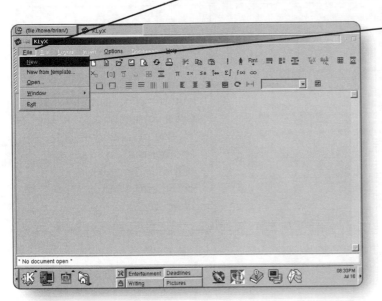

**5. Click** on **New**. The Save As dialog box will open, and the cursor will be at the end of the directory path in the Location text box.

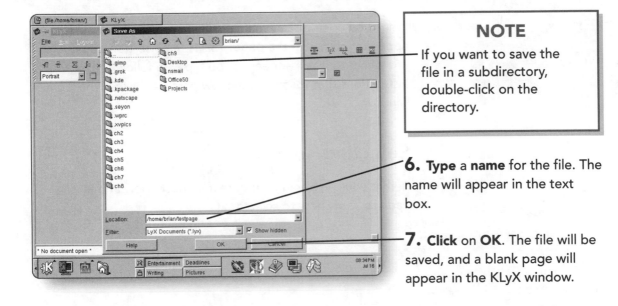

**NOTE**

If you want to save the file in a subdirectory, double-click on the directory.

**6. Type** a **name** for the file. The name will appear in the text box.

**7. Click** on **OK**. The file will be saved, and a blank page will appear in the KLyX window.

You'll notice that the file name appears in the title bar. You'll also find information about the file in the status bar at the bottom of the window.

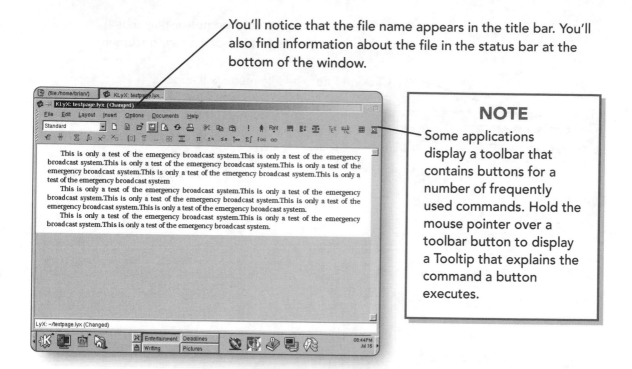

## Working with Text

When you open a blank page, notice a vertical bar in the upper-left corner of the page. This is the insertion point, and it is where text will appear as you type. To follow the instructions that follow, type a few paragraphs into the KLyX window.

## Selecting Text

Before you can begin editing text in most applications, you need to know how to select text.

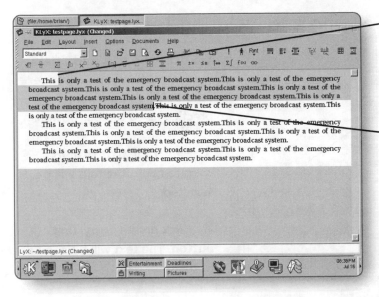

**1. Click** and **hold** the **mouse pointer** at the place where you want to begin the selection. The insertion bar will appear in the selected position.

**2. Drag** the **mouse** to the **end** of the selection. The selected text will be highlighted.

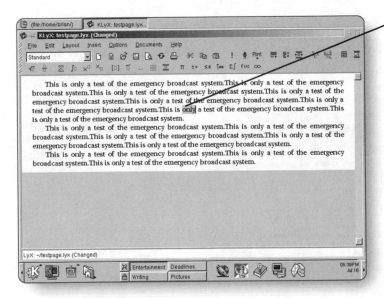

**3. Double-click** on a **word**. The word will be selected.

# Copying and Deleting Text

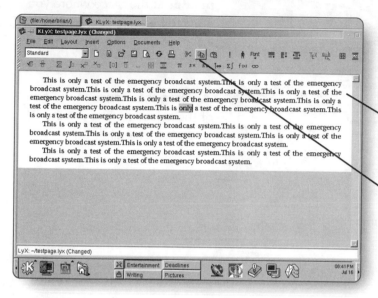

You'll use the copy and delete functions when you rearrange text. You'll also get some practice using toolbar buttons.

**1.** **Select** the **text** that you want to copy. The text will be selected.

**2.** **Click** on the **Copy Text button**. The text will be copied to the Clipboard.

**3.** **Click** on the **place** where you want to place a copy of the text. The insertion bar will appear in the selected position.

**4.** **Click** on the **Paste Text button**. The text will be copied to the new position.

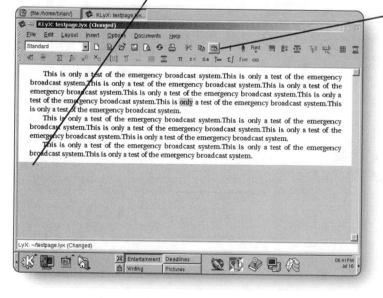

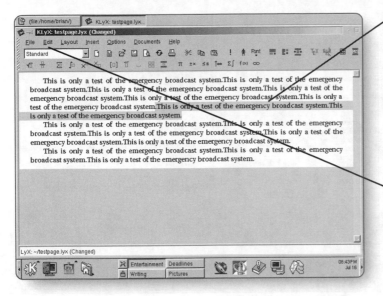

**5. Select** the **text** that you want to delete. The text will be selected.

**6. Press** the **Delete key**. The text will be deleted.

### TIP

If you made a mistake and want to reverse the last action you performed, open the Edit menu and click on the Undo command. You can undo more than one action.

# Saving a File

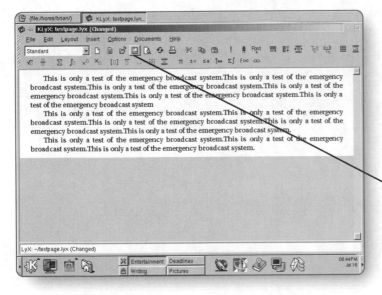

The importance of saving your work can never be emphasized enough. Anyone who uses a computer has lost valuable work at one time or another. Save your work regularly; it only takes a few mouse clicks to save hours of work.

**1. Click** on the **Save button**. Any changes you made to the file since you opened it will be saved.

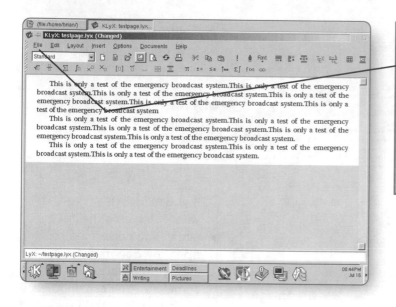

**TIP**

If you want to have another copy of a document, open the File menu and select Save As. You can then save the document using a different file name.

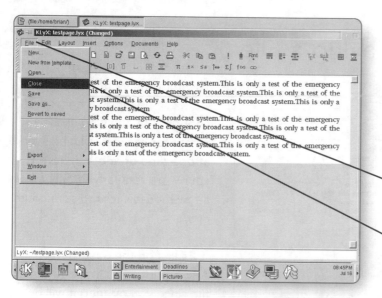

# Closing a File

When you are finished working with a document, you can close the file. It's easy to close the file but still leave your application open.

**1. Click** on **File**. The File menu will appear.

**2. Click** on **Close**. The file will close and the KLyX window will stay open.

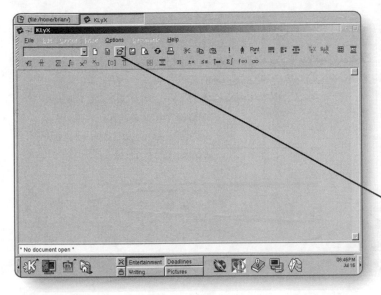

# Opening an Existing File

You can open any document that you've saved. You'll need to go back to the file system and remember where you put the file.

**1. Click** on the **Open button**. The Open dialog box will open.

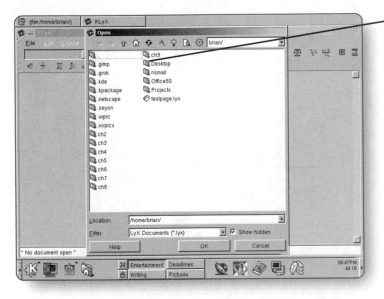

**2. Double-click** on the **directory** where the file is located. The list of files contained in that directory will appear.

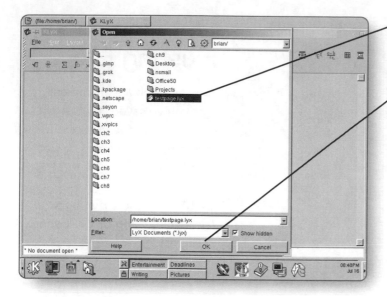

**3. Click** on the **file** that you want to open. The file will be selected.

**4. Click** on **OK**. The file will appear in the application window and you can resume working on the file.

# 11

# Drawing with The GIMP

The GIMP, or GNU Image Manipulation Program, is a sophisticated graphics program that can be used to color correct scanned photographs, draw pictures, combine and crop images to make a single image, and undertake other artistic ventures. The GIMP contains a toolbox where you can select the tools and operations you want performed. The GIMP also contains a drawing canvas window where you can create and edit images. Drawings created or edited in The GIMP can be saved in many formats for use in other applications or operating systems. In this chapter, you'll learn how to:

- Start a new drawing in The GIMP
- Draw basic shapes
- Add text to a picture
- Save a drawing to use later

# Getting Started with The GIMP

If you installed OpenLinux using the recommended packages option, The GIMP is one of the graphics applications that you installed. The GIMP is a very powerful program that can handle any graphics task you may toss its way. You'll find all sorts of fun art tools in The GIMP toolbox, so take a break and play for a while.

## Opening The GIMP

The first time you use The GIMP, you'll need to set up some directories that the program needs to operate. You don't need to do much more than give The GIMP setup routine the okay to do so. When this is done, The GIMP will start and you can begin exploring all the tools in the toolbox.

**1.** **Click** on the **Application Starter**. The main menu will appear.

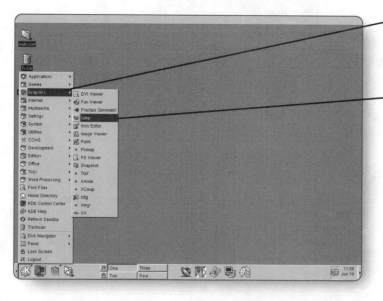

**2.** **Move** the **mouse pointer** to Graphics. The Graphics menu will appear.

**3.** **Click** on **Gimp**. The GIMP Installation dialog box will open.

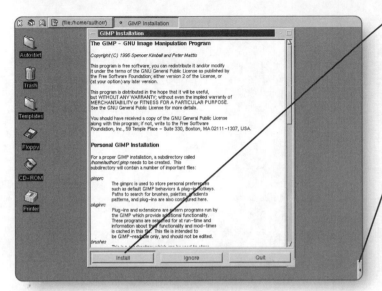

**4. Click** on the **Install button**. The Installation Log dialog box will open.

### TIP

If you need more screen space, zip up the Panel with a click. Click on it a second time, and it will reappear.

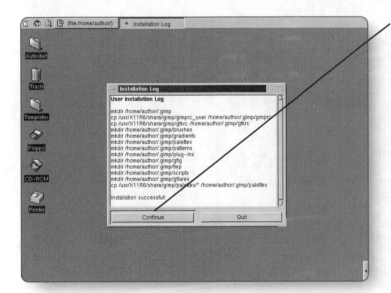

**5. Click** on the **Continue button**. The GIMP Startup screen will appear.

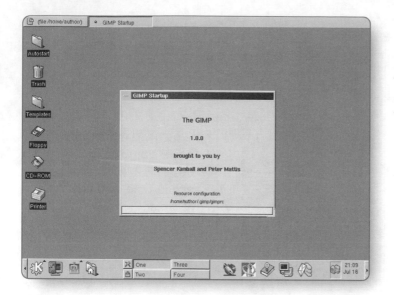

You'll see the program loading and all of the plug-ins being installed. When the startup is finished, The GIMP toolbox will appear onscreen, along with a Tip of the Day dialog box.

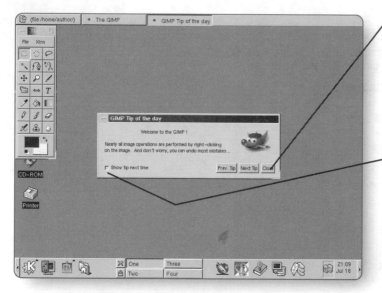

**6.** **Click** on the **Close button** on The GIMP Tip of the day dialog box. The dialog box will close.

### NOTE

If you don't want to read the tips of the day, click on the Show tip next time button. You can also read more tips by clicking on the Prev. Tip and Next Tip buttons.

## Creating a New Canvas

It's time to open a workspace on your screen to begin your work of art. Before you begin, you'll need to decide on the canvas size on which to create your artwork, whether you want to work in grayscale (shades of black and white) or in color, and the background color or lack of color.

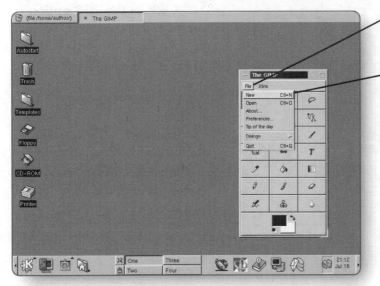

**1. Click** on **File**. The File menu will appear.

**2. Click** on **New**. The New Image dialog box will open.

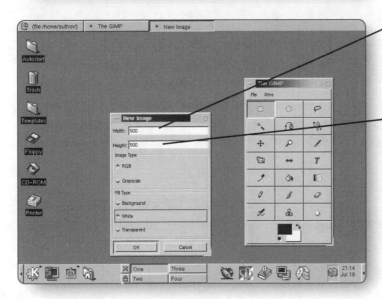

**3. Double-click** in the **Width text box**, and **type** the **number** of pixels wide you want the new picture.

**4. Double-click** in the **Height text box**, and **type** the **number** of pixels high you want the new picture.

> ### NOTE
> A pixel is the smallest sized dot that can be displayed on a monitor. Your monitor's dot pitch determines the pixel size.

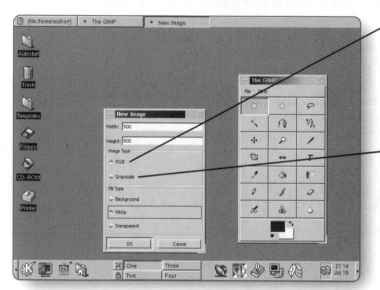

**5a.** **Click** on the **RGB option button** if you want to work in color. The option will be selected.

**OR**

**5b.** **Click** on the **Grayscale option button** if you want to work in shades of black and white. The option will be selected.

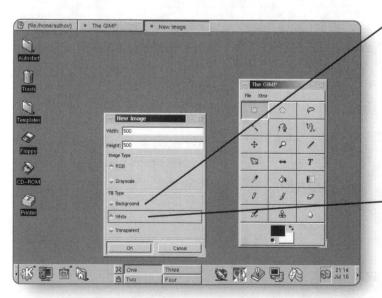

**6a.** **Click** on the **Background option button** if you want to use a specific color as the background for your image. You can select the color from the color selector in the toolbox. The option will be selected.

**OR**

**6b.** **Click** on the **White option button** if you want a white background for your picture. The option will be selected.

**OR**

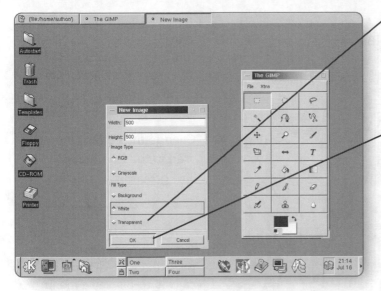

**6c. Click** on the **Transparent option button** if you do not want any background to appear behind your picture. The option will be selected.

**7. Click** on **OK**. The paint window will appear with a blank canvas on which to begin your work.

## Getting Familiar with The GIMP Toolbox

The GIMP toolbox is where you will find all of the painting, selection, and transformation tools. You can customize each tool by double-clicking on it.

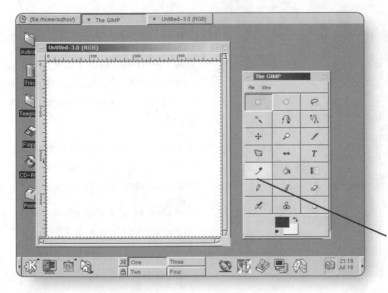

Before you can draw an object (such as a line or a filled box), you'll want to select the color in which you want the object to appear. You can select colors from a color selection tool or from another image or object that is open in The GIMP. You can also choose from a number of patterns and gradients as fills for objects you create.

- Use the Color Picker to select a color from any image open in The GIMP.

● When you create an object, such as a circle or square, use the Bucket Fill tool to add color to the inside area of the object.

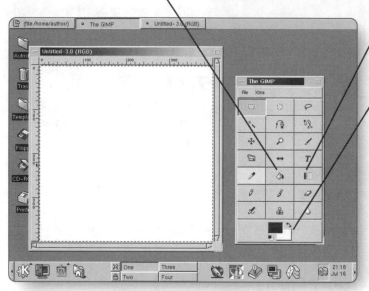

● The Gradient Fill tool uses a blend of colors to fill an object.

● Change the colors currently used in the Foreground/Background Color Selector.

---

**TIP**

There's another color palette. Right-click on the canvas to display a menu, move the mouse pointer to Dialogs and then click on Palette.

---

When you want to place shapes on the canvas, there are several drawing tools available.

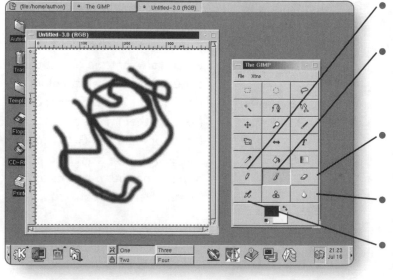

● The Pencil tool creates solid lines on the canvas.

● The Paintbrush tool can create lines with fuzzy edges, patterns, and multicolored images.

● Use the Eraser tool when you want to use a brush stroke to remove part of an image.

● The Blur tool can soften the edges in a picture.

● The Airbrush tool gives a line a splattered effect.

**TIP**

To adjust the size and shape of the brush stroke, open the File menu on the toolbox, move the mouse pointer to Dialogs and then click on Brushes.

If you want to make changes to an entire image or to just part of the image, you must first select the area with which you want to work. You may need to select an area in order to change the brightness. Or maybe you need to move part of an image to another position on the picture. There are several tools you can use to select parts of an image

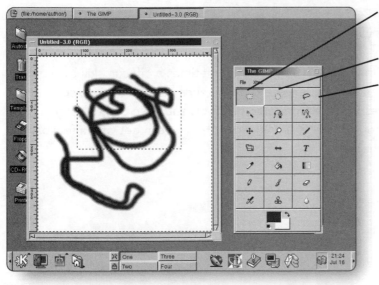

- Select a rectangular area on the picture.

- Select an elliptical area.

- Select an area by drawing around it.

- Select an area that contains the same color.

- Use Bezier curves to select an area and to adjust the selection outline.

- When you want The GIMP to guess at the outline of a selection area, use the Intelligent Scissors.

# Creating Great Graphics with The GIMP

The best way to get started with a graphics program is to play with its basic tools. Get comfortable drawing lines with pencils and brushes.

## Drawing Shapes

Drawing with a mouse is sometimes a difficult skill to acquire, but with patience and persistence you can achieve some great results. The GIMP also has tools and Help tips to get you going; so let's see how creative you can get with a few basic shapes.

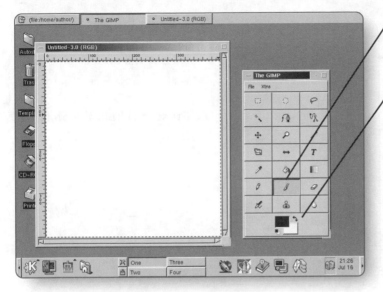

**1. Click** on the **Brush tool** in the Toolbox. The tool will be selected.

**2. Click** on the **Foreground Color Selection box.** The Color Selection dialog box will open.

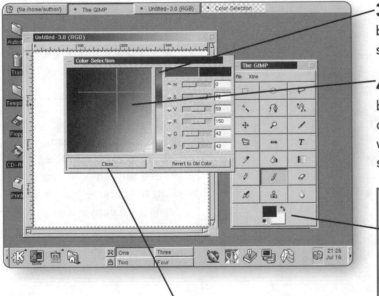

**3. Click** on a **color** in the color bar. The color for the brush stroke will be selected.

**4. Click** on a **color** in the color box if you want to change the color tone. The selected color will change to the selected shade.

### NOTE

You can see a preview of the color in the Foreground color box in the toolbox.

**5. Click** on the **Close button** when you have selected a color you like. The Color Selection dialog box will close and you can now draw a line.

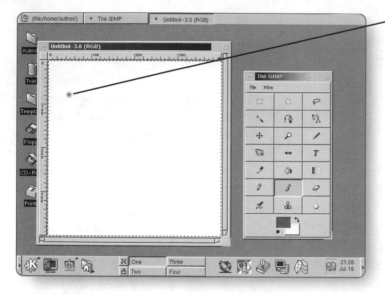

**6.** **Click** on the **place** where you want to begin a straight line. A dot will appear on the canvas.

**7.** **Press and hold** the **Shift key**.

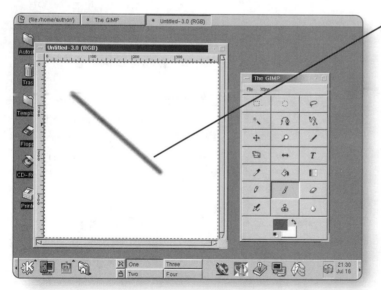

**8.** **Click** on the **place** where you want the line to end. The line will appear on the canvas in the color you selected.

---

### TIP

If you want a freeform line, click and hold the mouse button while you drag the mouse pointer across the canvas.

---

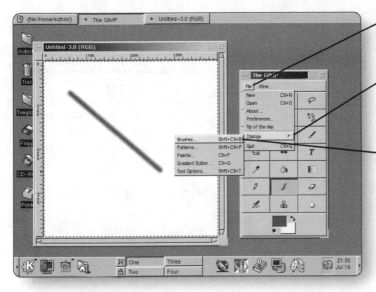

**9. Click** on **File**. The File menu will appear.

**10. Move** the **mouse pointer** to **Dialogs**. A second menu will appear.

**11. Click** on **Brushes**. The Brush Selection dialog box will open.

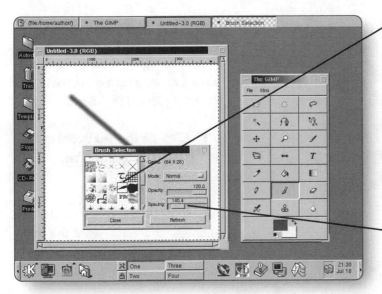

**12. Scroll** through the **list** of brushes and **click** on a **brush**. The brush will be selected.

### NOTE
If you click and hold on a brush, you'll see a larger image.

**13. Click and drag** the **Spacing slider** to change the spacing of the brush stroke. The spacing will be changed.

### NOTE
You can close the Brush Selection dialog box when you are finished working with it. You can create more brush strokes later by leaving the dialog box open.

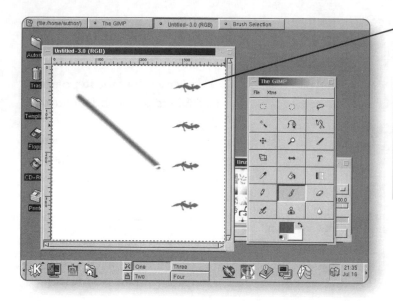

**14.** **Draw** a **different line**. The line will appear on the canvas.

### TIP

If you want to remove a shape you just created, press the Ctrl and Z keys simultaneously.

## Adding Text to Your Picture

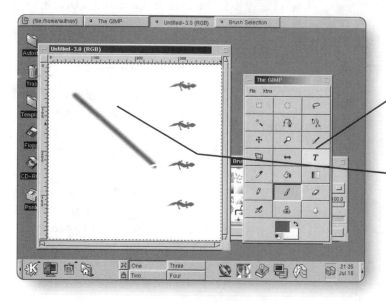

The Text tool enables you to use any available font and create a text object on the canvas.

**1.** **Click** on the **Text tool** in the toolbox. The tool will be selected.

**2.** **Click** on the **place** on the canvas where you want the text to begin. The Text Tool dialog box will open.

**3.** **Click** in the **preview box** and **type** the **text** that you want to appear on the canvas.

**4.** **Click** on the **font** that you want to apply to the text. The text in the preview box will change to show the selected font.

**5.** **Double-click** in the **size text box**, and **type** the **number** of pixels high you want the text.

**6.** **Click** on **OK**. The text will appear on the canvas. When the text appears on the canvas, it will be selected.

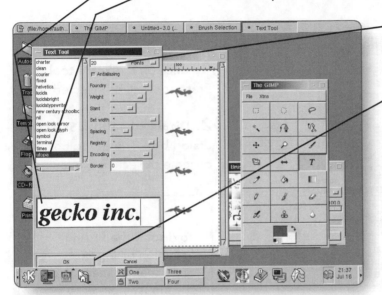

**7.** **Hold** the **mouse pointer** over the text. The mouse will change to a four-sided arrow.

**8.** **Click and drag** the **text** to a new position on the canvas. The text will be moved.

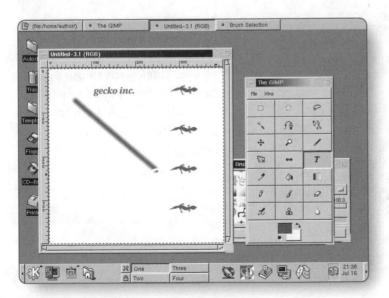

## Making Changes to Your Picture

There are a few lines on your canvas—nothing complex, just something with which to practice. Now let's experiment with erasing unwanted objects and moving a few things around.

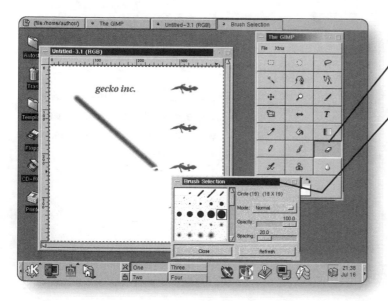

### *Erasing an Object*

**1.** **Click** on the **Erase tool**. The Erase tool will be selected.

**2.** **Display** the **Brush Selection dialog box**. The dialog box will become the active window.

---

**NOTE**

To display the Brush Selection dialog box, open the File menu, move the mouse pointer to Dialogs, and click on Brushes.

---

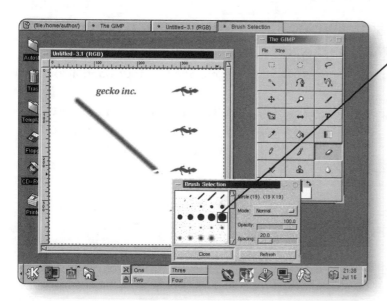

**3.** **Click** on the **brush** you want to use. You'll want to use a brush size that will adequately cover the area you wish to erase. The brush will be selected.

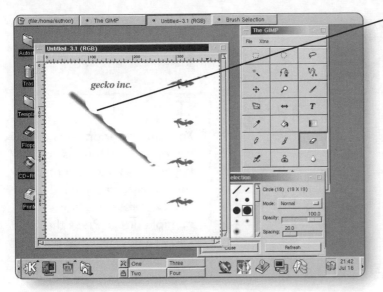

**4.** **Click and drag** the **mouse pointer** over the area on the canvas that you want to erase. The object will disappear.

**5.** **Change** the **brush size** if the coverage of the eraser is not working the way you want.

**6.** **Click and drag** the **mouse pointer** over those areas that you want to erase. The object will disappear.

If you come to an area where you need to see the picture up close to do the work, you'll need to use the Zoom feature.

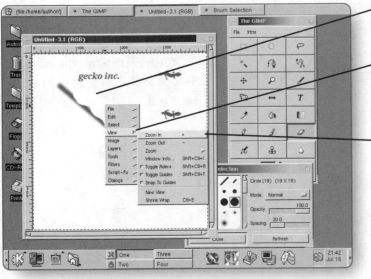

**7.** **Right-click** on the **picture**. A menu will appear.

**8.** **Move** the **mouse pointer** to **View**. The View menu will appear.

**9.** **Click** on **Zoom In**. You'll see more of the picture.

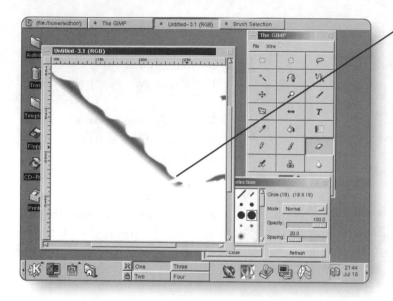

**10. Continue erasing** the unwanted object. The erased image will be removed.

### TIP

You can also zoom in and out of your picture using keyboard shortcuts. Press the = key to zoom in. You can press this key multiple times. Press the – key to get back to your original view.

## Moving an Object

Before you can move an object, you must first select it. This section will show you an easy way to move your artwork around on the page.

**1. Click** on the **Rectangular Select tool**. The tool will be selected.

### NOTE

If you want to select a round shape, use the Elliptical Select tool. You can also use the Hand-Drawn Select tool to draw your own outline around an object.

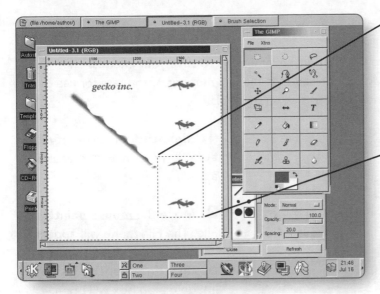

**2. Click and hold** at the **upper-left corner** of the object you want to select, and **drag** the **mouse pointer** to the lower-right corner. An outline will appear around the object.

**3. Release** the **mouse button**. An outline will appear around the object.

**4. Place** the **mouse pointer** over the object you just selected. The mouse pointer will change to a four-pointed arrow.

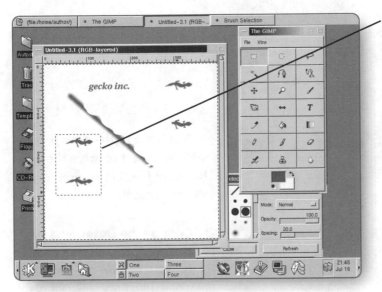

**5. Click** and **hold** on the **object**, and **drag** it to a **new position**. The object will move with the mouse pointer.

**6. Release** the **mouse button** when the object is in the desired location.

# Saving Your Work

The GIMP offers several ways to save your images. The program can save the file in a number of formats for use by other programs or on the Web.

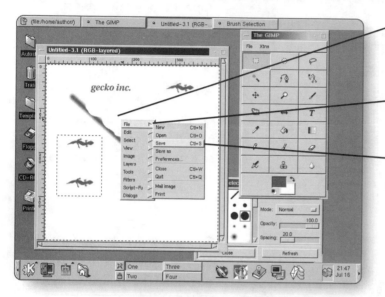

**1. Right-click** on an **empty area** of the canvas. A menu will appear.

**2. Move** the **mouse pointer** to File. The File menu will appear.

**3. Click** on **Save**. The Save Image dialog box will open.

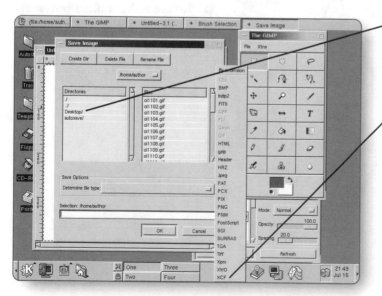

**4. Navigate** to the **directory** in which you want to store the file. The list of files in the directory will appear in the Files list.

**5. Click** on the **Determine file type drop-down** list, and **click** on the **XCF option**. This is The GIMP's native file format. If you want to work with the file in The GIMP again, use this format.

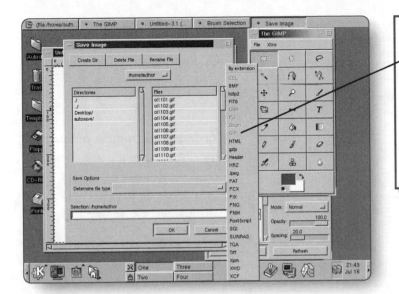

## NOTE

If you want to use the file in a Web page, use either the GIF or Jpeg option. If you are sending the file to a commercial printer, use the Tiff or PostScript format.

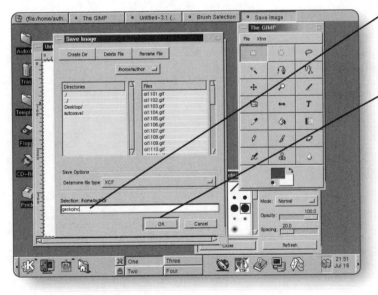

**6. Click** in the **Selection text box**, and **type** a **name** for the file.

**7. Click** on **OK**. Your file will be saved.

When you are finished working with the file, you can close it.

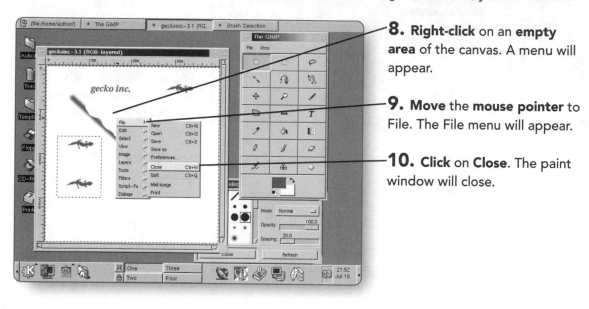

**8. Right-click** on an **empty area** of the canvas. A menu will appear.

**9. Move** the **mouse pointer** to File. The File menu will appear.

**10. Click** on **Close**. The paint window will close.

# 12

# Getting Organized with KOrganizer

Some days it's just too hard to remember everything that needs to be done. Keeping a calendar is the first step toward getting organized. Linux comes installed with several applications that can help you keep your personal and business life organized. KOrganizer will help you keep track of appointments, recurring events, and your to-do list. After you learn about KOrganizer's basic functions, you can begin to explore how to use KOrganizer to schedule activities with a group. If you have a 3COM PalmPilot, KOrganizer is the perfect companion for keeping your desktop and palmtop schedules synchronized. In this chapter, you'll learn how to:

- Add appointments to the calendar
- Schedule upcoming events
- Keep a to-do list

# Starting the KOrganizer

Like the other Linux programs that you've seen throughout this book, the KOrganizer can be found on the main menu. If you use the KOrganizer frequently, you may want to make it an icon on the Panel, or you can put it in your Personal menu with other important applications and files.

**1.** **Click** on the **Application Starter**. The main menu will appear.

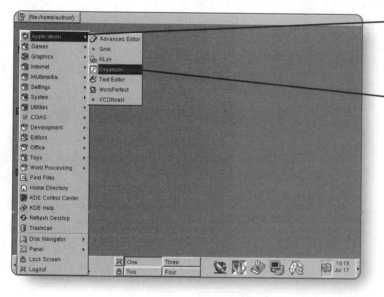

**2.** **Move** the **mouse pointer** to **Applications**. The Applications menu will appear.

**3.** **Click** on **Organizer**. The KOrganizer will appear.

# Understanding the KOrganizer Window

You'll notice that the KOrganizer window is divided into three sections. There's a calendar that also acts as a navigation tool. There's an events view that displays a single day or multiple days, and also shows any appointments scheduled. In addition, you'll see a to-do list where you can make notes to yourself about items that need your attention. You can see active items on the to-do list no matter which day you are viewing.

## Clicking Through the Years

The Date Navigator enables you to flip between the pages in your calendar. You can easily flip to another day in the same month, a different month, and even a whole new year. When you open KOrganizer, the current date will display.

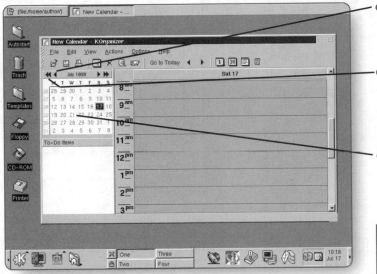

- Click on the single arrow to move to the previous month or the next month.

- Click on the double arrow to move to the same month of the previous year or the same month of the upcoming year.

- Click on a number to change to a different date in the displayed month.

### NOTE

Hold the mouse pointer over the buttons to see the Tooltips.

## Changing the Events View

When you first open KOrganizer, the events view displays the current date, broken into hours. The toolbar contains a number of buttons that can change the time period that will display in the events view.

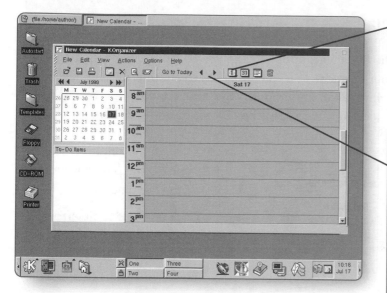

**1. Click** on the **Schedule View button**. The events view will change to display the current Monday through Friday workweek.

## TIP

The Previous and Next buttons on the toolbar will move you to the next date if you have only a single date displayed, or you will move to the next week if you are looking at one of the week views.

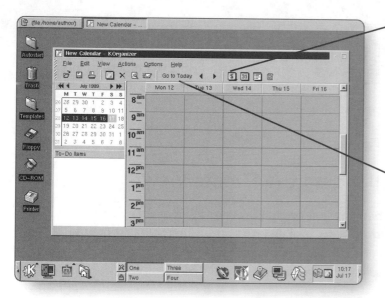

**2. Click** on the **Schedule View button**. The events view will change to display the current week beginning on Monday and ending on Sunday.

## NOTE

Click on the Go to Today button on the toolbar to return to the current date.

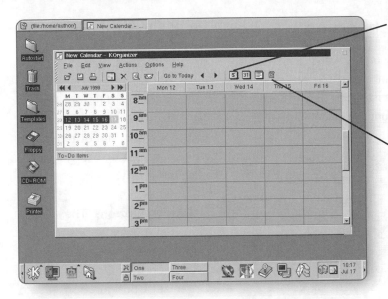

**3. Click** on the **Schedule View button**. You'll be returned to the beginning events view that shows only the current day.

## TIP

If you'd rather see your appointments in a list format, click on the To-Do List View button.

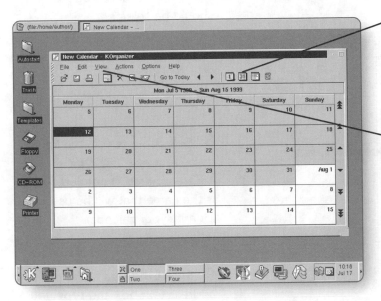

**4. Click** on the **Month View button**. The current month will display in the events view.

## NOTE

You can also change the view by opening the View menu and selecting a view from the list.

# Changing the Look of KOrganizer

You may want to change some of KOrganizer's default settings. KOrganizer starts the week out on a Monday, and it starts your day at 8 a.m. If your clients are in a different time zone, you'll need to start your day before the crack of dawn.

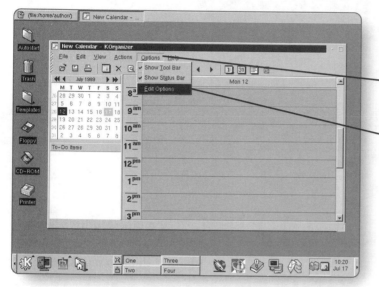

Explore some of the other settings and set up KOrganizer to fit your lifestyle.

**1. Click** on **Options**. The Options menu will appear.

**2. Click** on **Edit Options**. The KOrganizer Configuration Options dialog box will open, and the Personal category should be selected.

**3. Select** the **text** in the Your name text box and **type** a different **name**, if needed. This is the name that will be used to identify your calendar information.

**4. Select** the **text** in the Email address text box and **type** your **e-mail address**. This is important if you will be using KOrganizer for group scheduling activities.

**5. Click** on the **Time & Date category**. The Time & Date options will appear.

**6. Click** on the **up and down arrows** next to the Default Appointment Time text box to change the default selected time that any appointment will start. The default time will change.

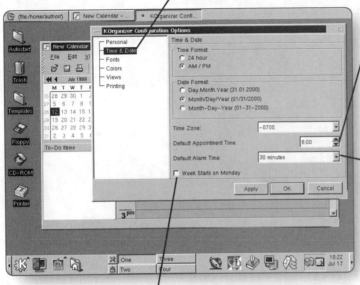

**7. Click** on the **down arrow** next to the Default Alarm Time list box and **click** on the **amount of time** before a scheduled appointment or event that you want to be reminded of. The reminder time will change.

**8. Click** in the **Week Starts on Monday check box** if you want your weeks to start on Monday. The box will be cleared.

**9. Click** on the **Views category**. The Views options will appear.

**10. Click** on the **up and down arrows** next to the Day Begins At text box to change the time when your day starts. The time will change.

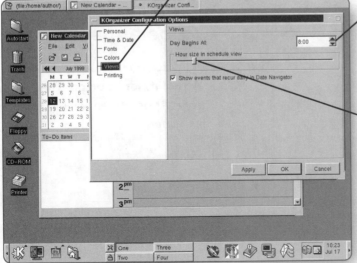

**11. Click and drag** on the **Hour size in schedule view slider** to change the height allocated to each hour in the events view. Drag the slider to the left to make the size smaller. Drag the slider to the right to make the size larger.

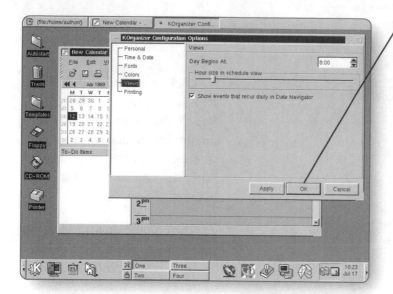

**12.** **Click** on **OK**. Your changes will be made.

# Working with an Appointment Book

If you have a reason for being at a designated place at a certain time on a specific date, keep track of it in the calendar.

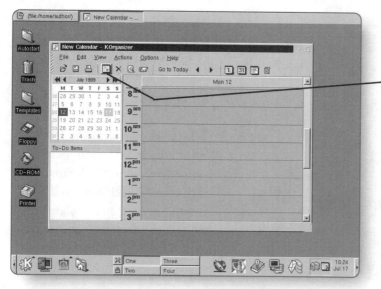

## Creating a New Appointment

**1.** **Click** on the **New Appointment button**. The New Appointment dialog box will open.

**2. Click** in the **Summary text box** and **type** a **description** of the appointment, persons attending the appointment, or notes needed for the appointment.

**3. Click** in the **Start time text box** and **type** the **date** on which the appointment is scheduled to begin. Use slashes, for example mm/dd/yy.

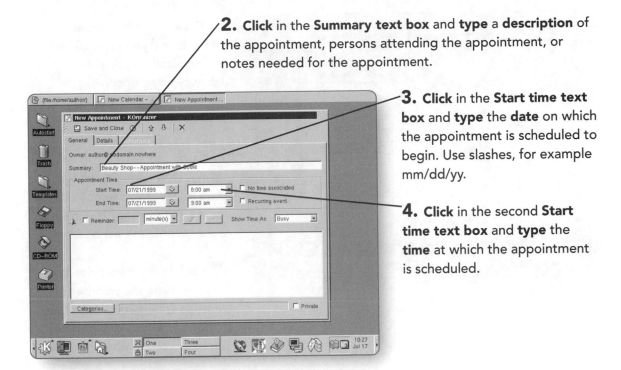

**4. Click** in the second **Start time text box** and **type** the **time** at which the appointment is scheduled.

**5. Click** in the **End time text boxes** and **type** the **date and time** at which the appointment is scheduled to end.

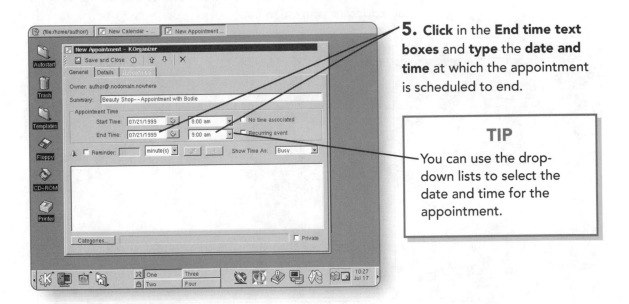

## TIP

You can use the drop-down lists to select the date and time for the appointment.

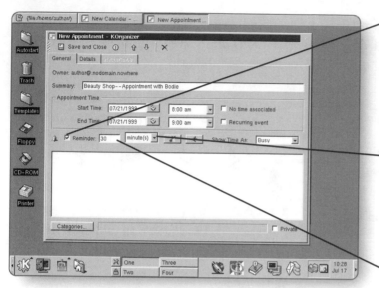

**6.** **Click** in the **Reminder check box** if you want to be automatically notified in advance of an upcoming appointment. A check will appear in the box.

**7.** **Click** on the **Minutes list box button** and **click** on the **time interval** you want to use for the notification. The interval will appear in the list box.

**8.** **Click** in the **Reminder text box** and **type** the **number** of intervals (selected in step 7) in advance that you'd like to be reminded of the appointment.

**9.** **Click** on the **Save and Close button**. The appointment will be added to your calendar.

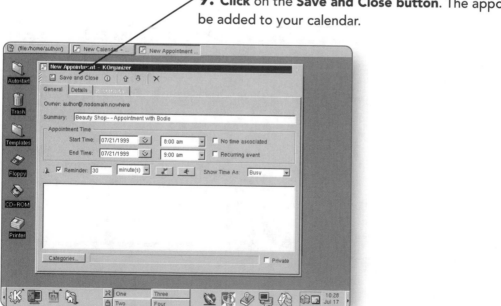

**10. Click** on the **date** on which you scheduled the appointment. Your appointment will appear in a box on the Day View of the calendar. If you added a notification alarm to the appointment, a bell icon will appear in the appointment box.

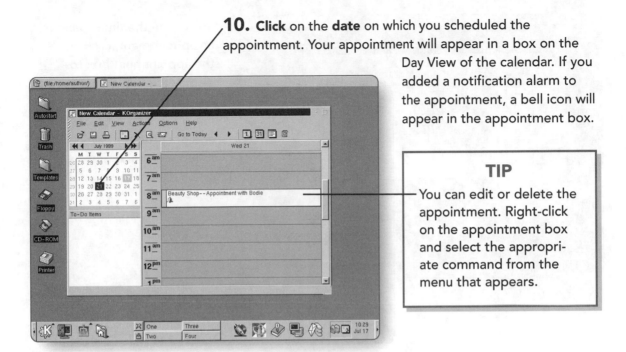

## TIP

You can edit or delete the appointment. Right-click on the appointment box and select the appropriate command from the menu that appears.

## Editing an Appointment

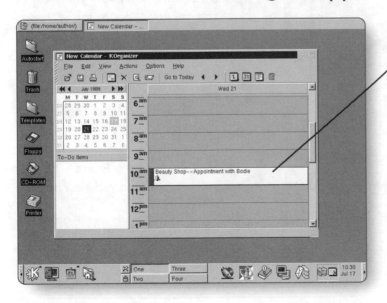

Here are a few tips for editing appointments.

- To move an appointment to a different time during the same day, click and hold inside the appointment box and drag until the appointment box is moved to the desired location.

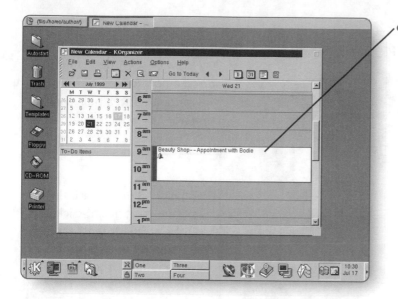

● To change the time span for an appointment, click inside the appointment box to display the box outline. Click and drag the top outline to move the start time or click and drag the bottom outline to move the end time.

# Working with Recurring Events

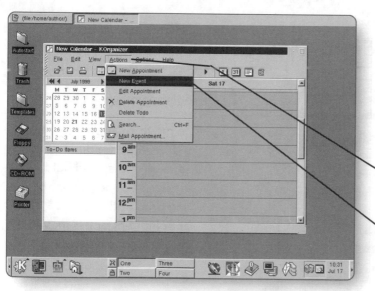

Are you looking for an easy way to remind yourself to send mom a birthday card every year? Let the calendar keep track of these important dates for you. It will even give you advance notice so you can do some shopping.

**1. Click** on **Actions**. The Actions menu will appear.

**2. Click** on **New Event**. The New Appointment dialog box will open.

**3. Click** in the **Summary text box** and **type** a **description** of the event.

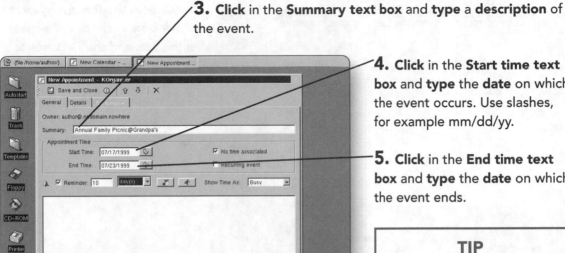

**4. Click** in the **Start time text box** and **type** the **date** on which the event occurs. Use slashes, for example mm/dd/yy.

**5. Click** in the **End time text box** and **type** the **date** on which the event ends.

**TIP**

You can use the drop-down lists to select the date and time for the appointment.

**6. Click** in the **Reminder check box** if you want to be automatically notified in advance of an upcoming appointment. A check will appear in the box.

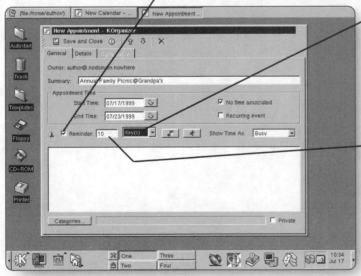

**7. Click** on the **Reminder list box button** and **click** on the **time interval** you want to use for the notification. The interval will appear in the list box.

**8. Click** in the **Reminder text box** and **type** the **number** of intervals (selected in step 7) in advance that you'd like to be reminded of the appointment.

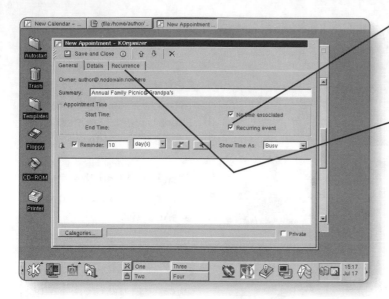

**9.** **Click** in the **Recurring event check box**. A check will appear in the box and the Recurrence tab will become active.

**10.** **Click** on the **Recurrence tab**. The Recurrence tab will come to the top of the stack.

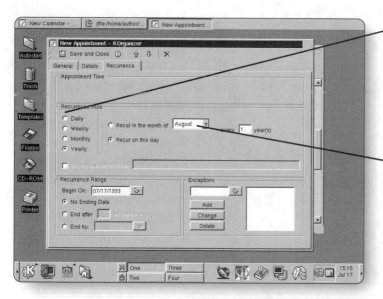

**11.** **Click** on a **Recurrence Rule option button**. The option will be selected and the rules section will change according to the recurrence schedule option selected.

**12.** **Set** the **parameters** for the recurring event. The recurrence rule will be set.

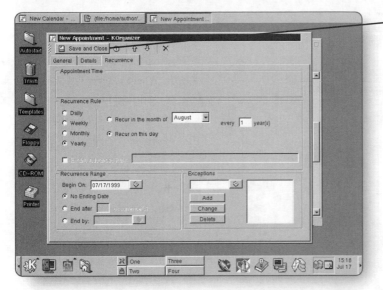

**13. Click** on the **Save and Close button**. The event will be set.

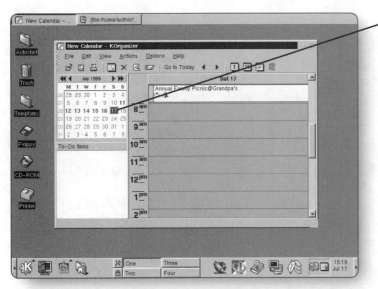

**14. Click** on the **date** that the event is scheduled to occur. You'll see the event in the events view. You can make changes to the event just the same way as you would make changes to an appointment.

# Creating a To-Do List

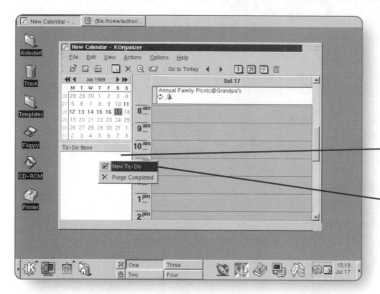

If you need to keep a list of reminders so that you pick up a few supplies on the way into the office, or pick up the laundry from the cleaners, use the To-Do List.

**1.** **Right-click** in the **To-Do Items box**. A menu will appear.

**2.** **Click** on **New To-Do**. A blank field will be created in which you can enter the task you need to do or the item you need to remember.

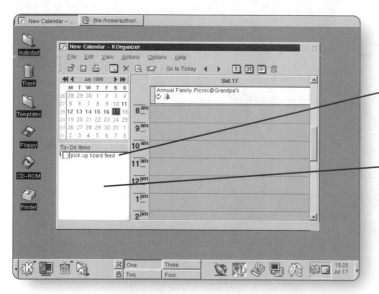

**3.** **Click** on the blank **to-do field**. The cursor will appear next to the empty check box.

**4.** **Type** a **description** of the to-do item. The to-do item will appear in the to-do field.

**5.** **Click** outside the to-do item in an **empty area** of the To-Do List. The to-do item will be created.

---

### NOTE

If you need to edit this description later, double-click on the description.

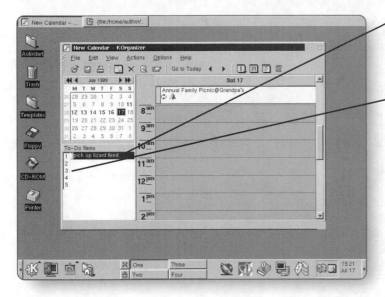

**6. Double-click** in the **first To-Do Item column**. A list of priorities will appear.

**7. Click** on a **priority**, with 1 being the highest priority and 5 being the lowest priority. The priority will be selected.

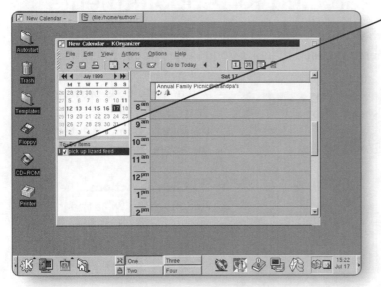

**8.** When you have completed a to-do item, **double-click** in the **second column**. The to-do item will be marked as completed.

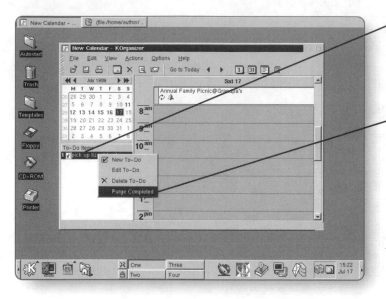

**9.** When you want to clear all the completed to-do items, **right-click** on a **completed to-do item**. A menu will appear.

**10. Click** on **Purge Completed**. All the entries that you marked as completed will be removed from the To-Do List.

# Searching for Appointments

When you need to find a certain appointment or event, there's no need to look through every page. You can let KOrganizer search for you. All you need to do is provide a few descriptive words that match the description you entered for the appointment or event.

**1. Click** on **Actions**. The Actions menu will appear.

**2. Click** on **Search**. The korganizer dialog box will open.

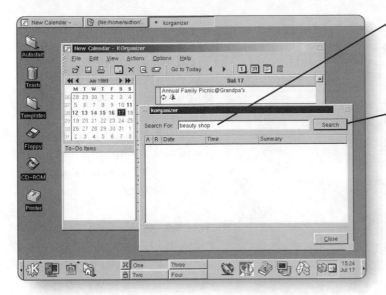

**3. Type information** that describes the appointment you want to find. The text will appear in the text box.

**4. Click** on the **Search button**. The search will begin and any matching results will appear in the bottom section of the dialog box.

### NOTE

If you need to know more about the appointment, double-click on the appointment. The Edit Appointment dialog box will open.

**5. Click** on the **Close** button. The korganizer dialog box will close.

# Saving the Calendar Information

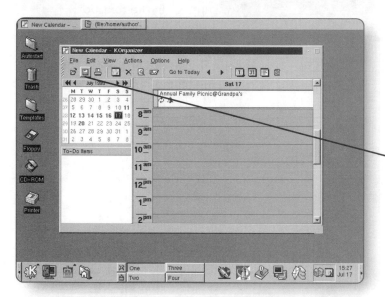

Before you can close KOrganizer, you'll need to save all the information you entered. If you're working with the calendar a lot, you may want to hit that Save button often.

**1. Click** on the **Save This Calendar button**. The calendar will be saved using the default name. It is now safe to close KOrganizer.

# 13

# Exploring WordPerfect

If you installed OpenLinux using the recommended installation plus commercial packages, you'll find an icon on the Panel that looks like the nib of a fountain pen. This is your shortcut to WordPerfect. If WordPerfect isn't installed, you'll want to refer to Appendix B, "Installing Software," to find out how to install WordPerfect. WordPerfect is a popular word processing application that runs on many different operating systems. It also has the capability of handling many different file formats. If you've been using another word processing program, you can use all your files in WordPerfect. In this chapter, you'll learn how to:

- Open WordPerfect
- Find help sources inside the program
- Change text and document formatting
- Check your document for grammar and spelling

# Getting Started with WordPerfect

If you're switching from another word processing program to WordPerfect, you'll want to take a little time to get familiar with the differences between your old program and WordPerfect. A good way to do this is to browse through the menu system and read the help files.

## Opening the Program

The first time you open WordPerfect, you'll be asked for a license key. You'll need to go to the Corel Web site at

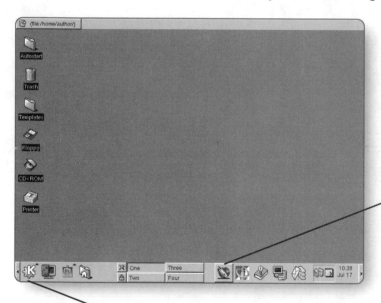

**http://linux.corel.com**. Scroll to the bottom of the page and click on the *register now* link. You'll be asked to fill out a survey, but you only need to fill in those items preceded by an asterisk (*). After you submit the survey, you'll get your registration key number.

**1.** **Click** on the **WordPerfect icon** on the Panel. A warning dialog box will open.

**NOTE**

If you don't see a WordPerfect icon on the Panel, open the Application Starter and move the mouse pointer to Applications. You should find WordPerfect there.

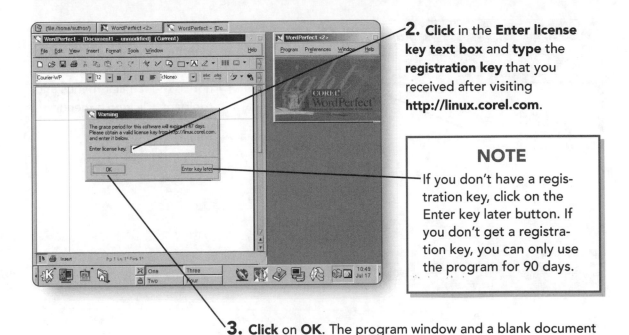

**2. Click** in the **Enter license key text box** and **type** the **registration key** that you received after visiting **http://linux.corel.com**.

> **NOTE**
>
> If you don't have a registration key, click on the Enter key later button. If you don't get a registration key, you can only use the program for 90 days.

**3. Click** on **OK**. The program window and a blank document window will open.

## Exploring WordPerfect

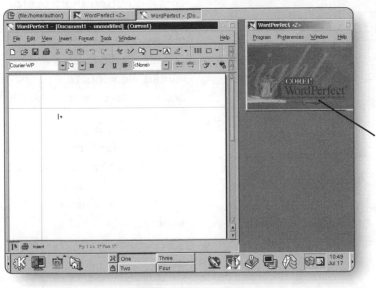

Before you dive into WordPerfect, open a few menus to see what tasks the program can perform. Hold the mouse pointer over a button to display a Tooltip.

- The Program window contains commands to create and open documents, set program preferences such as timed backups and color schemes, arrange windows, and close the program.

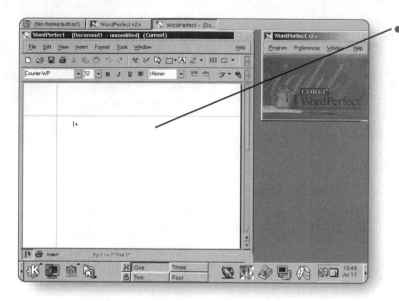

- The Document window is where you will be performing most of your work. You'll notice the familiar menus and toolbars. Click on a menu to open it.

- You'll find all of the available commands in the menus. If a menu command has an arrow to the right, click on the command to display a second menu.

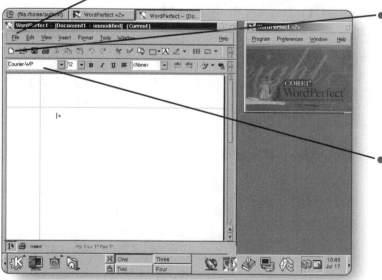

- The WordPerfect toolbar contains button shortcuts to commonly used commands for saving and printing files, copying and undoing, adding various elements to a page, and changing views.

- The Property bar contains commands for formatting text. You can change the look of the font, paragraph alignment, and insert symbols.

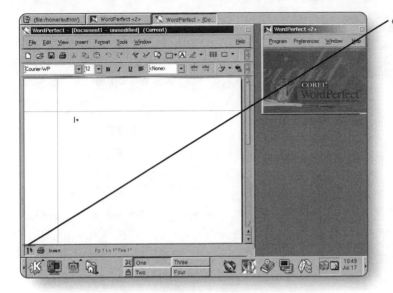

• The Application bar contains information about the document with which you are working. You'll see the cursor position and the printer status. You can change the information that displays on the Application bar. Right-click on the bar and select Settings.

# Finding Help

To help you use WordPerfect, the following are a few places within the program where you can find more help.

## Asking the PerfectExpert

The PerfectExpert is an easy way to get fast answers. The PerfectExpert contains help files for commonly sought help topics. It can also help you perform tasks such as creating a new document, formatting the document, or adding a special toolbar to the Document window.

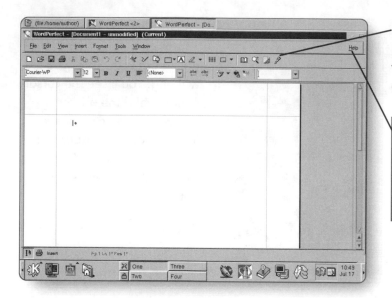

**1. Click** on the **PerfectExpert button** on the WordPerfect toolbar. The Corel PerfectExpert dialog box will open.

### NOTE

You can also find the PerfectExpert in the Help menus.

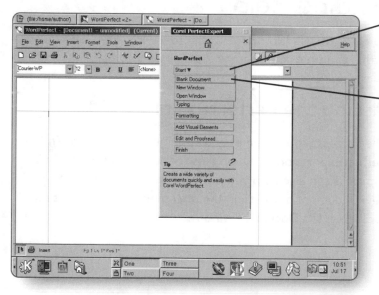

**2. Click** on the **down arrow** next to a Help topic. A list of subtopics will appear.

**3. Click** on a **topic**. The command will be executed or a dialog box will open.

### NOTE

If a dialog box opens, you can click on the Close button to close the dialog box without making any changes.

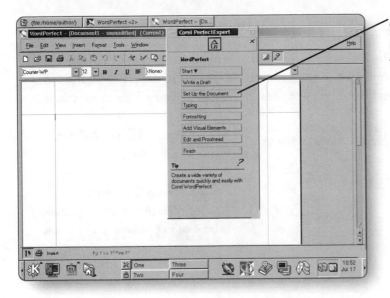

**4. Click** on a **topic**. A second page of options for the selected topic will appear.

**5. Click** on a **subtopic** to see a dialog box where you can change options. A dialog box will appear.

**6. Click** on the **Home button.** The initial list of Help topics will appear.

**7. Click** on the **Close button** when you are finished. The Corel PerfectExpert dialog box will close.

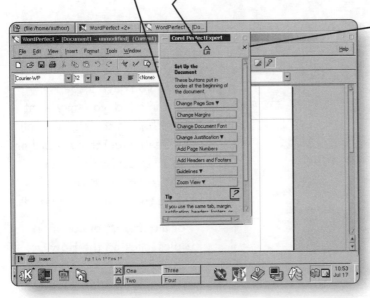

# Looking Up Other Help Sources

The Help Contents is your other source of information contained in the program. It gives you access to all the Help features and Help files. It even provides a Search function.

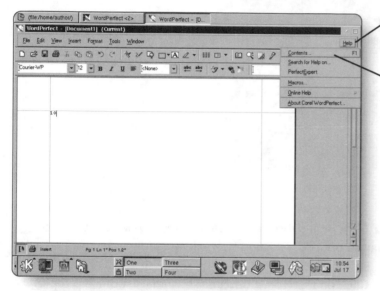

**1. Click** on **Help**. The Help menu will appear.

**2. Click** on **Contents**. The Corel WordPerfect Help dialog box will appear.

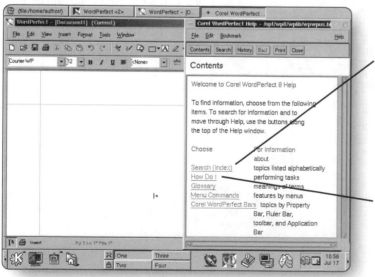

The Help Contents gives you access to all of the help files.

● When you have a specific topic in mind, you may want to perform a search. Just tell the Search function a word or two to describe what you want to do and it will find topics that match your needs.

● For a quick list of common topics, click on the How Do I link.

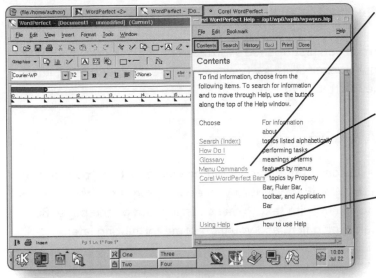

- If you want to know what function a particular menu command performs, check out the Menu Commands section.

- To read a description of the toolbars and toolbar buttons, click on the Corel WordPerfect Bars section.

- Before you begin, read the section on Using Help if you're not sure how to navigate around the help windows.

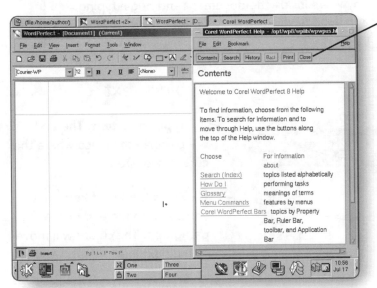

**3.** When you're finished browsing the help topics, **click** on the **Close** button. The Help window will close.

# Starting Your First Document

When you first opened WordPerfect, a blank document was also opened. This is where you will create your memo, letter, newsletter, or report.

## Working with Text

Text is one of the more common elements that you'll be using in the WordPerfect word-processing program. There are lots you can do with text to make it stand out on the page. But start typing first, and you'll do some formatting later.

---

### TIP

If the Shadow Cursor is turned on, you can click anywhere inside the document and begin typing. You don't have to start at the top of the page.

---

### *Typing Text*

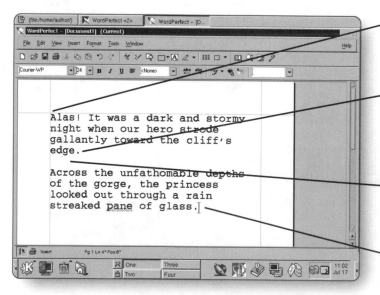

**1. Type** some **text**. The text will begin in the place where the cursor is located.

**2. Press** the **Enter key** when you come to the end of the paragraph. The cursor will move to the next line.

**3.** If you want more space between paragraphs, **press** the **Enter** key a second time.

**4. Type** additional **paragraphs** as needed. The text will appear as you type.

## *Selecting Text*

Before you can edit or format text, you'll need to select the text. Here are a few selection techniques for you to try out.

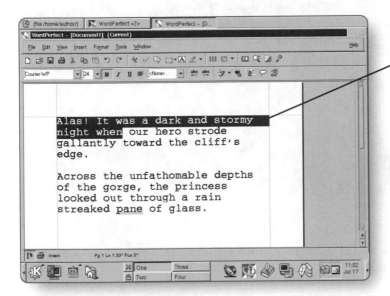

- To select one word, double-click on the word.

- To select a sentence, click three times on the sentence.

- To select a paragraph, click four times on the paragraph.

- To select a block of text, click and hold at the beginning of the text you want to select, and then drag the mouse pointer to the end of the text. Release the mouse button when the text is selected.

## *Formatting Text*

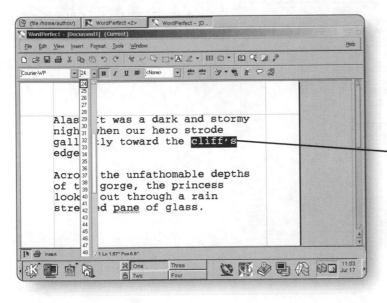

You can make many changes to the way text looks. You can change the font size, the font style, and the typeface.

**1. Select** the **text** you want to change. The text will be selected.

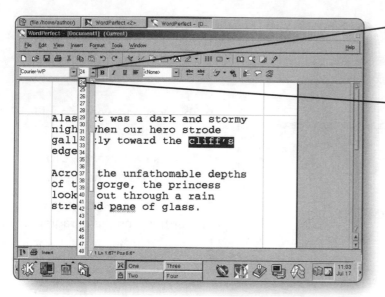

**2. Click** on the **arrow** next to the Font Size list box. A list of available font sizes will appear.

**3. Click** on a **size**. The text will change to the selected size.

**4. Select** the **text** you want to change. The text will be selected.

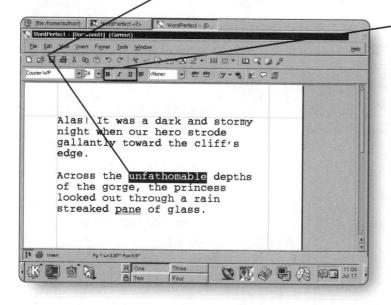

**5. Click** on the **Bold, Italics, or Underline button**. The text style will be changed depending on your selection.

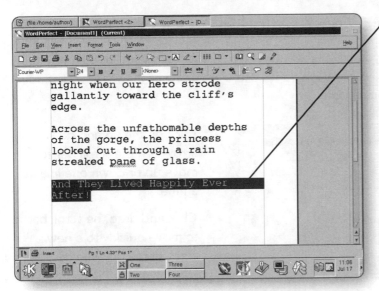

**6. Select** the **text** you want to change. The text will be selected.

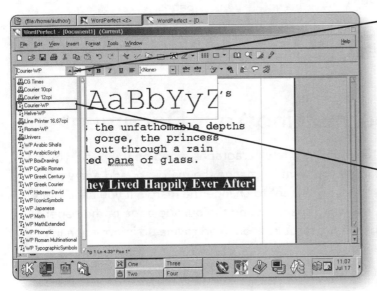

**7. Click** on the **arrow** next to the Change Font list box. A list of available fonts will appear. You'll notice that a preview pane appears next to the list box, so you can see what the font looks like.

**8. Click** on a **font**. The selected text will change to the new typeface.

## Moving Around in a Document

If you have typed several pages of text, you'll need a way to move between pages. Here are a few of the window features you can use.

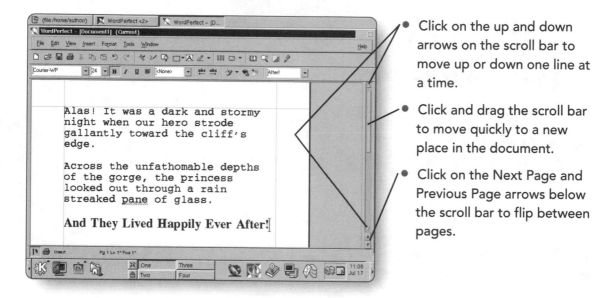

- Click on the up and down arrows on the scroll bar to move up or down one line at a time.

- Click and drag the scroll bar to move quickly to a new place in the document.

- Click on the Next Page and Previous Page arrows below the scroll bar to flip between pages.

# Formatting Your Document

After you have a few paragraphs typed on the page, you may find that you want to change the margin or add a few tab markers. You'll want to change the margin if you need more or less white space around the outside edge of the paper. Tabs are great tools if you need to line up information in columns.

## Turning On the Ruler

The Ruler enables you to make changes to the document margins and tabs quickly. The Ruler does not display in the document window by default; you must turn it on first.

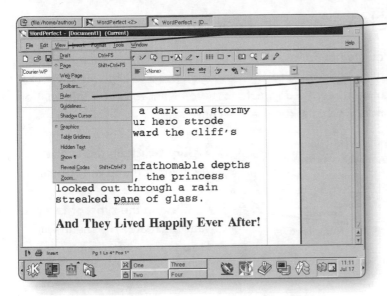

**1.** **Click** on **View**. The View menu will appear.

**2.** **Click** on **Ruler**. The Ruler will appear at the top of the document, just below the toolbars.

---

**TIP**

You can select multiple tabs. Press and hold the Shift key and drag the mouse pointer over the tabs you want to select.

## Setting Tabs

The Ruler enables you to set different types of tabs and also to remove tabs. Here are a few tips for working with tabs.

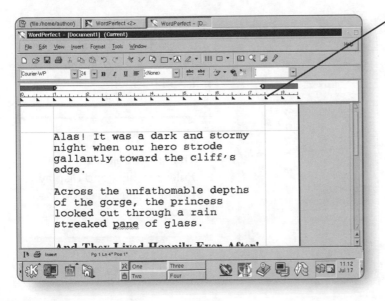

- To delete any extra tabs from the Ruler, click and hold on the tab marker and drag the tab off the Ruler.

- To move a tab to a new position, click and hold on the tab marker and drag the tab to the place where you want it to be.

- To create a new tab position, click on the place where you want the tab positioned.

## Changing Tab Markers

You are not limited to using the left tab. There are other tab styles from which to choose. If you need to align numbers in a column, use the decimal tab. If you want to center information under a tab marker, use the center tab.

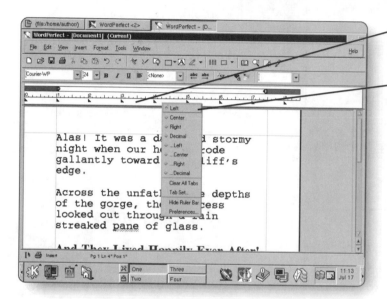

**1. Right-click** on the **tab line** of the Ruler. A menu will appear.

**2. Click** on the **type of tab** you want to create. The menu will disappear and you can create the tab.

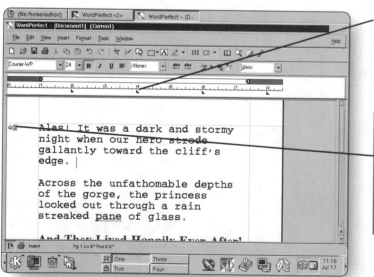

**3. Click** on the **place** where you want to set the tab. A tab marker will appear in the selected position.

### NOTE

The arrow below the Ruler can hide and display the Ruler. Just click on the arrow.

## Changing Margins

The new document you created probably had margins set at one inch all the way around the page. If this won't suit your purposes, here's how you can change the amount of white space at the edges of the page.

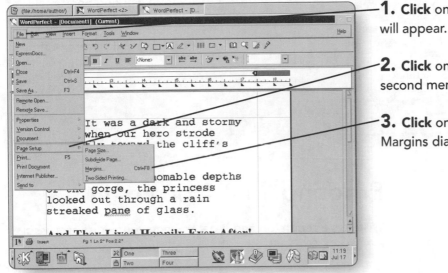

**1. Click** on **File**. The File menu will appear.

**2. Click** on **Page Setup**. A second menu will appear.

**3. Click** on **Margins**. The Margins dialog box will open.

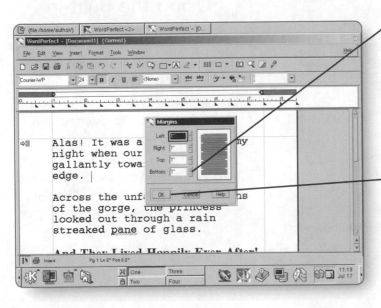

**4. Click** on the **up and down arrows** next to the margin that you want to change until the amount of space you want to set for the margin displays. The margin size will change in the preview pane.

**5. Click** on **OK**. The margins will be changed.

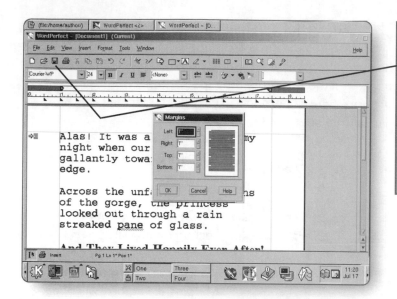

**NOTE**

Have you saved your document yet? Click on the Save button. It's a good idea to click on the Save button often while you're working on a document.

# Proofing Your Document

Writing's a tough job and it helps when your word processor provides a few tools to make the process go more smoothly.

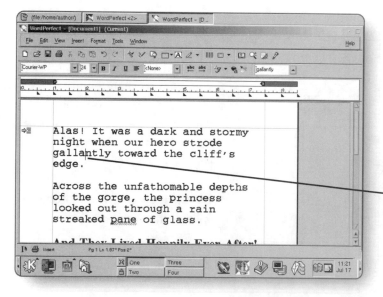

## Using the Built-in Thesaurus

Sometimes you may not like a particular word that you used, but can't think of a different word to use. WordPerfect can help you out with this.

**1. Click** on the **word** that you'd like to replace with a different word of the same meaning. The word will appear in the Suggestions list box.

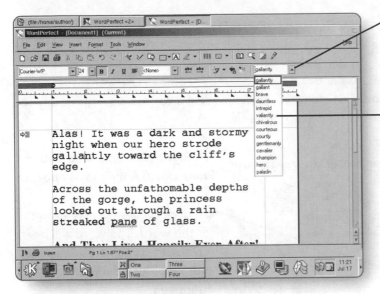

**2. Click** on the **arrow** next to the Suggestions list box. A list of alternate words with the same meaning will appear.

**3. Click** on the **word** that you want to use to replace the original word. The word in the document will be replaced.

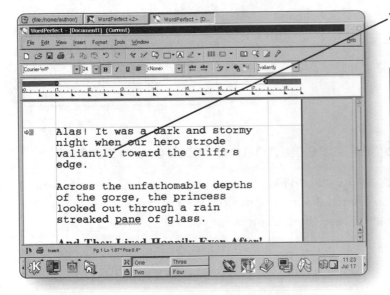

You'll see the new word in the document.

**TIP**

If you're not happy with this word, click on the Reverse button on the toolbar to revert back to the original word and try again.

## Correcting Grammar Errors as You Type

You may notice a blue line under some of the words that you type. This indicates a grammatical error. Here's a quick way to correct grammar on-the-fly.

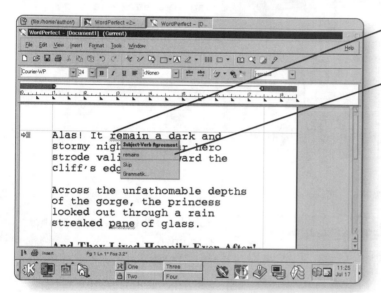

**1.** **Right-click** on a **blue underlined word**. A menu will appear.

**2.** **Click** on the **correct usage** for the word. The word will be replaced with the correct usage and the blue underline will disappear.

### TIP

You can correct spelling errors on-the-fly. Right-click on any words that are underlined in red.

## Spell Checking the Entire Document

It's always a good idea to spell check your document before you print it. But even with a good spell checker, you'll still want to read the document for yourself.

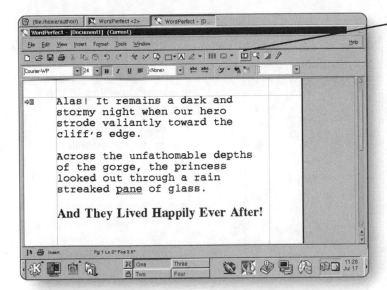

**1. Click** on the **Check and Correct Spelling button** on the toolbar. WordPerfect will begin to check your document and when it finds a misspelled word, the Spell Checker dialog box will open with the first misspelled word displayed in the Replace With text box.

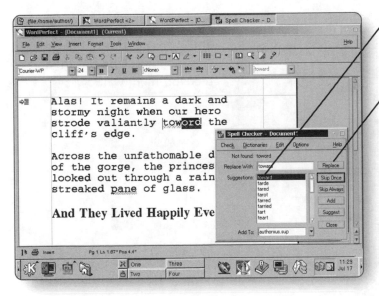

**2. Click** on the **correct spelling** in the Suggestions text box. The word will be selected.

**3. Click** on the **Replace button**. The misspelled word in the document will be replaced with the correct spelling. If there are any other misspellings, the process will continue. When no other misspelled words can be found, a confirmation dialog box will open.

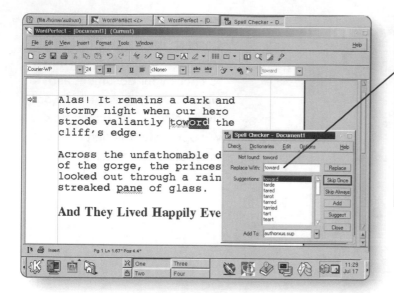

**TIP**

If the correct spelling is not listed, you can type the correct spelling in the Replace With text box. Or, if you want to use the word as displayed, click on the Skip Once or Skip Always button.

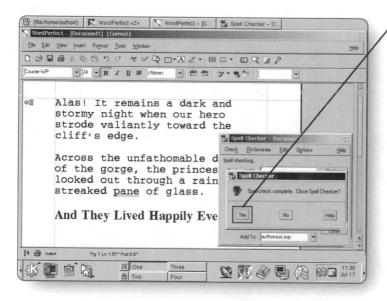

**4. Click** on the **Yes button**. The Spell Checker dialog box will close and you'll be returned to the Document window.

# Working with WordPerfect's Graphics Tools

WordPerfect contains a few tools to help you add a little creative break to your documents. You can easily add lines and shapes, such as boxes and circles. You can also add clip art or images that you created in a computer graphics program.

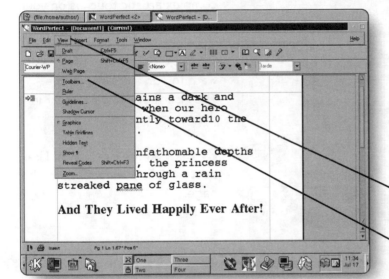

## Displaying the Graphics Toolbar

To see some of the fun art tools, you'll first need to display the Graphics toolbar.

**1. Click** on **View**. The View menu will appear.

**2. Click** on **Toolbars**. The Toolbars dialog box will open.

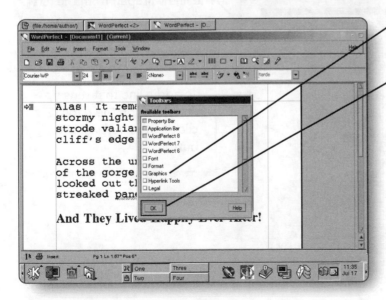

**3. Click** on **Graphics**. The option will be selected.

**4. Click** on **OK**. The Graphics toolbar will appear in the Document window.

# Adding Simple Graphical Touches

If you look across the Graphics toolbar, you'll see a number of elements that you can add to your documents. Let's play with a few simple elements; then you can challenge your skills later and try adding a few more complex artistic touches on your own.

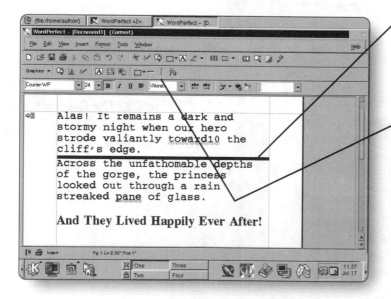

**1. Click** in the **place** where you want to add a horizontal line. The insertion bar will appear in the selected place.

**2. Click** on the **Horizontal Line button**. A line will appear on the page.

The line will span from the left margin to the right margin.

---

**NOTE**

To add a line that runs up and down on the page, click on the Vertical Line button.

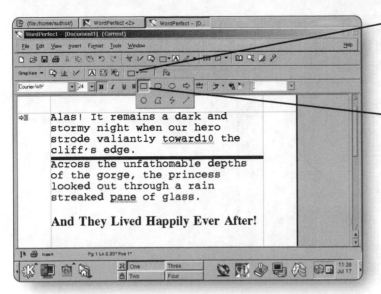

**3. Click** on the **down arrow** next to the Draw an Object button. A list of predefined objects will appear.

**4. Click** on an **object**. The object will be selected and the mouse pointer will change to a crosshair.

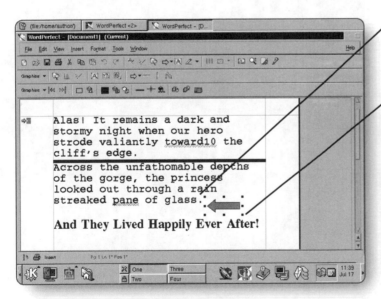

**5. Click and hold** on the **place** where you want to start the object.

**6. Drag** the **mouse pointer** to the place where you want to end the object. An outline of the object will appear in the document.

**7.** When the object is the desired size, **release** the **mouse button**. The object will be created.

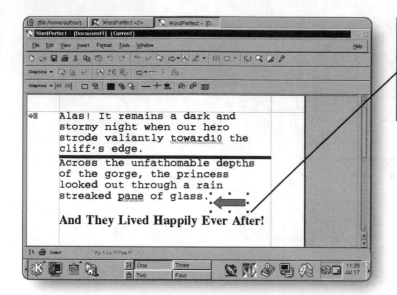

**TIP**

Click and hold on the resize handles to change the size of the object.

# 14

# Printing Files

Before you can print any of the files you created in the various Linux programs, you'll need to tell Linux a few things about your printer. After these introductions have been made, you can easily put an icon on your desktop that will print any files that you drop on the printer icon. If you work with Hewlett Packard printers, OpenLinux contains a special tool that enables you to change the printer settings so you can easily change from draft mode to presentation mode, or from 300 dpi resolution up to 600 dpi. In this chapter, you'll learn how to:

- Set up a printer that is attached to your computer
- Print files using drag and drop
- Change settings for HP printers

# Configuring a Local Printer

To access the Caldera Open Administration System, you'll need to be logged in as root. And, as the standard caution goes, please be careful while you're in root.

## Setting Up the Printer

As you move through the printer configuration process, some of the required information will be filled in for you. Other information that you need to configure the printer can be selected from lists.

**1. Click** on the **Caldera Open Administration System icon** on the Panel. The Caldera Open Administration System menu will appear.

**2. Move** the **mouse pointer** to Peripherals. The Peripherals menu will appear.

**3. Click** on **Printer**. The COAS su wrapper dialog box will open.

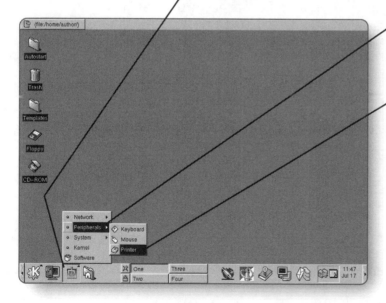

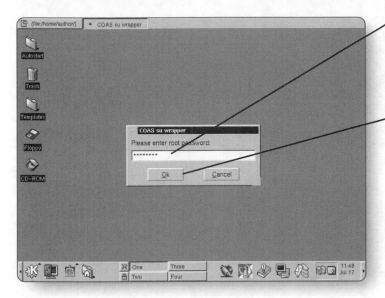

**4.** **Type** the **root password**. The password will appear as a series of asterisks (*) in the text box.

**5.** **Click** on **OK**. The Welcome to COAS dialog box will open.

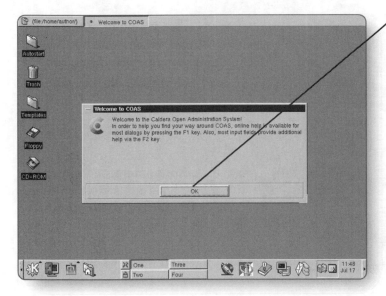

**6.** **Click** on **OK**. The Printer configuration dialog box will open.

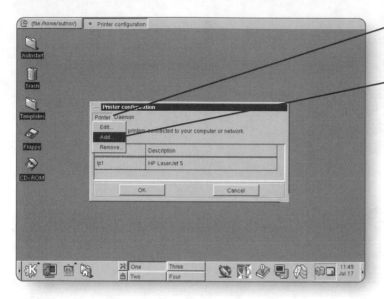

**7. Click** on **Printer**. The Printer menu will appear.

**8. Click** on **Add**. The Select printer model dialog box will open.

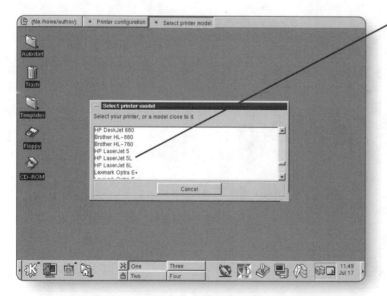

**9. Click** on the **printer** in the list that matches your printer. The Printer name dialog box will open.

### NOTE

Many printers emulate other printers, and most of those can emulate the HP printers. If your printer is on the list, select it; if not, try to find one that closely matches it.

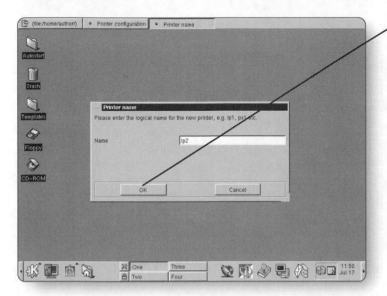

**10. Click** on **OK**. The Printer attributes dialog box will open.

**NOTE**

Make a note of the printer name. You'll need this so that you know which printer to send your print jobs.

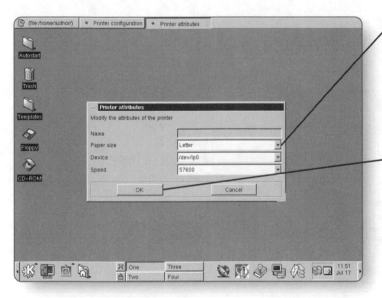

**11.** If you will be using a different size paper on which to print, **click** on the **down arrow** next to the Paper size list box and **click** on a **paper size**. The size will appear in the list box.

**12. Click** on **OK**. The Save dialog box will open.

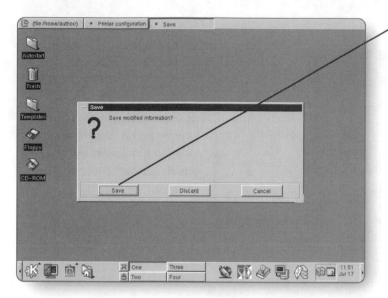

**13.** Click on **Save**. The Create printer queue dialog box will open.

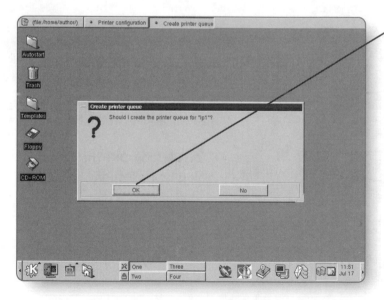

**14.** Click on **OK**. You'll see a series of Starting and Stopping Service screens flash across your screen. Don't worry, it's just your printer configuration file being processed. When the process is complete, you'll be returned to the Printer configuration dialog box.

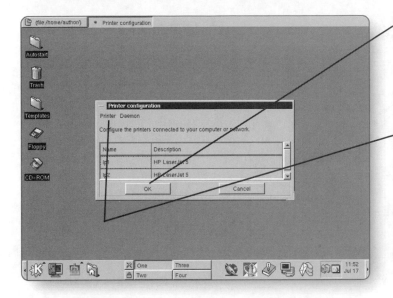

**15. Click** on **OK**. You're now ready to put the printer on the desktop.

## Placing the Printer on the Desktop

Now that the system knows that there is a printer attached, all users will have access to it. Before they can have access to the printer, they'll need to add a printer icon to their desktop. After they have the icon, it's a matter of drag and drop to print a file.

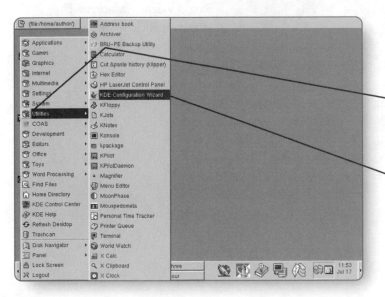

**1. Click** on the **Application Starter**. The main menu will appear.

**2. Move** the **mouse pointer** to **Utilities**. The Utilities menu will appear.

**3. Click** on **KDE Configuration Wizard**. The KDE Setup Wizard will start.

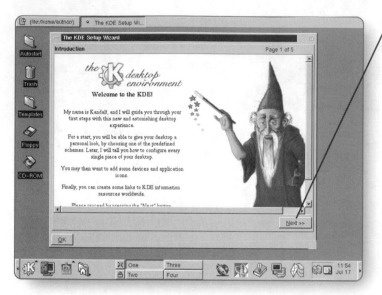

**4. Click** on the **Next button** until you get to the Printer integration page (it's on page 4). The Printer integration page will appear.

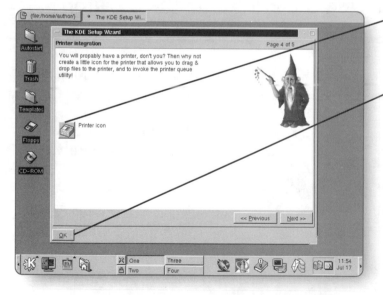

**5. Click** on the **Printer icon**. An icon will be added to the desktop.

**6. Click** on **OK** on the KDE Setup Wizard window. The wizard will close and you can begin printing files.

# Printing Your Files

Even in an electronic world, there's room for paper. When you want to see your document in print, invoke the printer daemon. Think of the printer daemon as a copy of a print command that packages up your print job and escorts it to the printer.

## Printing Made Quick and Easy

It's time to practice your square dance skills. Shuffle to the drag and drop beat, and release the file you want to print over to the Printer icon.

**1. Open** the **File Manager**. The File Manager will open and your home directory will be displayed.

**2. Navigate** to the **directory** that contains the file that you want to print. The list of files in the directory will appear in the right pane.

**3. Click and hold** on the **file** that you want to print. The file will be selected.

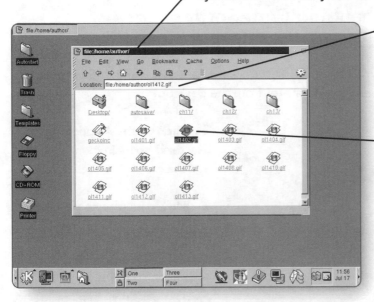

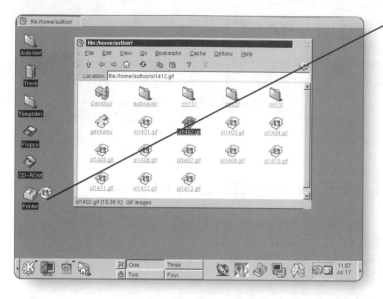

**4. Drag** the **file** until it is over the Printer icon. You'll see an icon representing the file over the printer.

**5. Release** the **mouse button**. The file will be sent to the print queue and will begin printing shortly.

## Changing Print Settings for HP LaserJet Printers

If you have a Hewlett Packard LaserJet printer, you can easily manage your printer from the desktop.

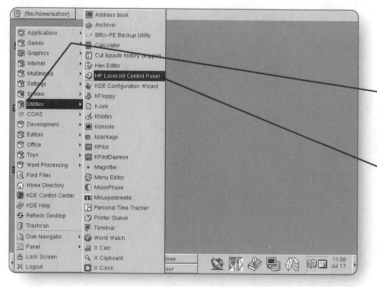

**1. Click** on the **Application Starter**. The main menu will appear.

**2. Move** the **mouse pointer** to **Utilities**. The Utilities menu will appear.

**3. Click** on **HP LaserJet Control Panel**. The Ljet Tool dialog box will open and the Paper tab should be at the top of the stack.

**4.** If you need to change the paper size, **click** on the **down arrow** next to the Format list box and **click** on the **paper size** on which you want to print the document. The paper size will appear in the list box.

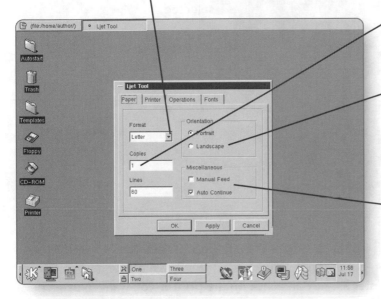

**5.** To print multiple copies of a document, **type** the **number** of copies in the Copies text box.

**6.** **Click** on the **Landscape option button** if you want to change the orientation of the page. The option will be selected.

**7.** If you will be using the printer's manual feed tray, **click** in the **Manual Feed check box**. A check mark will appear in the box.

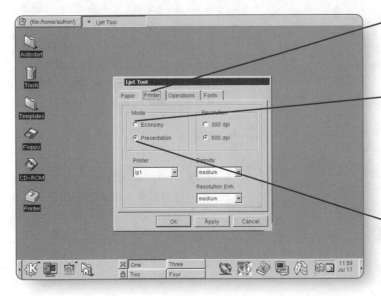

**8.** **Click** on the **Printer tab**. The Printer tab will come to the top of the stack.

**9a.** If you want to print a rough draft, **click** on the **Economy option button**. The option will be selected.

**OR**

**9b.** If you want a quality printout, **click** on the **Presentation option button**. The option will be selected.

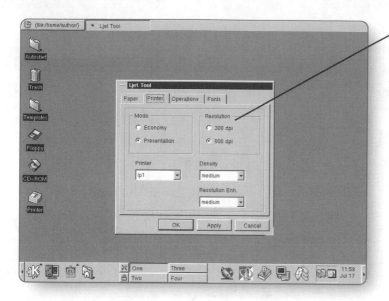

**10. Click** on the **Resolution option button** that corresponds to the resolution at which you want to print. The option will be selected.

**11.** If there is more than one printer attached to your computer or network, **click** on the **down arrow** next to the Printer list box and **click** on the **printer** you want to use. The printer will appear in the list box.

**12.** To adjust the darkness and lightness of the printed page, **click** on the **down arrow** next to the Density list box and **click** on the desired **density**. The density will appear in the list box.

**13. Click** on **OK** when you are finished making changes. The dialog box will close, and you can try out the new print settings.

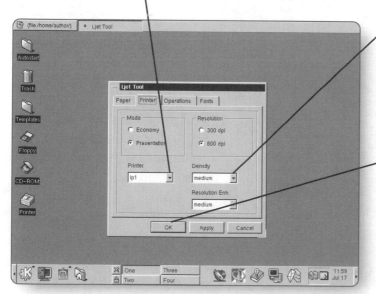

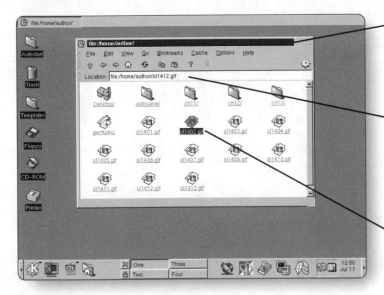

**14. Open** the **File Manager**. The File Manager will open and your home directory will be displayed.

**15. Navigate** to the **directory** that contains the file that you want to print. The list of files in the directory will appear in the right pane.

**16. Click and hold** on the **file** that you want to print. The file will be selected.

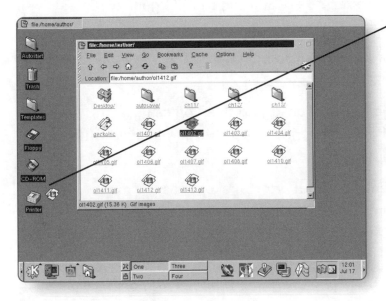

**17. Drag** the **file** until it is over the Printer icon. You'll see an icon representing the file over the printer.

**18. Release** the **mouse button**. The file will be sent to the print queue and will begin printing shortly.

# Part III Review Questions

1. Which menu command and toolbar button will create a new document file for you? *See "Creating a New File" in Chapter 10*

2. How do you make a second copy of an open document? *See "Saving a File" in Chapter 10*

3. How do you create a blank canvas with The GIMP? *See "Getting Started with The GIMP" in Chapter 11*

4. Where do you go to change the color used by a brush in The GIMP? *See "Creating Great Graphics with The GIMP" in Chapter 11*

5. Which program that was installed with OpenLinux can help you keep your life organized? *See "Starting the KOrganizer" in Chapter 12*

6. How do you add an appointment to KOrganizer? *See "Working with an Appointment Book" in Chapter 12*

7. Where do you get the registration key so that you can use WordPerfect beyond the trial period? *See "Getting Started with WordPerfect" in Chapter 13*

8. Which window elements in WordPerfect make it easy to move around your document? *See "Starting Your First Document" in Chapter 13*

9. Which user has the authority to set up a printer so that all users on the system have access to it? *See "Configuring a Local Printer" in Chapter 14*

10. What is the easiest way to print files stored on your computer? *See "Printing Your Files" in Chapter 14*

# PART IV

# Tuning Up OpenLinux

# 15

# Getting On
# the Internet

Before you can take Linux on the Internet and explore the
World Wide Web, you need to set up a dialer. The KDE
Interface uses the Kppp dialer to set up your connection and to
dial your ISP (*Internet Service Provider*). This is a simple
interface and will get you online in just a few minutes. After
you're online, you can browse Web sites, check your e-mail,
discuss your Linux problems and questions in the newsgroups,
and whatever else catches your fancy. In this chapter, you'll
learn how to:

- Create an Internet connection using Kppp
- Dial your ISP

# Creating the Connection

After an account is set up with an ISP and you have all the
required information, you can create the dial-up connection.
This section will show how to configure the most common
connection, a PPP (*Point-to-Point Protocol*). You might want
to check out the OpenLinux hardware compatibility list to
make sure your modem is compatible with OpenLinux. You'll
find the list at **www.calderasystems.com/products/
openlinux/hardware.html**.

**1.** **Click** on the **Application Starter**. The main menu will
appear.

**2.** **Move** the **mouse pointer** to **Internet**. The Internet menu
will appear.

**3.** **Click** on **Kppp**. The kppp
dialog box will open.

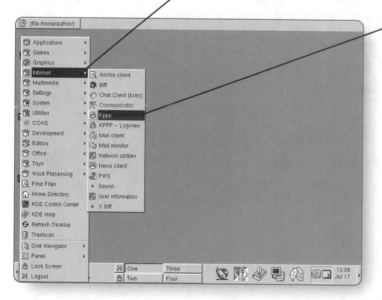

### NOTE

You might see a dialog
box that tells you about
the Quickhelp feature. To
use Quickhelp, right-click
on a button or option in
any dialog box.

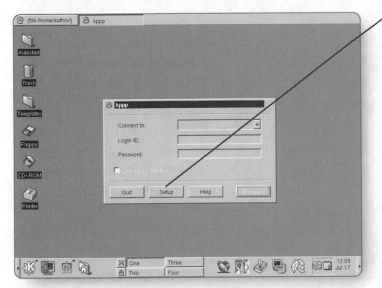

**4. Click** on the **Setup button**. The kppp Configuration dialog box will open and the Accounts tab should be at the top of the stack.

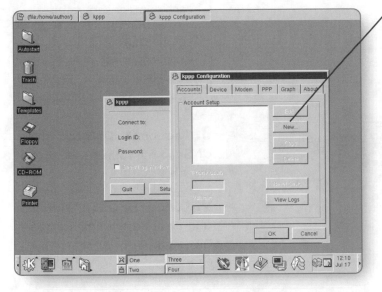

**5. Click** on the **New button**. The New Account dialog box will open and the Dial tab should be at the top of the stack.

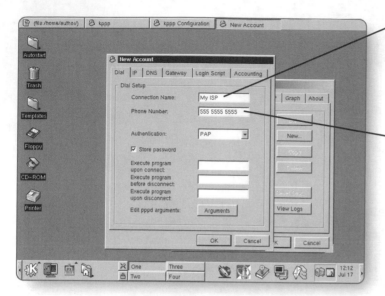

**6. Click** in the **Connection Name text box** and **type** a descriptive **name** for the Internet Connection. You could use the name of your ISP.

**7. Click** in the **Phone Number text box** and **type** the **phone number** you need to dial to connect to your ISP; you can use dashes in the phone number.

### TIP

If your ISP has several phone numbers that you can use to connect to the Internet, you can type each number separated by a colon. When the first number fails to connect, kppp will use the next number.

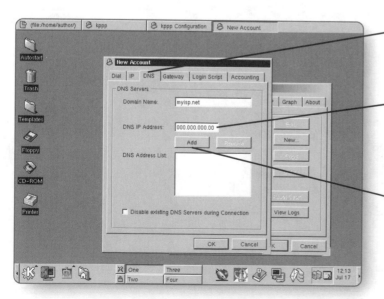

**8. Click** on the **DNS tab**. The DNS tab will come to the top of the stack.

**9. Click** in the **DNS IP Address text box** and **type** the primary **DNS number** given to you by your ISP.

**10. Click** on the **Add button**. The DNS IP Address will be added to the DNS Address List.

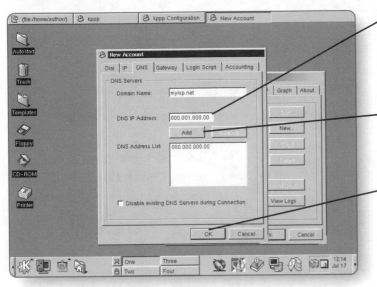

**11.** **Click** in the **DNS IP Address text box** and **type** the secondary DNS **number** given to you by your ISP.

**12.** **Click** on the **Add button**. The address will be added to the DNS Address List.

**13.** **Click** on **OK**. You will be returned to the kppp Configuration dialog box.

**14.** **Click** on the **Device tab**. The Device tab will come to the top of the stack.

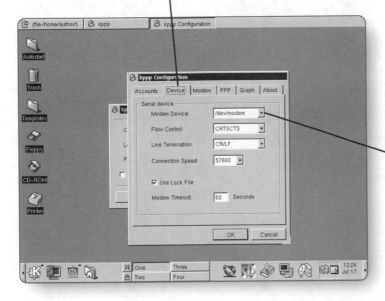

**NOTE**

If you are using an external modem, make sure it is turned on.

**15.** **Click** the **down arrow** next to the **Modem Device list box** and **click** on the **port** to which your modem is connected. The modem port will appear in the list box.

**TIP**

In Linux, com port 1 becomes /dev/ttyS0, com port 2 becomes /dev/ttyS1, serial port 1 becomes /dev/cua0, and serial port 2 becomes /dev/cua1.

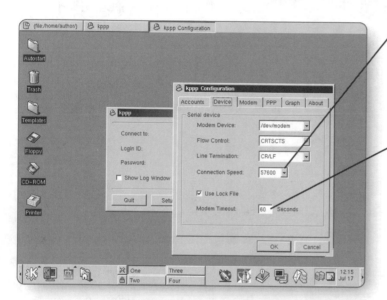

**16.** Click the **down arrow** next to the **Connection Speed list box** and **click** on the **speed** of your modem. The speed will appear in the list box.

**17.** **Double-click** in the **Modem Timeout text box** and **type** the **amount** of time you want the modem to wait for a connection to your ISP to be made. After the designated amount of time, the dialer will try to connect to your ISP again.

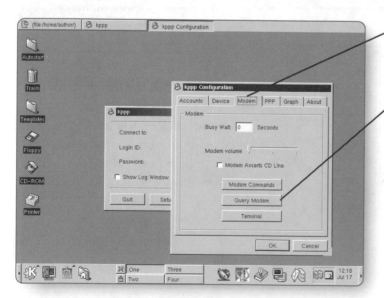

**18.** Click on the **Modem tab**. The Modem tab will come to the top of the stack.

**19.** Click on the **Query Modem button**. The ATI Query dialog box will open and will test the modem. When the test is complete, the Modem Query Results dialog box will open.

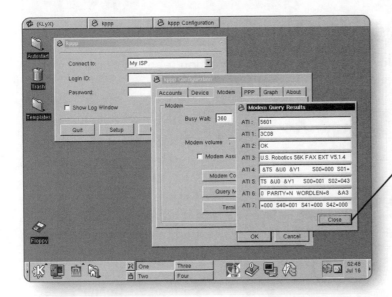

**TIP**

If you receive an error message, click on the Device tab and try a different modem port.

**20. Click** on **Close**. You will be returned to the Modem tab of the kppp Configuration dialog box.

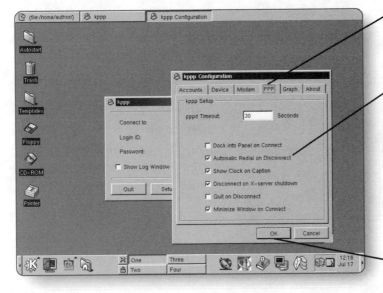

**21. Click** on the **PPP tab**. The PPP tab will come to the top of the stack.

**22. Click** on the **Automatic Redial on Disconnect check box** if you want the kppp dialer to reconnect you to your ISP if you are unexpectedly disconnected from the Internet. A check mark will appear in the box.

**23. Click** on **OK**. You will be returned to the kppp dialer and you'll be ready to give your connection a test drive.

# Making the Connection

Now that you've got the connection set up, it's time to give your dial-up connection a try.

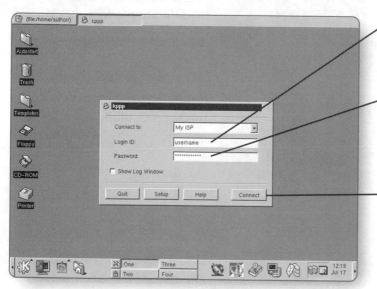

**1.** **Click** in the **Login ID text box** and **type** the **username** required by your ISP.

**2.** **Click** in the **Password text box** and **type** the **password** needed to authenticate your connection.

**3.** **Click** on the **Connect button**. The Connecting to dialog box will open.

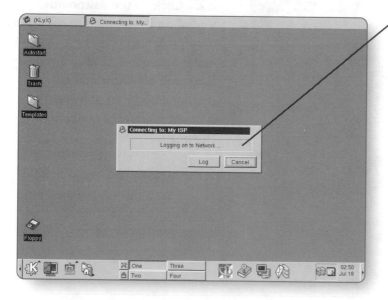

You can watch as your modem attempts to connect to your ISP. You'll get a connection dialog box when the connection is made. You're ready to surf!

# 16

# Browsing the Internet

Now that you've made the connection to your Internet Service Provider, you'll need a Web browser, e-mail program, and newsgroup reader so that you can travel on the Web and stay in contact with other people. You'll find all these capabilities, and more, in Netscape Communicator. In this chapter, you'll learn how to:

- Use Netscape Navigator to visit Web sites
- Create a list of bookmarks to store often-visited Web sites
- Set cookie preferences
- Save Web pages

# Using the Netscape Navigator Web Browser

Netscape Navigator is one of several Linux Web browsers that you can use to surf the Web. If you come from a Windows or Macintosh background, you'll find Navigator to be a familiar face and a quick way to get up and running on the Web.

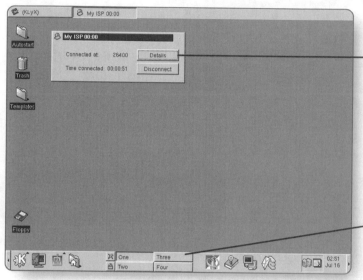

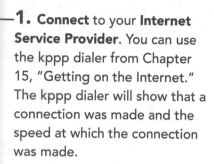

**1. Connect** to your **Internet Service Provider**. You can use the kppp dialer from Chapter 15, "Getting on the Internet." The kppp dialer will show that a connection was made and the speed at which the connection was made.

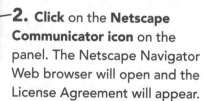

**2. Click** on the **Netscape Communicator icon** on the panel. The Netscape Navigator Web browser will open and the License Agreement will appear.

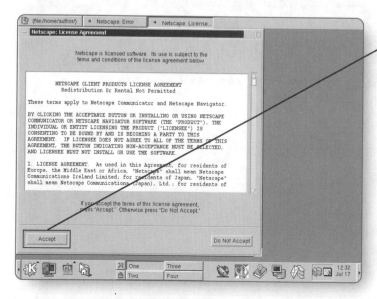

**3. Click** on **Accept**. An Error window will appear letting you know where the cache directory for your user account has been created.

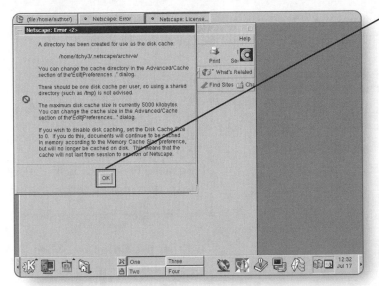

**4. Click** on **OK**. The dialog box will close and the home page for the Netscape Product Registration will appear in the browser window.

## Accessing Web Pages

Begin by typing a Web address, or URL (Uniform Resource Locator), into the Netsite text box. You may know of different addresses that you'd like to try, but if not, try the Prima Tech Home Page at **www.prima-tech.com**.

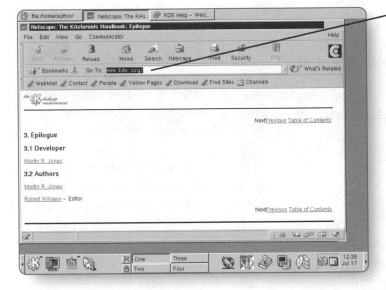

**1. Double-click** in the **Location box**. The URL that is currently in the Location box will be selected.

### NOTE

The name of the Location text box will change as you work with the browser. You may see the text box labeled as Netsite, Go To, or Location. Don't worry about the name. Just remember that this text box takes to you whichever Web site you select.

**2. Type** the **URL** of the Web page you want to visit. The first URL will disappear and the URL you type will display.

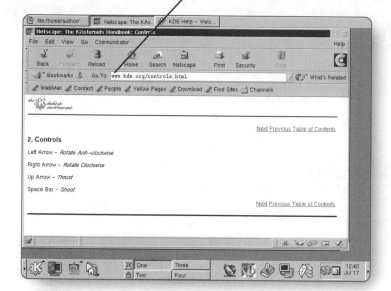

**3. Press** the **Enter key** when you are finished typing the URL. The Web page will appear in the browser window.

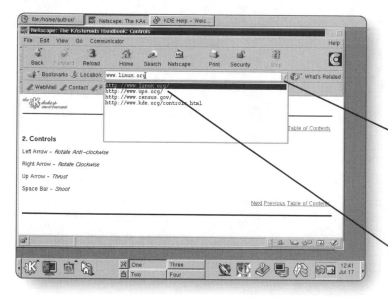

If you've typed Web addresses previously in the Location box, Navigator keeps track of these Web addresses in the Location box drop-down list.

**4. Click** on the **down arrow** to the right of the Location box. A list of URLs that you previously typed in the Location box will appear.

**5. Click** on a **URL**. The associated Web page will appear in the browser window.

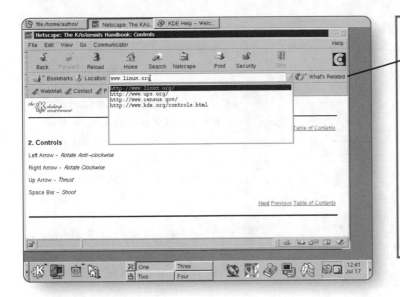

**TIP**

If you're searching for information and a page that you are visiting is close, but not quite what you were looking for, click on the What's Related button. A list of Web sites, similar to the one currently displayed in the browser window, will appear.

## Changing Your Home Page

The home page is the first Web page you see when you open the Navigator browser. The first time you use Navigator, a home page is selected for you. You can change it to something that is more useful or interesting to you.

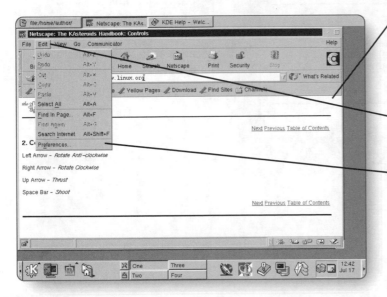

**1. Open** the **Web page** that you want to use as a home page. The Web page will appear in the browser window.

**2. Click** on **Edit**. The Edit menu will appear.

**3. Click** on **Preferences**. The Preferences dialog box will open.

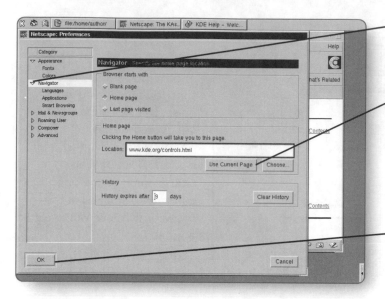

**4. Click** on the **Navigator category**. The Specify the home page location pane will appear.

**5. Click** on the **Use Current Page button**. The URL in the Location text box will change to match the URL of the page displayed in the browser window.

**6. Click** on **OK**. The Preferences dialog box will close and you'll return to the browser window.

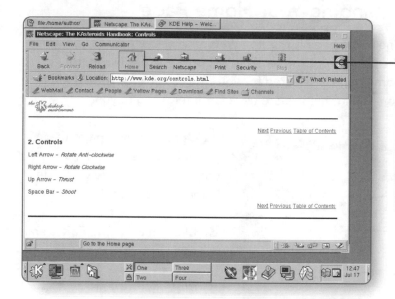

### NOTE

When you're cruising around the Web, you can return to your home page easily with just a click of the Home button. Your default home page will appear in the browser window.

# Keeping a List of Frequently Visited Web Sites

If you visit a number of Web sites on a regular basis, you'll want to keep of list of those sites for future reference. A tool called Bookmarks will keep all the Web pages organized in one convenient place. If you don't want one big list of bookmarks, you can create folders in which to file the bookmarks.

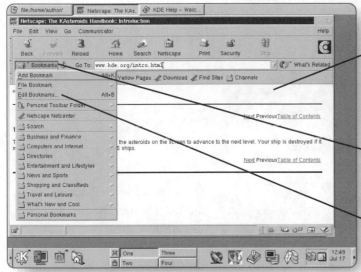

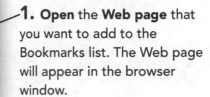

**1. Open** the **Web page** that you want to add to the Bookmarks list. The Web page will appear in the browser window.

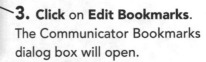

**2. Click** on the **Bookmarks button**. The Bookmarks menu will appear.

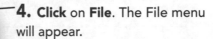

**3. Click** on **Edit Bookmarks**. The Communicator Bookmarks dialog box will open.

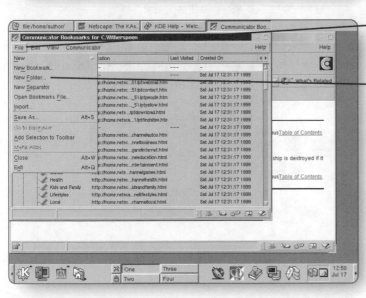

**4. Click** on **File**. The File menu will appear.

**5. Click** on **New Folder**. The Bookmark Properties dialog box will open.

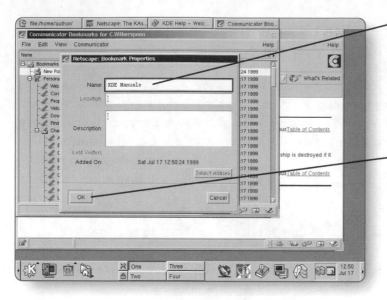

**6. Select** the **text** in the Name text box and **type** a **name** for the folder in which you want to place some of your bookmarks. The new folder name will appear in the text box.

**7. Click** on **OK**. The folder will be created.

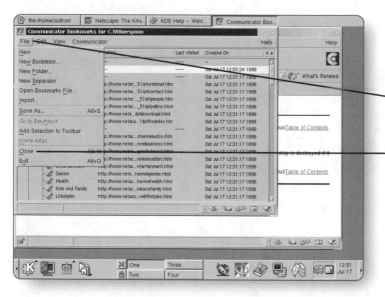

The new folder will appear in the Bookmarks list and will be selected.

**8. Click** on **File**. The File menu will appear.

**9. Click** on **Close**. The Communicator Bookmarks dialog box will close.

**10. Click** on the **Bookmarks button**. The Bookmarks menu will appear.

**11. Click** on **File Bookmark**. A second menu will appear.

**12. Click** on the **folder** into which you want to place the bookmark. The bookmark will be stored in the selected folder.

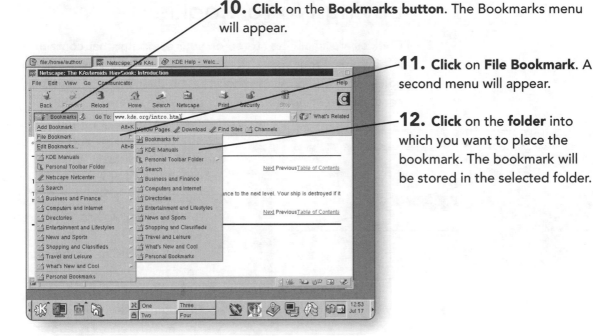

**13. Click** on the **Bookmarks button** to access a bookmark. The Bookmarks menu will appear.

**14. Click** on the **folder** that contains the bookmark that you want to view. A list of the Web sites contained in the folder will appear.

**15. Click** on the **Web site**. The Web site will appear in the browser window.

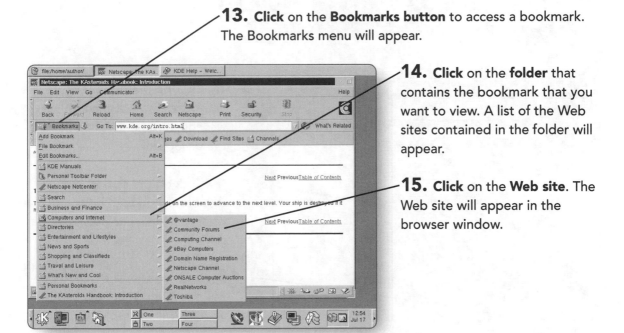

# Saying No to Cookies

Cookies are small files stored on your computer that contain information about your visits to a Web site. They may allow you to continue browsing the site from the place where you concluded your previous visit, or they may remember information that you supplied to the site on a previous visit. You can decide individually or universally whether to accept cookies that ask to be downloaded to your computer.

**1.** **Click** on **Edit**. The Edit menu will appear.

**2.** **Click** on **Preferences**. The Netscape Preferences dialog box will open.

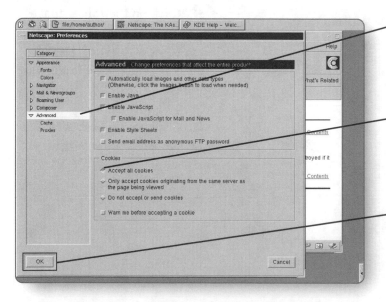

**3.** **Click** on the **Advanced category**. The Advanced pane will appear on the right side of the dialog box.

**4.** **Click** on the **option button** that corresponds to how you want to handle cookies. The option will be selected.

**5.** **Click** on **OK**. The dialog box will close, and your new cookie settings will be applied.

# Saving and Printing Web Pages

As you surf the Web, you'll encounter many interesting and informative Web sites. You may want to store some of these informative Web pages for future reference.

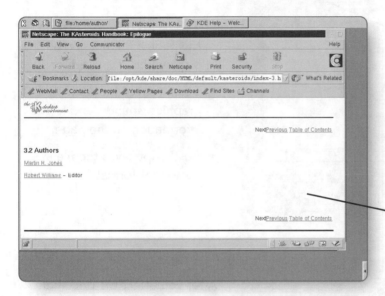

## Saving Web Pages

Saving a Web page enables you to keep a permanent copy of the Web page on your computer. By doing this, you can view the page in any application that can read HTML, PostScript, or text files.

**1. Display** the **Web page** that you want to save. The Web page will appear in the browser window.

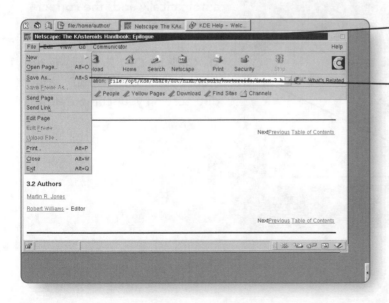

**2. Click** on **File**. The File menu will appear.

**3. Click** on **Save As**. The Save As dialog box will open.

**4. Navigate** to the **directory** in which you want to save the Web page. The directory will be selected.

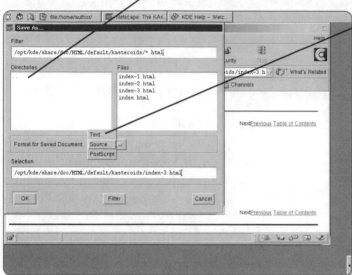

**5. Choose** one of the following **options** from the Format for Saved Document list box:

• Text saves only the text on the page so that it can be displayed in a text editor.

• Source saves the text, graphics, sounds, and HTML information on the page.

• PostScript saves the file in PostScript format.

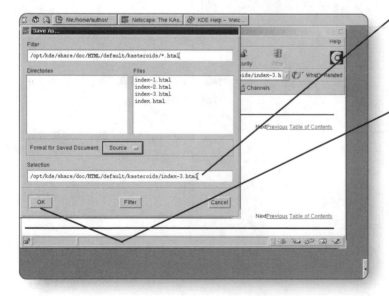

After you select the document format, the Save As dialog box automatically adds the correct extension to the file name.

**6. Click** on **OK**. The file will be stored in the designated directory on your computer.

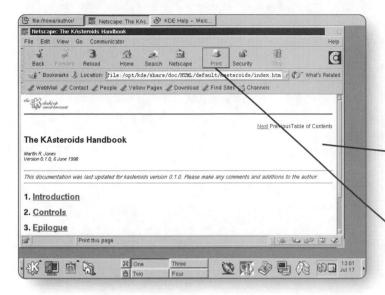

# Printing Web Pages

Even though we live in an electronic world, it is sometimes more convenient to have a paper copy of a document.

**1. Display** the **Web page** that you want to print. The page will appear in the browser window.

**2. Click** on the **Print button**. The Print dialog box will open.

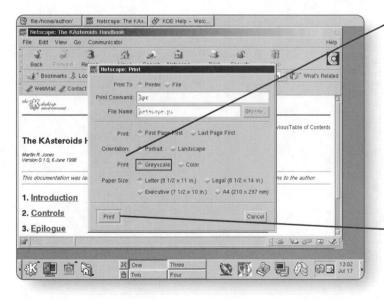

**3. Click** on a **Print option button**. The option will be selected.

- If you will be printing to a laser printer, click on the Greyscale option button.

- If you will be printing to a color ink jet printer, click on the Color option button.

**4. Click** on **Print**. The Web page will be sent to your printer and a paper copy will appear.

# 17

# Working with E-mail

E-mail has been the most popular network application since the very beginning of computer networking. A few university computers were connected together by the government in the ARPANET project in the late 1960s to test a new method of data transmission called "Packet-switching." E-mail turned out to be an unplanned side benefit of packet-switching networks. This chapter will show you how to take advantage of the fruits of that breakthrough by setting up an e-mail account and learning to use the KDE mail client. In this chapter, you'll learn how to:

- Set up the KDE mail client
- Send, receive, and reply to messages
- Maintain an address book

# Setting Up Mail Accounts

Setting up Internet tools and configuring them may seem a little daunting to someone who has not had much experience with doing it, but it is handled nicely by KDE. There is a configuration tool to guide you as you go along, so let's get started.

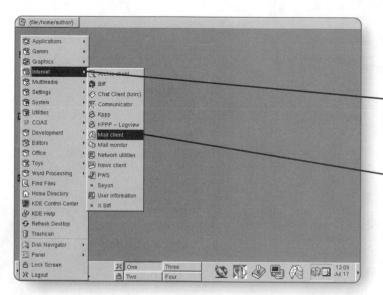

**1.** **Click** on the **Application Starter**. The main menu will appear.

**2.** **Move** the **mouse pointer** to **Internet**. The Internet menu will appear.

**3.** **Click** on **Mail client**. The Settings dialog box will open. The Identity tab should be at the top of the stack, and your name should appear in the Name text box.

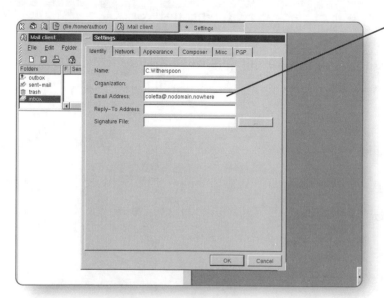

**4.** **Click** in the **Email Address text box**. The cursor will become an insertion bar.

**5.** **Type** your **e-mail address**. The e-mail address will be changed.

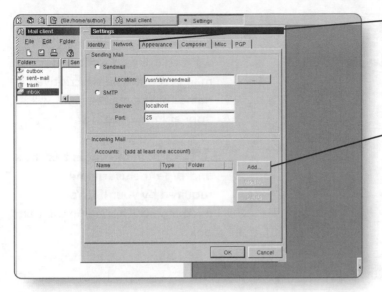

**6. Click** on the **Network Tab**. The Network Tab will come to the top of the stack. This is where you will create your incoming mail account.

**7. Click** on the **Add** button in the Incoming Mail section. The Select Account dialog box will open.

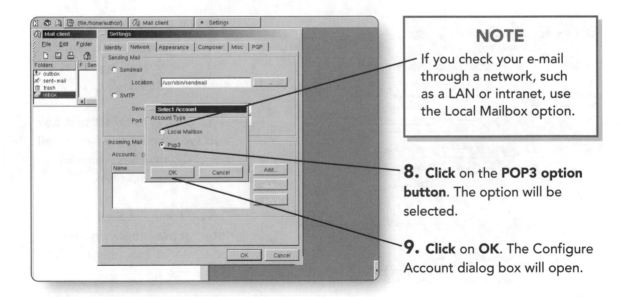

### NOTE

If you check your e-mail through a network, such as a LAN or intranet, use the Local Mailbox option.

**8. Click** on the **POP3 option button**. The option will be selected.

**9. Click** on **OK**. The Configure Account dialog box will open.

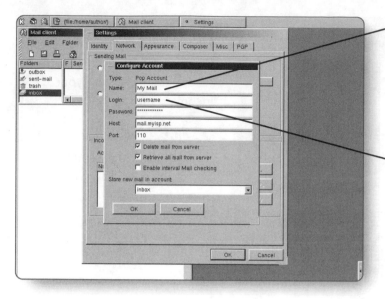

**10. Click** in the **Name text box** and **type** the **name** you want to use to describe your mail account. The descriptive name for the mail account will appear in the text box.

**11. Click** in the **Login text box** and **type** the **username** required by your ISP. Your username will appear in the text box.

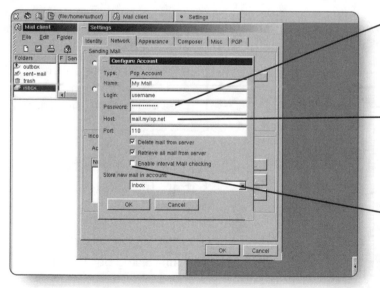

**12. Click** in the **Password text box** and **type** your **password**. You password will appear as a series of asterisks(*).

**13. Click** in the **Host text box** and **type** the name of your **mail host**. The mail host name will appear in the text box.

**14. Click** in the **Enable Interval Mail checking** option box. Interval mail checking will be selected.

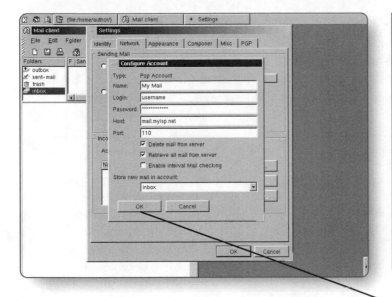

**TIP**

Interval mail checking will cause the Mail Client to poll the mail server after an elapsed time and download any incoming messages that are in your mailbox. This polling will keep your ISP from dumping you as an inactive connection when you need to step away from your computer for a little while.

**15. Click** on **OK**. You will be returned to the Settings dialog box.

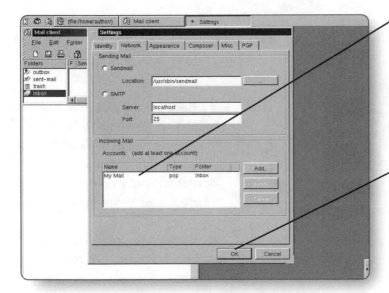

Your newly configured mail account will display in the Incoming Mail Accounts window. If you're connected to your ISP, the mail client will call up your mail account and download your mail.

**16. Click** on **OK**. The Settings dialog box will close.

# Receiving Messages

When the Settings dialog panel in the last section disappeared, it left the KDE Mail Client open on the desktop with your mail messages displayed.

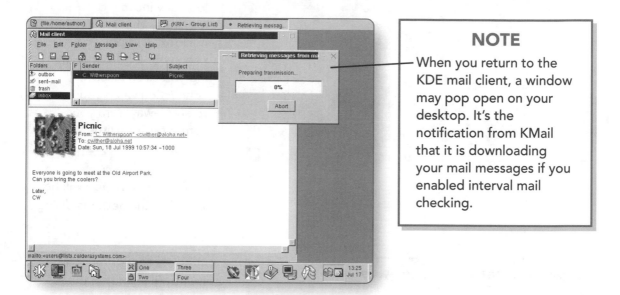

### NOTE

When you return to the KDE mail client, a window may pop open on your desktop. It's the notification from KMail that it is downloading your mail messages if you enabled interval mail checking.

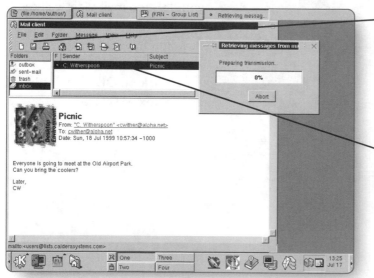

**1. Click** on the **Get new mail button** on the toolbar. The Message download dialog box will open, and KMail will download your mail messages from your ISP's mail server.

**2. Click** on the **message** that you want to read. The message will appear in the preview pane.

# Sending Messages

The KDE Mail Client is a well-thought-out tool and everything that you need is just a click away. It is a simple matter to open a composer window and compose a new e-mail message.

## Sending a New Message

For those already familiar with e-mail, the KMail Composer probably looks very much like the composer in the e-mail program you were using before. All the things that the Composer can do are in the menus on the menu bar. The toolbar buttons automate some processes and make components more accessible. To begin composing your message, follow these steps.

**1. Click** on the **Compose new message button** on the toolbar. The Choose Signature File browser will open.

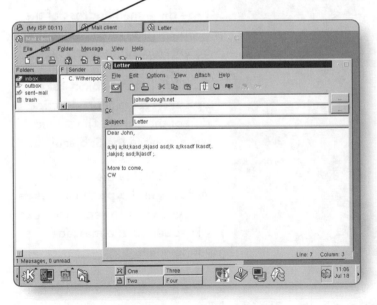

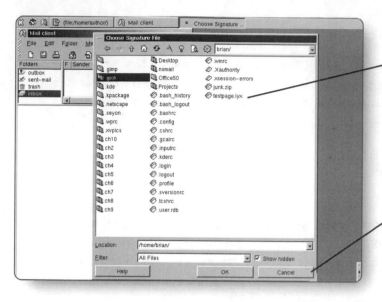

**2. Click** on **Cancel**. The Signature File browser will disappear, and the KMail Composer will open.

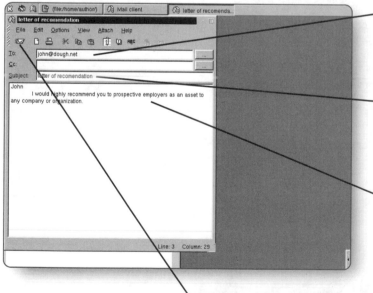

**3. Click** in the **To text box** and **type** the **e-mail address** of the recipient. The e-mail address will be entered in the text box.

**4. Click** in the **Subject text box** and type a short description of the e-mail. The subject will appear in the Subject line.

**5. Click** inside the **Message Window** and **type** the **message** that you want to send. The text will appear in the message window.

**6.** When you have completed the message, **click** on the **Send message button**. The KMail Composer window will close, and the message will be sent.

# Maintaining an Address Book

When you need a way to keep track of those e-mail addresses that you use frequently, keep them in the KMail Addressbook.

## Opening the Addressbook

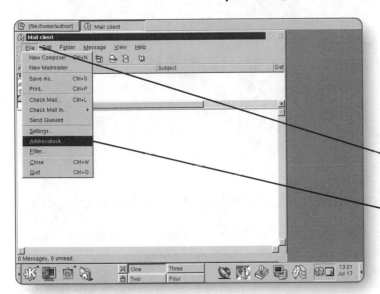

You can use the KDE Mail client address book to keep track of your e-mail contacts. Taking the time now to learn about the address book features will make the job of sending e-mail a snap.

**1. Click** on **File**. The File menu will appear.

**2. Click** on **Addressbook**. The Addressbook Manager window will open.

## Adding an Address

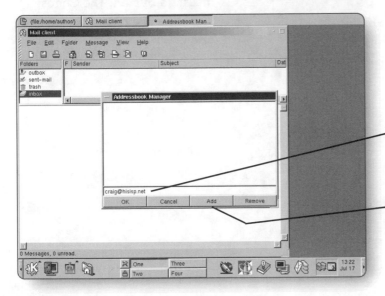

Adding new e-mail addresses to the Addressbook is a simple process.

**1. Click** in the **text box** above the button bar and **type** an **e-mail address**.

**2. Click** on the **Add button**. The e-mail address will be added to the address book.

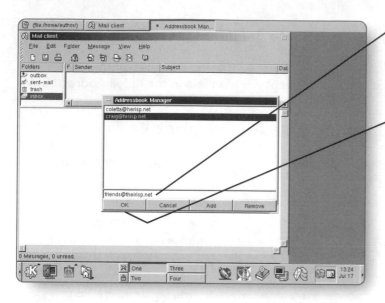

**3. Add** additional **e-mail addresses** to the address book. The list of e-mail addresses will increase.

**4.** When you are finished, **click** on **OK**. The Addressbook Manager window will close, and you can now use the address book to send a message.

## Sending E-mail with the Addressbook

Now that you've saved a few e-mail addresses, you can make the task of sending messages a little easier.

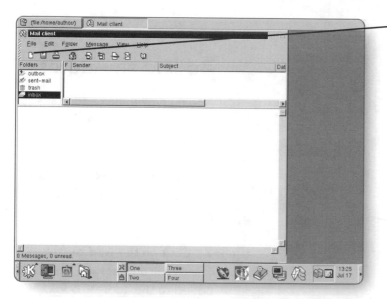

**1. Click** on the **Compose new message button**. The Choose Signature File dialog box will open.

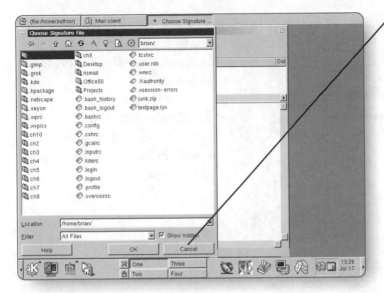

**2. Click** on **Cancel**. The dialog box will disappear, and a KMail Composer window will open.

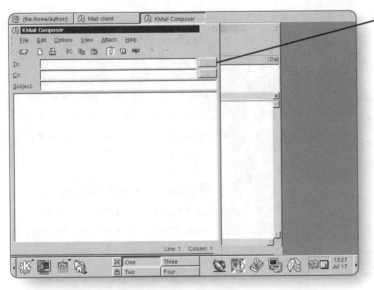

**3. Click** on the **button** to the right of the To text box. The Addressbook will open.

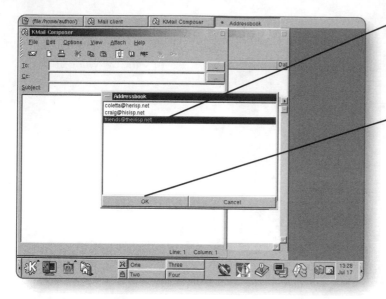

**4.** **Click** on the **e-mail address** to which you want to send the message. The e-mail address will be selected.

**5.** **Click** on **OK**. The Addressbook will close and the e-mail address will appear in the To text box.

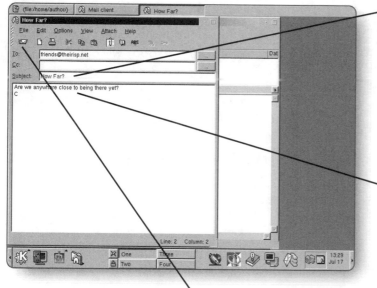

**6.** **Click** in the **Subject text box** and **type** a **subject** for the message. The subject of the e-mail message will appear in the text box. This lets the recipient know what the message is about before they read it.

**7.** **Click** in the **Message area** and **type** your **letter**. You're now ready to send the message to its intended recipient.

**8.** **Click** on the **Send message button**. The message will be on its way to the recipient.

# 18

# Lurking the Newsgroups

Usenet newsgroups are an unbelievably rich source of current information and interest for just about any subject you can name. If you want to learn more about Linux, check out the Linux-related newsgroups. You can usually find someone willing to help you solve a problem, answer a question about how to use a software program, or discuss the future of Linux. Newsgroups are a great way to meet people, and the News client can get you started. In this chapter, you'll learn how to:

- Set up access to a news server
- Subscribe to newsgroups
- Read and respond to newsgroup messages

# Setting Up a News Client

Before you can get to any of the newsgroups, you'll need to connect to your ISP and set up access to their newsgroup server.

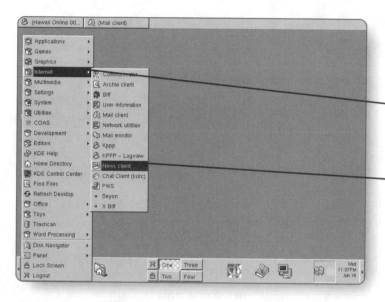

**1. Click** on the **Application Starter**. The main menu will appear.

**2. Move** the **mouse pointer** to **Internet**. The Internet menu will appear.

**3. Click** on **News client**. If this is the first time you have used the News client, you will be asked for some information before proceeding.

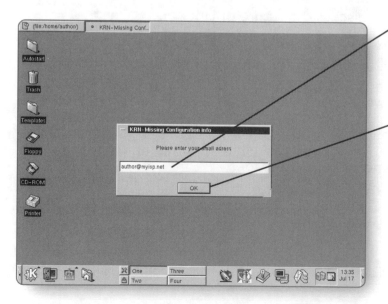

**4. Clear** the **information** in the text box and **type** your **e-mail address**. Your e-mail address will appear in the text box.

**5. Click** on **OK**. Another dialog box will open asking for your real name.

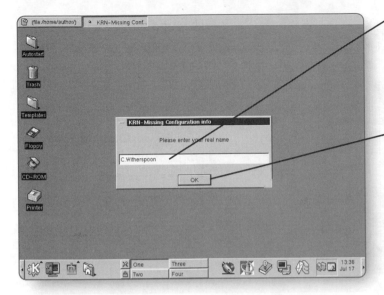

**6. Type** your **name** in the text box. The name that will be used in the headers of any messages you post in the newsgroups will appear in the text box.

**7. Click** on **OK**. Another dialog box will open asking for your organization's name.

### TIP

If you want to be incognito while surfing the newsgroups, use a fictitious name.

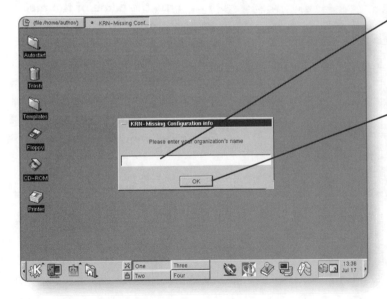

**8. Type** the **name of the company** for which you work, if desired. You can leave this field blank.

**9. Click** on **OK**. Another dialog box will open asking for the name of the news server to which you want to subscribe.

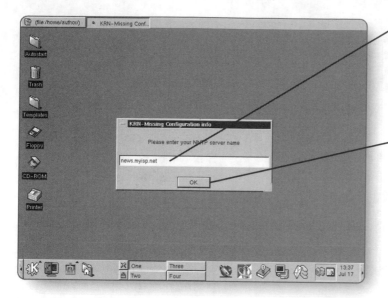

**10.** **Type** the **name of the news server** to which you want to connect. The news server name will appear in the text box.

**11.** **Click** on **OK**. Another dialog box will open asking for the name of your ISP's SMTP server.

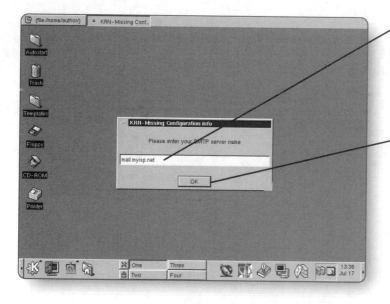

**12.** **Type** the **name of the mail server** through which you send your e-mail. The name of your outgoing mail server will appear in the text box.

**13.** **Click** on **OK**. The KRN-Group List window will appear.

# Getting the Newsgroups

After you have set up the news server, it's time to get the list of newsgroups and begin lurking.

## Downloading the List of Newsgroups

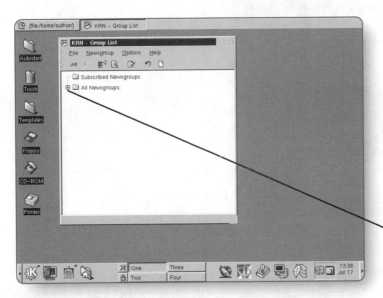

Before you can read any newsgroup messages, you'll need to download the entire list of newsgroups. After this list is downloaded, you'll always have access to it. In the future, the only part of the list that you'll need to download will be from any new newsgroups that appear.

**1.** **Click** on the **plus sign** next to All Newsgroups. An error dialog box will open telling you that you do not have a list of newsgroups yet.

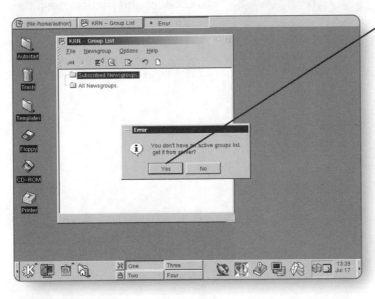

**2.** **Click** on **Yes**. The Krn-Question dialog box will open asking whether you want to connect to the news server.

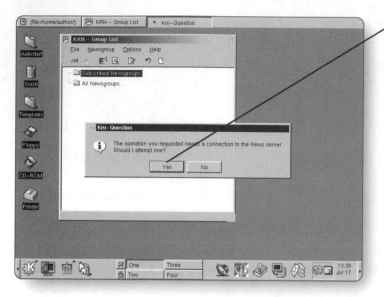

**3. Click** on **Yes**. The connection will be made to the server and the list of newsgroups will begin downloading.

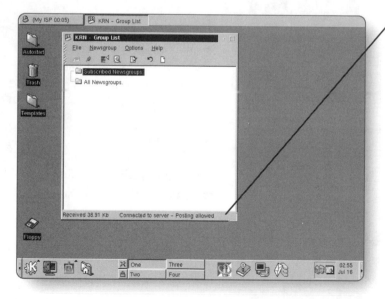

This will take some time to complete. There are thousands of newsgroup names and the list you are getting is just the names and headers that you will need to connect and participate in the groups.

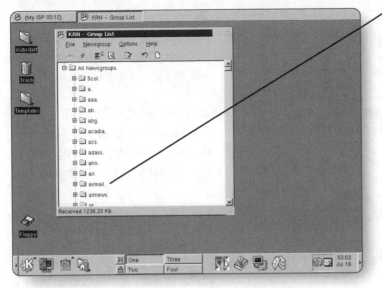

After the list finishes downloading, all of the newsgroups will be listed in the tree directory shown in the KRN-Group List window.

## Subscribing to Newsgroups

Subscribing to newsgroups isn't like subscribing to magazines and having them delivered to your doorstep. The magazines aren't always free and you can't really interact with the people who write magazine articles. The newsgroups to which you subscribe do get delivered right to your doorstep though (through the News client), and they get updated automatically whenever you go online. And, you are encouraged to converse with the posters of newsgroup messages.

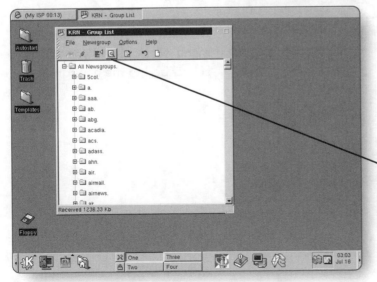

**1. Click** on the **Find Group button** on the toolbar. The KRN-Find a Newsgroup dialog box will open.

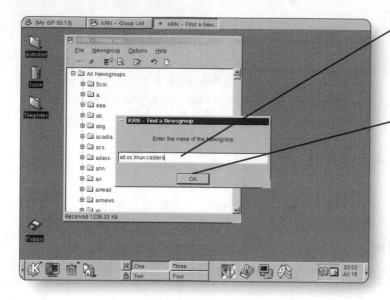

**2. Type** the name of the **newsgroup** for which you are looking. The newsgroup name will appear in the text box.

**3. Click** on **OK**. The KRN-Group List window will expand the tree directory and highlight the newsgroup you named.

### NOTE

You could also just browse through the list of newsgroups. Just click on a plus sign to expand the list, or click on the minus sign to collapse the list.

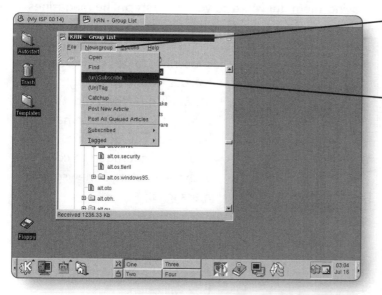

**4. Click** on **Newsgroup** in the menu bar. The Newsgroup menu will appear.

**5. Click** on **(un)Subscribe**. The menu will close and you will be subscribed to the newsgroup.

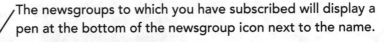

The newsgroups to which you have subscribed will display a pen at the bottom of the newsgroup icon next to the name.

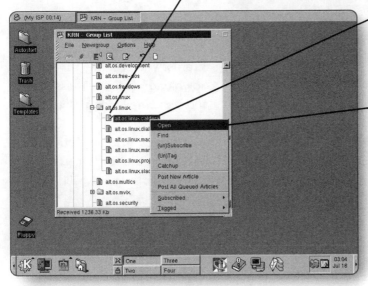

**6. Right-click and hold** on the subscribed **newsgroup** that you want to view. A menu will appear.

**7. Move** the **mouse pointer** to **Open** and release the mouse button. The News client will open.

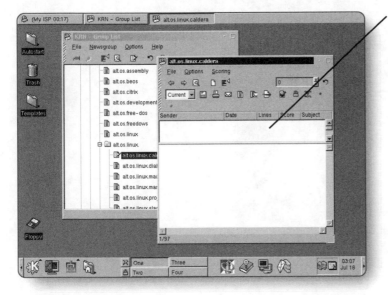

When the newsgroup opens, you won't see any messages. You'll need to do a little more downloading.

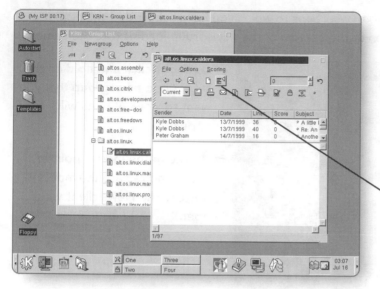

## Viewing the List of Messages

Now that you have an idea of which newsgroups might interest you, it's time to download the list of messages and do some lurking around.

**1.** **Click** on the **Get Article List button** on the toolbar. The KRN-Question dialog box will appear.

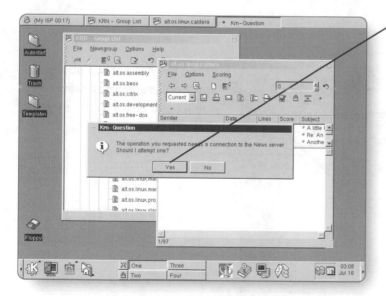

**2.** **Click** on **Yes**. The KRN Confirmation dialog box will open.

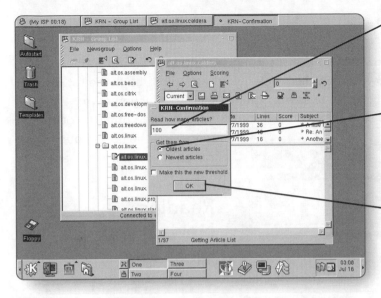

**3. Change** the default **number** of articles that will download at one time, if you want. The default will be changed.

**4. Click** on an **option button** to select whether newer articles or older articles will display first. The option will be selected.

**5. Click** on **OK**. The list of articles will begin downloading.

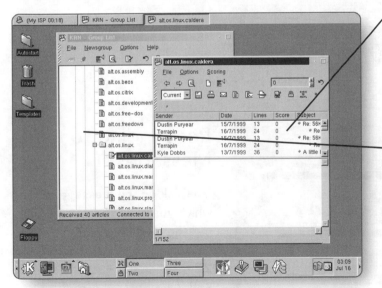

When the download is finished, the messages will be displayed in the message list in the News client window.

**TIP**

You can follow several newsgroups at one time. Go back to the KRN-Group List window and select another newsgroup. KRN will launch another News client window and display the articles for that newsgroup. No need to close one newsgroup to go look through another.

# Participating in Newsgroups

Now that you have subscribed to a Newsgroup and downloaded the articles, you can look through the list of articles for ones that interest you. Then, if you have something to offer the other readers of the newsgroup, you can post your own messages.

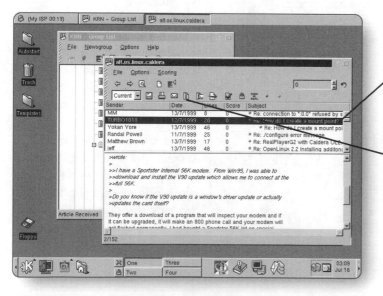

## Reading Newsgroup Messages

**1. Click** on an **article** in the article list. The article will appear in the message pane.

## Responding to Messages

**1. Click** on the **message** to which you want to respond. The message will be selected.

**2. Click** on the **Post a Followup button**. A mail message window will open.

**3. Type** a **reply message** in the Message area.

**4. Click** on the **Send Message button**. The message will be sent. After some time, you'll see your message in the message list.

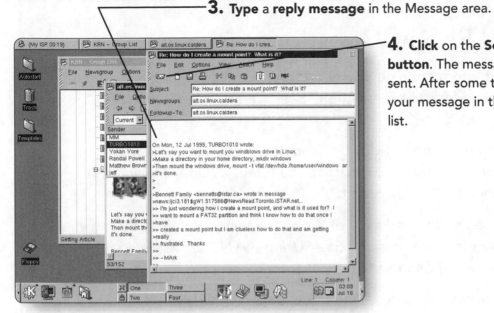

# Part IV Review Questions

1. What information do you need from your ISP before you can create a dial up Internet connection? *See "Creating the Connection" in Chapter 15*

2. Which is the easiest dial up program (packaged with OpenLinux) that you can use to connect to the Internet? *See "Making the Connection" in Chapter 15*

3. Where can you find a list of Web sites that you visited during your current Internet session? *See "Using the Netscape Navigator Web Browser" in Chapter 16*

4. Where do you go to change how the browser handles cookies? *See "Saying No to Cookies" in Chapter 16*

5. In addition to Netscape Communicator, what other e-mail application is available with OpenLinux? *See "Setting Up Mail Accounts" in Chapter 17*

6. How can you make it easier to send e-mail to those people with whom you correspond frequently? *See "Maintaining an Address Book" in Chapter 17*

7. What information do you need to access a news server? *See "Setting up a News Client" in Chapter 18*

8. How do you subscribe to a newsgroup? *See "Getting the Newsgroups" in Chapter 18*

9. How do you post a followup message to a Newsgroup? *See "Participating in Newsgroups" in Chapter 18*

10. How can you remain anonymous in Newsgroups? *See "Setting Up a News Client" in Chapter 18*

# PART V

# Appendixes

# A

# Installing OpenLinux

There are many ways to use the Linux operating system. Linux is primarily known as a server operating system that can run networks, Web sites, and FTP servers. Linux is also popular as a workstation operating system for graphics, Internet, and productivity applications. This book assumes that you are using OpenLinux as a workstation. When you install OpenLinux, you have the option of installing OpenLinux as the sole operating system for the computer, or you can run OpenLinux on the same machine that has Microsoft Windows installed. Before you begin the installation process, please read this appendix and the Caldera OpenLinux 2.2 Getting Started Guide. In this chapter, you'll learn how to:

- Determine which installation method you want
- Prepare for the installation process
- Create a separate partition in which to install Linux
- Install the Caldera OpenLinux operating system

# Understanding Your Installation Options

Before you install OpenLinux for the first time, you'll need to make a few decisions and do some research.

## Using OpenLinux as the Sole Operating System

If you want to use OpenLinux as the only operating system on your computer, you can skip some of the preparatory work (that is, partitioning your hard drive) that is needed if you want to use Windows and OpenLinux on the same computer. If you have an old computer that needs a new life, you might want to consider this option. If you choose this method, you'll need to determine your system devices. When you've done this, insert the Caldera OpenLinux 2.2 CD-ROM into your computer's CD-ROM drive and insert the Boot/Install Disk that came with the boxed Caldera OpenLinux into your floppy drive. Turn off the power to your computer, wait 15 seconds, and then turn on the power. Your computer will restart. When your computer restarts, you'll see the system startup process. After OpenLinux determines the computer's hardware, the installation process will begin.

## Sharing Your Computer with Windows

If you want to get a little more complex, you can use both OpenLinux and Microsoft Windows on the same computer. This takes some extra work, but the tools that are supplied with OpenLinux make this a much simpler task. You can't use OpenLinux and Windows at the same time, but you can shut down one operating system and start up the other. Before you begin, you'll need to determine your computer's system devices and partition your hard drive. This appendix assumes you will be sharing your computer between OpenLinux and Windows.

# Getting Ready

Before you begin, you'll want to do some planning and organizing. You'll need to write down a few important facts about your computer's configuration.

## Determining Your System Devices

Even though OpenLinux has the ability to automatically detect and configure itself properly, you need to collect some basic information about the hardware installed on your computer. This information can be found in the manuals that came with the computer or with the particular peripheral. It can also be obtained from the manufacturer or vendor. Or, if you have Microsoft Windows on your computer, you can look in the System Properties.

**1.** **Click** on **Start** on the Windows Taskbar. The Start menu will appear.

**2.** **Move** the **mouse pointer** to **Settings**. The Settings menu will appear.

**3.** **Click** on **Control Panel**. The Control Panel will appear.

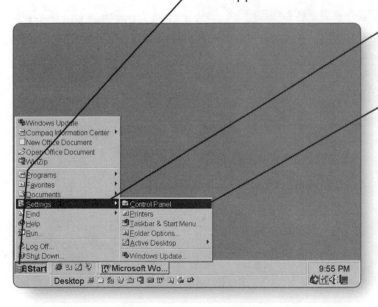

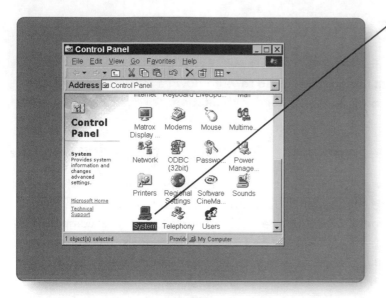

**4. Double-click** on the **System icon**. The System Properties dialog box will open.

**5. Click** on the **Device Manager tab**. The Device Manager tab will come to the top of the stack.

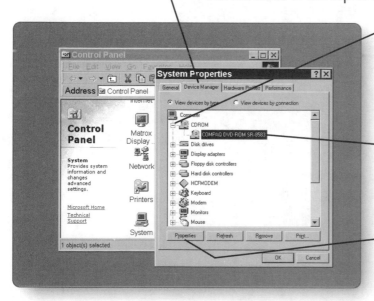

**6. Click** on the **Plus sign** next to a device. The device type will expand to show the devices of that type that are installed on your computer.

**7. Click** on the **device** about which you need hardware information. The device will be selected.

**8. Click** on the **Properties button**. The Properties dialog box for the selected device will open.

**9. Collect** the **information** about the devices attached to your computer. The following information for each device is needed during the installation process:

- Mouse: What kind of mouse do you have? A PS-2 compatible mouse or a serial mouse; with one, two, or three buttons? To which com port is your mouse attached?

- Keyboard: You'll need to know the model of the keyboard and the language layout you are using.

- Video card: You'll need the make and model and how much memory it has. (Most video cards are auto-detected.)

- Monitor: You should know your monitor's make and model number and the vertical and horizontal refresh rate parameters.

**10.** You may also want to collect information about the following devices. You may need this information after you start working with OpenLinux.

- Hard drives: Write down the number of hard disk drives, how they are numbered, what size they are, and whether they are IDE or SCSI.

- CD-ROM drives: Write down the interface type (IDE, SCSI, or other) and be sure to write down the manufacturer and model number of any in the Other category.

- Modem: Take down the make, model number, and speed.

- Sound, video, and game controllers: Find out the names of the manufacturers and the model numbers.

- Network adapters: You will need the information about your card's make and model if you want to be connected to a network.

- SCSI controllers: Jot down the make and model numbers.

Now that you know all about your system devices, you'll need to go to the Caldera OpenLinux hardware compatibility page at **www.calderasystems.com/products/openlinux/ hardware.html**. This Web page will give you a hint as to whether you may have a problem with the OpenLinux installation. Another place you may want to check out is the Caldera OpenLinux newsgroup at **alt.os.linux.caldera**. This newsgroup is a great source of information. You can learn a lot from other people's experiences.

## Loading the Install Preparation Components into Microsoft Windows

The components that you'll be installing in the Windows operating system will help you set up Linux, so that it can live on the same computer with Windows, and on the same hard drive.

**1.** **Place** the **OpenLinux CD number 1** into your computer's CD-ROM drive. The OpenLinux Tools menu will appear.

## NOTE

If your CD-ROM does not automatically open this page, open Windows Explorer and display the contents of the winsetup folder on the CD-ROM. Then, double-click on the setup.exe file.

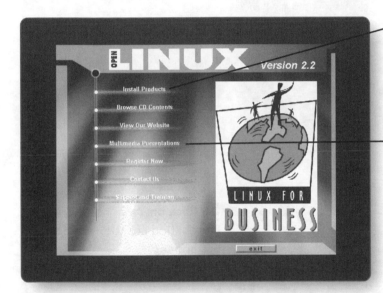

**2.** **Click** on **Install Products**. The Install Products menu will appear.

## TIP

You may want to explore OpenLinux further before you begin the installation. Click on Multimedia Presentations.

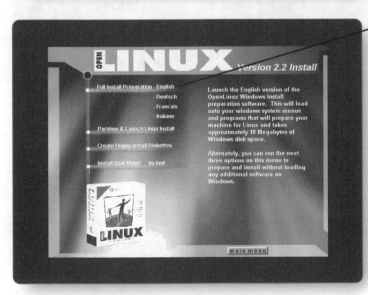

**3.** **Click** on **Full Install Preparation–English**. The Welcome window of the preparation process will appear.

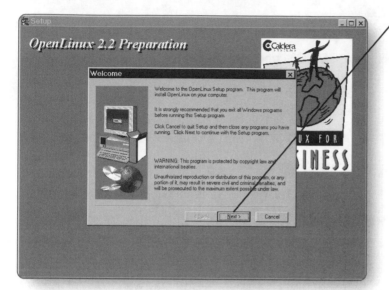

**4. Click** on **Next**. The Software License Agreement window will appear.

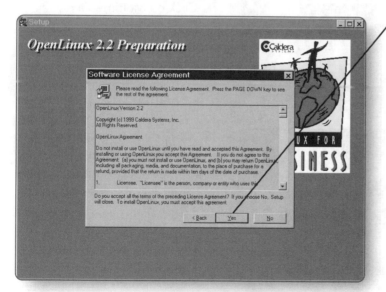

**5. Click** on **Yes**. The Choose Destination Location window will appear.

### NOTE

It is recommended that you not change the default installation directory.

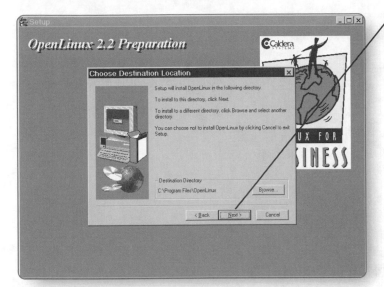

**6. Click** on **Next**. The Select Program Folder window will appear.

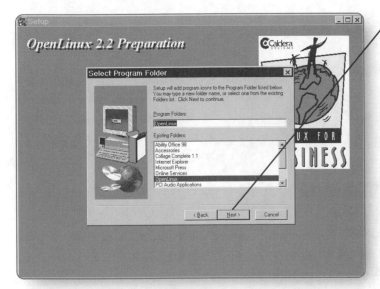

**7. Click** on **Next** to accept the default folder location. The components will be installed on your computer. When the installation of the components is complete, you'll see the Install Products menu again.

**8.** **Click** on the **main menu button** at the bottom of the screen. You'll be returned to the OpenLinux Tools menu.

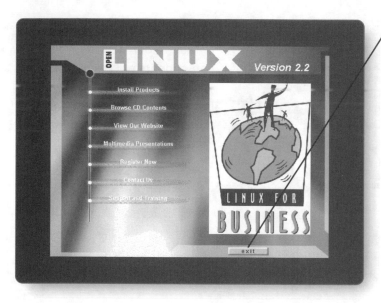

**9.** **Click** on the **exit button**. You'll be returned to Windows and the installation of the components will be complete. You're now ready to use the components to create installation and module disks, and to partition your hard drive.

## Creating Boot Disks

If your computer will not automatically boot from a CD-ROM, you'll need an installation disk. If you purchased the Caldera OpenLinux boxed set, a Boot/Install disk will be included. If you don't have one, you can create one. And it's also a good idea to make a modules disk. This will help you out if you have problems later with OpenLinux.

### *Creating the Installation Disk*

**1.** **Place** a blank, formatted **disk** into your floppy disk drive.

**2.** **Click** on the **Start button** on the Windows taskbar. The Start menu will appear.

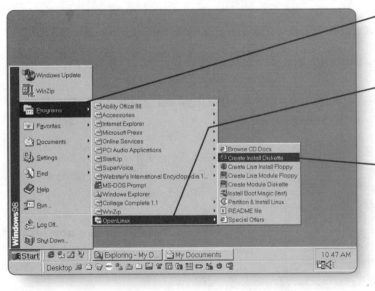

**3.** **Move** the **mouse pointer** to Programs. The Programs menu will appear.

**4.** **Move** the **mouse pointer** to OpenLinux. The OpenLinux menu will appear.

**5.** **Click** on **Create Install Diskette**. The Rawrite program will start.

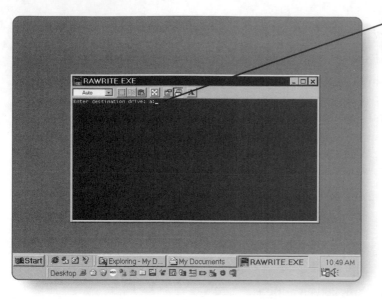

**6. Type a:** and **press** the **Enter** key. The Rawrite program will begin creating the installation disk. When Rawrite is finished, the program window will close.

**7. Remove** the **disk** from the floppy disk drive. You'll want to label this disk "Caldera OpenLinux 2.2 Installation Disk."

## Creating a Module Disk

**1. Place** a blank, formatted **disk** into your floppy disk drive.

**2. Click** on the **Start button** on the Windows taskbar. The Start menu will appear.

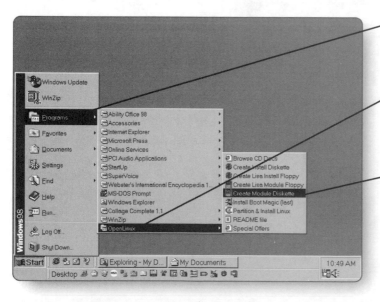

**3. Move** the **mouse pointer** to Programs. The Programs menu will appear.

**4. Move** the **mouse pointer** to OpenLinux. The OpenLinux menu will appear.

**5. Click** on **Create Module Diskette**. The Rawrite program will start.

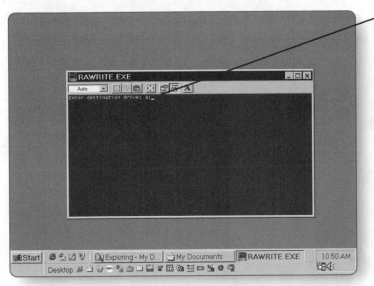

**6.** **Type a:** and **press** the **Enter** key. The Rawrite program will begin creating the modules disk. When Rawrite is finished, the program window will close.

**7.** **Remove** the **disk** from the floppy disk drive. You'll want to label this disk "Caldera OpenLinux 2.2 Modules Disk."

# Loading the OpenLinux Operating System

Now that you've installed all the software tools and boot disks that you'll need for the installation process, it's time to begin.

## Installing PartitionMagic

PartitionMagic is the software that will divide up your hard drive so that Linux can live on a separate area from Microsoft Windows. It is very important that you defragment your hard drive before you use Partition Magic. To use the Windows Disk Defragmenter, follow the Start button to Programs, then Accessories, and then System Tools.

**1. Click** on the **Start button** on the Windows taskbar. The Start menu will appear.

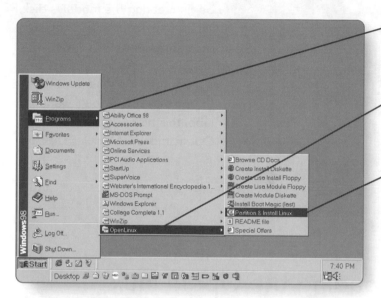

**2. Move** the **mouse pointer** to Programs. The Programs menu will appear.

**3. Move** the **mouse pointer** to OpenLinux. The OpenLinux menu will appear.

**4. Click** on **Partition & Install Linux**. The Welcome screen will appear.

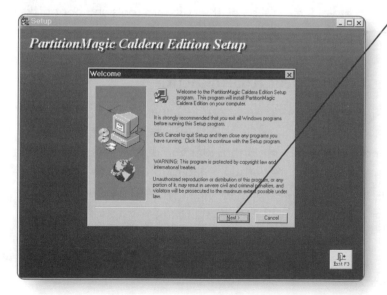

**5. Click** on **Next**. The Read Me screen will appear.

**6.** Read the **Read Me file**.

**7.** **Click** on **Next**. The Choose Destination Location screen will appear.

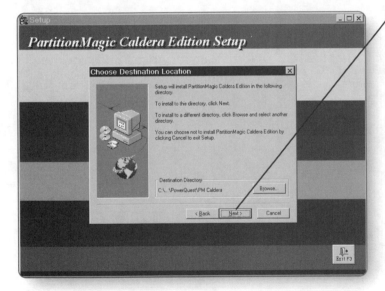

**8.** **Click** on **Next**. The Select program Folder screen will appear.

**9. Click** on **Next**. The installation will begin. When the PartitionMagic installation is complete, the Setup Complete screen will appear.

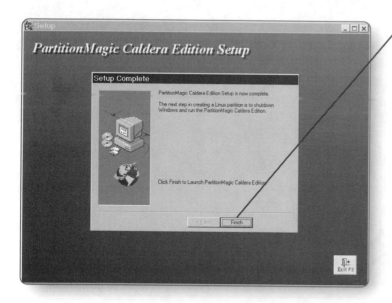

**10. Click** on **Finish**. Your computer will restart, and you'll be ready to partition your hard drive.

# Partitioning Your Hard Drive

When your computer reboots, the PartitionMagic program automatically starts, and you can select a partition size in which to install OpenLinux.

**1a.** **Click** on the **1.0 GB option button** in the Linux partition size section. You'll need at least 1 gigabyte to install the Linux operating system, all the applications, and still have room to add more applications and store your work. The option will be selected.

**OR**

**1b.** **Click** on the **Maximum option button** if you want to use all of the empty space on your hard drive for Linux. This will leave you with 100 MB of free space on the Windows partition. The option will be selected.

**2. Click** on **OK**. A confirmation dialog box will appear.

**3. Click** on **OK**. PartitionMagic will begin partitioning your hard drive. This should only take a couple of minutes. When the partition is built, the Partition Creation Complete dialog box will open.

**4. Click** on **OK**. Your computer will restart. When your computer returns, you'll be in Linux and ready to begin the installation process.

# Installing OpenLinux

Linux is a very flexible operating system that can be easily customized to meet your specific needs. Choices made during the installation process guide the setup program in selecting which software to load and configure. The installation process is enhanced by OpenLinux's ability to probe your computer and provide answers to some of its own questions. Many of the choices you need to make are selected for you as you progress through the installation.

When your computer reboots, a System startup screen will appear. You'll see a series of text lines appear inside the screen. You'll want to wait while the Linux kernel loads and you system hardware is checked. When this is finished, you'll be ready to begin the installation.

You'll then see a series of two screens where you can enter some basic information before the installation process begins. You'll need to choose your language and mouse type. On each screen of the installation process, you'll see specific directions on the right side of each screen. Read these instructions carefully. There is also a Help button at the lower-right corner of each screen. Click on this Help button to learn more about the specific task in the installation.

The next screen you will see is the Installation target screen. If you will be using OpenLinux as the sole operating system, click on the Entire Harddisk option button. If you will be sharing OpenLinux with Microsoft Windows, click on the Prepared Partition(s) option button.

Now that OpenLinux knows how you want the operating system installed, you'll need to specify where you want OpenLinux installed. If you are going to use OpenLinux as the sole operating system, you'll need to select the hard disk on which to install Linux. If you'll be sharing Linux with Windows, you'll need to specify the partition in which to install Linux. Most likely, these options will be selected for you. You'll just need to confirm the default settings.

Next, you'll need to decide how much of the Linux operating system you want installed on your computer. This book assumes that you will be installing using the All recommended packages option.

For the next few screens, you'll need the system device information that you collected in the "Getting Started" section of this appendix. OpenLinux's installation program will probe your hardware to determine what video equipment you have installed. In most cases, the probe will return all the information it needs about your video card and monitor. That is what we always want to happen, but there are exceptions, and sometimes you need to get a little more involved in the configuration process.

Caution! Of all the things that you need to do to install Linux, perhaps the most sensitive one is configuring an X server for your computer. It is possible to permanently damage your monitor and/or video card by entering the wrong information! If you are not truly knowledgeable about configuring video and operating systems, now is not the time to try guessing the answer. Now before you panic, the Caldera OpenLinux installation program has the ability to probe your system and autodetect all or most of the information needed. You then have to select only a few things from lists and the whole thing will flow smoothly along.

You will be asked to confirm your video card and monitor from a list. If your monitor is not listed, you'll need to enter your monitor's horizontal and vertical sync ranges.

You're almost at the end of the installation, and it's time to decide what screen resolution and color depth that you want to use. This list only contains those resolutions and color depths that are available for your video card and monitor. A minimum setup would be a resolution of 800x600 using 256 colors. If you want a better display, try 1024x768 at 16-bit color (or higher if you have it.)

You'll need to set a root password. It is important that you pick a good one that you will remember and that won't be easily compromised, because the root password allows the user entry to the entire system. You'll need to remember this password, so that you can log on to Linux when you need to perform root functions. You'll also be asked to set up a user account for yourself. This user account is where you will be doing your day-to-day work.

If you are setting up this machine as a stand-alone workstation and will be connecting to the Internet with a dial-up connection (that is, using a modem), select the No ethernet option button.

Lastly, you'll need to set the time zone in which you live. After you finish this, the installation will be completed. You can play a game of Tetris while this happens. When the installation is complete, remove the CD-ROM and the floppy disk.

# Switching Between OpenLinux and Windows

You're almost there; your last step is to set up BootMagic so that you can easily switch between OpenLinux and Microsoft Windows. After the OpenLinux installation is completed, you'll be presented with a graphical log on screen. Click on the Shutdown button. This will shut down the OpenLinux system and get you back to Microsoft Windows. You'll need to be in Windows to set up BootMagic.

**1.** **Click** on **Start** on the Windows taskbar. The Start menu will appear.

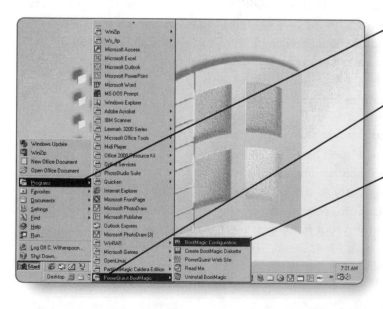

**2.** **Move** the **mouse pointer** to Programs. The Programs menu will appear.

**3.** **Move** the **mouse pointer** to PowerQuest BootMagic. A menu will appear.

**4.** **Click** on **BootMagic Configuration**. The BootMagic Configuration dialog box will open.

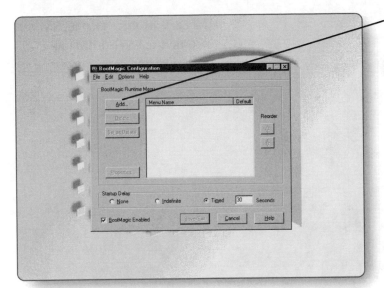

**5.** **Click** on the **Add button**. The BootMagic Add OS dialog box will open.

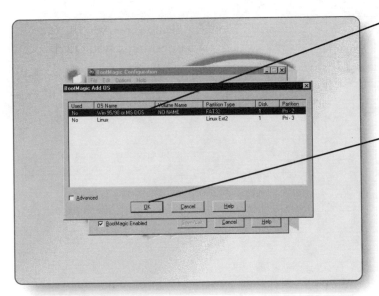

**6.** **Click** on **Win 95/98 or MS-DOS**. The option will be selected and Microsoft Windows will be the default operating system.

**7.** **Click** on **OK**. The BootMagic Menu Item Properties dialog box will open.

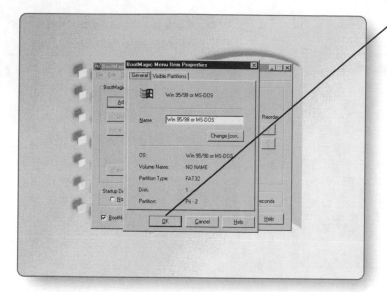

**8. Click** on **OK**. You will be returned to the BootMagic Configuration dialog box.

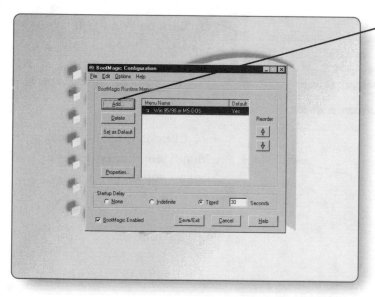

**9. Click** on the **Add button**. The BootMagic Add OS dialog box will open.

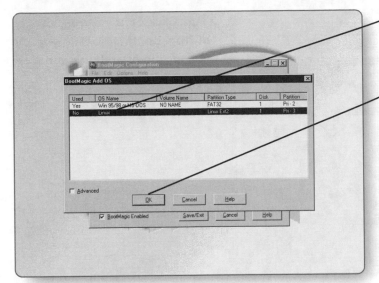

**10. Click** on **Linux**. The Linux operating system will be selected.

**11. Click** on **OK**. The BootMagic Menu Item Properties dialog box will open.

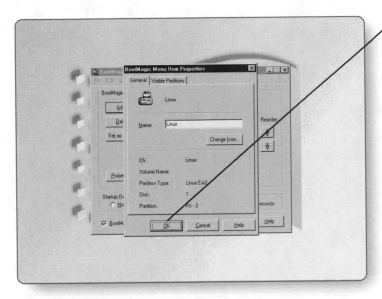

**12. Click** on **OK**. You will be returned to the BootMagic Configuration dialog box.

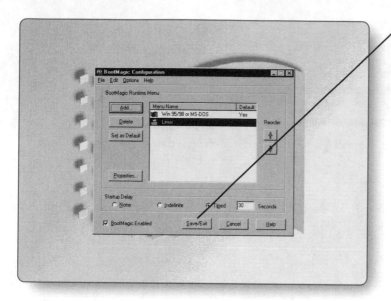

**13.** **Click** on the **Save/Exit button**. BootMagic is now ready to start the operating system of your choice whenever you restart your computer.

# B

# Installing Software

Depending on the installation method you chose for OpenLinux, you may not have all of the available software packages installed. You can use the kpackage utility to see what's installed on your computer. The kpackage utility also enables you (as root) to install any packages that you don't have. There may be software packages that you don't use and don't want cluttering up your system. This chapter will show you how to install and uninstall WordPerfect. There are other packages on the Caldera OpenLinux CD that you can install using this same method. In this chapter, you'll learn how to:

- Find information about installed packages
- Install an application
- Uninstall an application

# Finding Packages Using Kpackage

The kpackage utility is the tool that does the work of installing and uninstalling software. You can use kpackage to troubleshoot an installed application by verifying that all of the files installed with the application are still intact. And if they're not, then kpackage can be used to replace files for you.

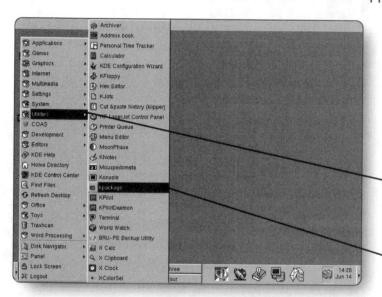

**1. Click** on the **Application Starter**. The main menu will appear.

**2. Move** the **mouse pointer** to **Utilities**. The Utilities menu will appear.

**3. Click** on **kpackage**. The kpackage utility will appear.

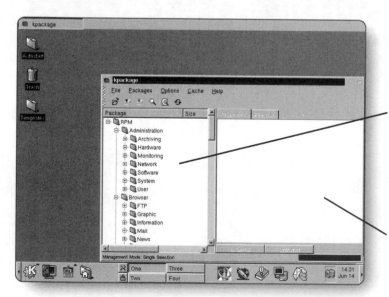

Take a moment to look over kpackage. The kpackage utility window is divided into two panels.

- The left panel displays a tree directory of all of the packages you have installed on your system. The listing is organized by software category.

- The right panel shows the contents of the directory that you select from the tree directory.

Take a short tour of the left panel, which contains the package directory tree, to get an idea of just how many things are installed on your system. You may find some interesting applications.

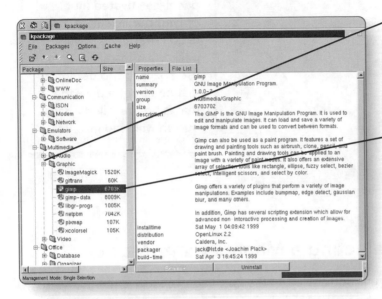

**4. Click** on the **plus sign** next to a package category. The tree will expand to show the installed packages in that category.

**5. Click** on a **package**. The right panel will display the Properties page for the application.

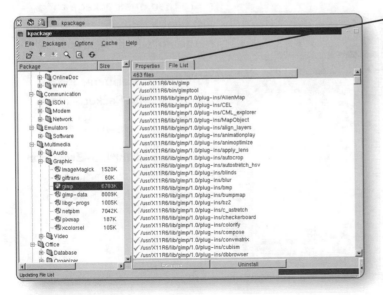

**6. Click** on the **File List tab** in the right panel. The right panel will display the file names of all of the files that are contained in the package.

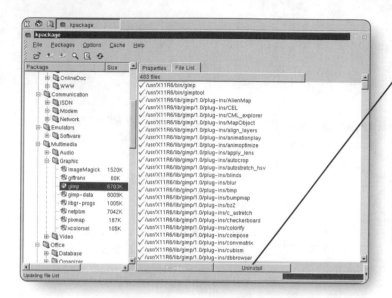

**TIP**

If the Uninstall button at the bottom of the right panel is activated (not grayed out) this is an indication that the software package is installed. If you use kpackage to get information about a package that is not installed, the button will read Install.

## Selecting a Management Mode

At the bottom left of the kpackage window is the Management Mode indicator. There are two possible modes: single selection and multiple selections. It is possible to select more than one package to install at a time. To change the mode, follow these steps.

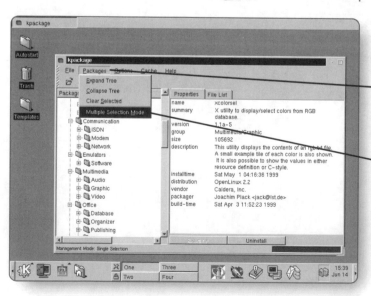

**1. Click** on **Packages** in the menu bar. The Package menu will appear.

**2. Click** on **Multiple Selection Mode**. The Mode indicator will change to Multiple Selection.

# Installing Applications

Installing applications to use with OpenLinux and KDE is managed quite painlessly by the kpackage utility, which will take care of all those pesky dependency problems and hook everything up just like it is supposed to be. The kpackage utility can be used not only to install software from a local source, such as a CD-ROM or a hard drive, but it can act as an FTP client to download packages off the Internet. For this installation, we are going to install the WordPerfect 8 application that came with your Caldera OpenLinux 2.2 installation disks.

## Installing WordPerfect

**1. Place** the **OpenLinux 2.2 Installation CD** (which is CD number 1) in your computer's CD-ROM drive.

**2. Click** on the desktop **CD-ROM icon**. The CD-ROM will be mounted and the File Manager window will open displaying the contents of the CD-ROM.

**3. Click** on the **Packages folder icon**. The contents of the /Packages directory will be displayed in the File Manager window.

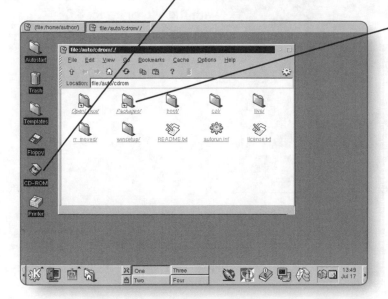

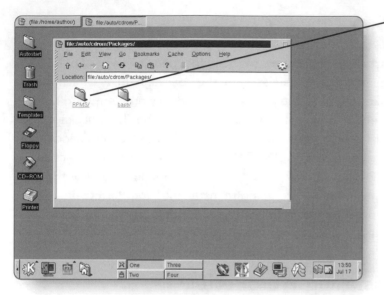

**4.** **Click** on the **RPMS folder icon**. The /RPMS directory contents will be displayed in the File Manager window.

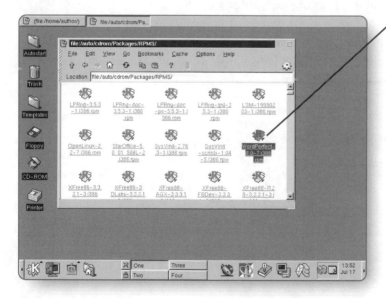

**5.** **Click** on the **WordPerfect-8.0-7.i386.rpm icon**. The kpackage utility will open automatically at the install panel with the WordPerfect 8.0 Properties page displayed.

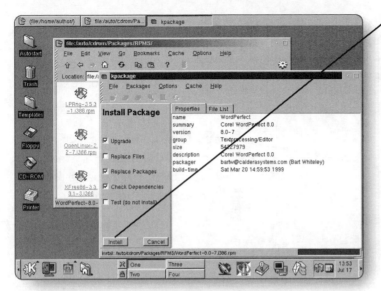

**6. Click** on **Install**. Kpackage will begin installing WordPerfect. When kpackage is finished installing WordPerfect, you will be returned to the kpackage utility with nothing displayed in the right panel.

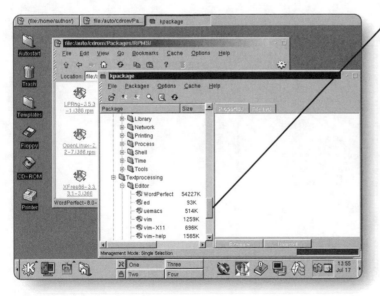

**7. Scroll** down to the bottom of the **tree directory** in the left pane. You'll see a category for Textprocessing.

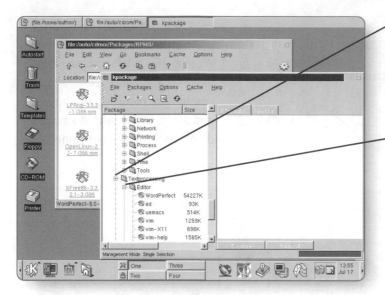

**8. Click** on the **plus sign** next to Textprocessing. The directory tree will expand, and you will see the categories of text processing applications.

**9. Click** on the **plus sign** next to Editor. The directory tree will expand, and you'll see a list of packages in the category.

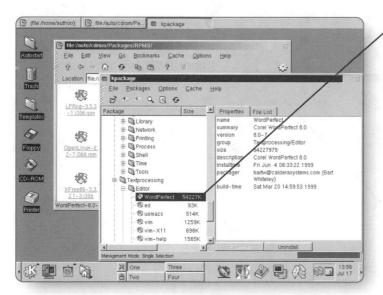

**10. Click** on **WordPerfect**. The properties and file list for WordPerfect will display in the right pane.

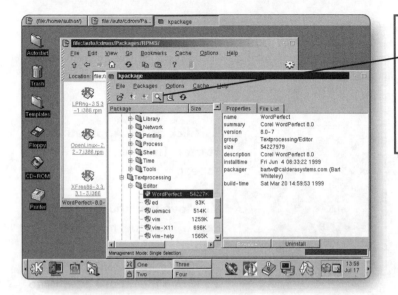

## TIP

If you can't find an installed package, click on the Find Installed Package button on the toolbar.

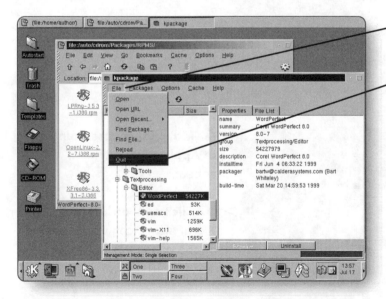

**11. Click** on **File**. The File menu will open.

**12. Click** on **Quit**. The kpackage utility will close.

**13. Unmount** the **CD-ROM drive** and **remove** the **CD** from the drive.

# Finding WordPerfect

Before you can begin using WordPerfect, you may want to place an icon on the panel. It'll make finding WordPerfect easier.

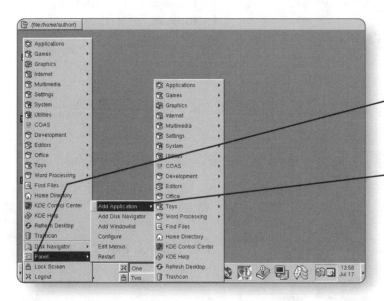

**1. Click** on the **Application Starter**. The main menu will appear.

**2. Move** the **mouse pointer** to **Panel**. The Panel menu will appear.

**3. Move** the **mouse pointer** to **Add Application**. The Add Application menu will appear.

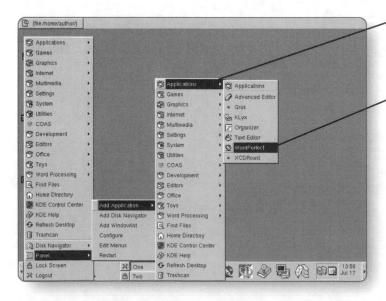

**4. Move** the **mouse pointer** to **Applications**. A menu will appear.

**5. Click** on **WordPerfect**. A WordPerfect icon will be placed on the panel.

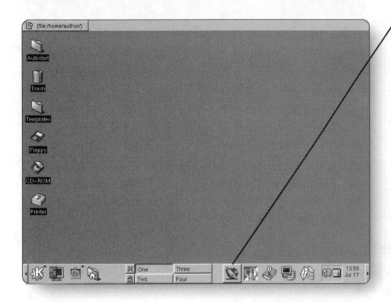

**6. Click** on the **WordPerfect icon**. WordPerfect will open on your screen.

### NOTE

To find out more about WordPerfect, turn to Chapter 13, "Exploring WordPerfect."

## Uninstalling Applications

Uninstalling applications is a straightforward process with kpackage. The uninstall will remove all of the application files and reset dependencies and clean up any bits left behind. We'll use WordPerfect again as an example.

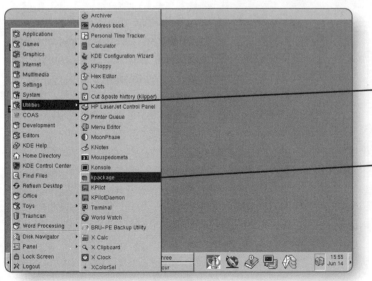

**1. Click** on the **Application Starter**. The main menu will appear.

**2. Move** the **mouse pointer** to **Utilities**. The Utilities menu will appear.

**3. Click** on **kpackage**. The kpackage utility will appear.

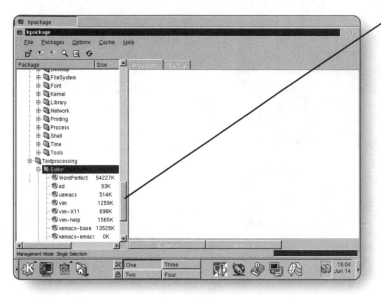

**4. Scroll** down to the bottom of the **tree directory** in the left pane. You'll see a category for Textprocessing.

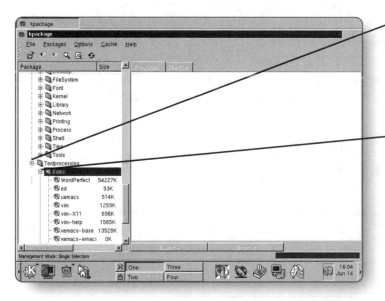

**5. Click** on the **plus sign** next to Textprocessing. The directory tree will expand, and you will see the categories of text-processing applications.

**6. Click** on the **plus sign** next to Editor. The directory tree will expand, and you'll see a list of packages in the category.

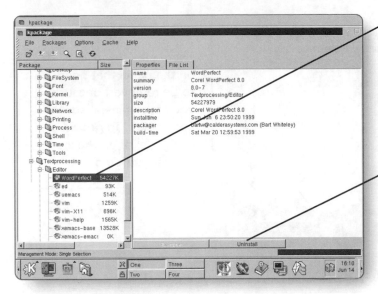

**7. Click** on **WordPerfect**. The right panel will display the Properties page for the WordPerfect package installed on your system, and the Uninstall button will be activated.

**8. Click** on **Uninstall**. The kpackage Uninstall dialog box will open.

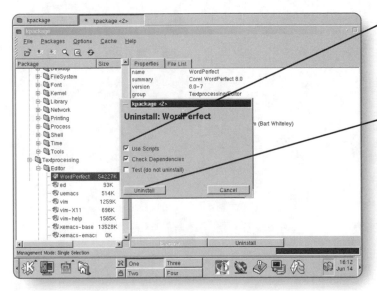

**9. Click** in the **Use Scripts** and **Check Dependencies check boxes**. Check marks will appear in the boxes.

**10. Click** on **Uninstall**. The Uninstall utility will take a few minutes to perform its function, and then you will be returned to the kpackage utility. The WordPerfect package will be removed from the tree directory.

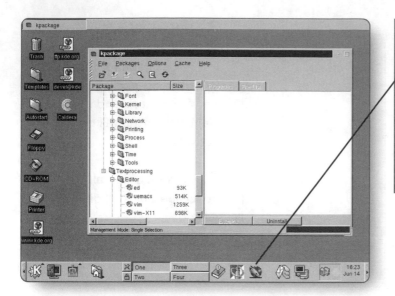

### TIP

There may be an icon left on the panel that needs to be removed because you have uninstalled the application. To get rid of it, right-click on the icon and select Remove.

# Glossary

## A

**Absolute pathname.** Specifies the exact directory in the directory tree where a file or subdirectory is stored. The absolute pathname includes the entire path that is required to access the file. The absolute pathname begins with the root directory.

**Access rights.** These are also known as file permissions. They enable you to define which users have access to which files, directories, and peripherals in the system, and the type of access each user is allowed.

**Active window.** The window in which an application will run, or in which a task will be performed.

**Anonymous FTP.** A way in which any person can access the public areas of an FTP site to transfer data files. To access these public areas, use "anonymous" as the user name and your e-mail address as the password.

**Application.** A software program that performs a specific task or function, such as word processing, bookkeeping, or graphics.

**Archive.** To put data files in a place where they are protected from loss. Use a backup program to copy the files onto a removable media that can be kept in a safe deposit box or fireproof safe.

## B

**Background process.** A function (such as a print job or automatic save) that does not require interaction from the user. When a function is running in the background, you can work with another application without any noticeable effect on performance.

**Backup.** To make a copy of files that are stored on your computer's hard drive onto another medium, such as floppy disk, magnetic tape, or CD-ROM. If the files on your hard disk become damaged or lost, you can restore the files from the backup.

**Boot**. The process your computer goes through when it is turned on so that the operating system loads.

**Boot disk**. A floppy disk that you create during the installation process so that you can start the OpenLinux operating system in the event that Boot Magic does not work on your system.

**Boot image floppy**. A floppy disk that will boot your computer and load a small Linux operating system. This floppy disk may be needed before you can install the entire Linux distribution.

## C

**Cache memory**. A storage area for data as it moves between the computer's RAM memory and the processor chip. Cache memory is needed to keep the processor working at full potential. Most computers have either 128K or 256K of cache memory. This speed indicates how fast the processor moves data in and out of cache memory.

**Command line**. This is a text-mode display in which you can type Linux commands and then press the Enter key to execute the commands. You can perform command-line operations from a terminal window, a terminal emulator, a console, or an x-term window. The easiest to work with is the x-term window, because you can open it inside the KDE interface and you don't have to log off from the interface to perform functions that cannot be executed with the interface.

**Current directory**. The directory or folder in which all file and directory commands operate. Your current directory will usually be your Home directory.

## D

**Daemon.** A process that sits in background and waits until something activates it. For example, the Update daemon starts on a regular cycle to flush the buffer cache; the Sendmail daemon starts when mail is sent over the network.

**Defragment**. A computer maintenance task that reorganizes the file system so that files can be located and displayed quickly and programs run efficiently. The program locates files that are scattered through out a hard drive, combines the pieces into one file, and prioritizes them on the hard drive according to usage.

**Desktop**. The background that displays behind all the different screen elements (such as windows, dialog boxes, and applications) used in the Linux operating system.

**Device drivers**. Small software programs that provide access to system devices and resources, such as disk drives, modems, graphics cards, and printers.

**Dial-up networking**. A method of connecting to the Internet or to some other computer or network through a dial-up modem.

**Directory**. A unique address in your computer's file system where files are stored. Linux uses several conventions for indicating the location of the directory in relation to other directories. Directories and subdirectories are separated by a forward slash (/), which is different from DOS and Windows systems. A single forward slash indicates that you are at the root directory. The current directory in which you are working is indicated by a single period (.). The directory above the directory in which you are working is indicated by two periods (..).

**Distribution**. A set of prepackaged Linux software made available by a vendor. The package contains the Linux operating system, the set of GNU software applications and utilities, and other software programs developed by the vendor.

**Dynamic IP address**. An Internet Protocol address assigned when the dial-up connection is made. This means that each time you connect to the Internet, you will get a different IP address.

# E

**Encryption**. A procedure used in cryptography to convert text into cipher to keep anyone but the intended recipient from reading the message. The many types of data encryption are the basis of network security. Data Encryption Standard and public key encryption are common.

**Executable file**. A single file used to open a program.

# F

**File**. A collection of data, such as a letter created in a word processing program or a scanned image of a photograph, that is stored on a hard drive or other storage medium.

**File permissions**. A way to protect files from being tampered with by other users on a computer or network. The user who creates the files owns the files and the directories in which the files are contained. The owner can specify which other users can access the files and the type of access.

**File server**. A computer that maintains data files and enables users and other computers in the network to access those files to which they have permission.

**File system**. The method and data structure that the Linux operating system uses to store files. The file system can be used to organize and manage files.

**Foreground process**. The application in which you are currently working. A foreground process receives input from the keyboard and the results are seen on the screen.

**Free Software Foundation**. A grant-sponsored group at MIT that develops and distributes software for UNIX operating systems. The Free Software Foundation has developed such products as X Windows, emacs, a C++ compiler, and the glib++ library. They are well known for all of their GNU software.

**FTP (File Transfer Protocol)**. A method of sending and receiving files across a computer network or the Internet.

## G

**GNU project**. A project sponsored by the Free Software Foundation to provide a freely distributable replacement for UNIX. Some of the more popular tools are the GNU C and C++ compilers, and the GNU EMACS editor.

**GUI (Graphical User Interface)**. A shell that runs over the Linux operating system. This shell enables a user to visually see the operating system in action. The shell uses windows, dialog boxes, icons, and other graphics to create an environment that is easier in which to work. A GUI also supports the use of the mouse to make tasks easier.

## H

**Home directory**. The place within the Linux file system where you store or save all of the files and directories (or folders) that you create.

## I

**Icon**. A small picture that represents a quick way to access applications, peripherals, files, and directories.

## K

**Kernel**. The center of the Linux operating system. This piece of software is responsible for the Linux file system and the timing activities of the operating system. Operating system utilities use kernel functions to perform work. The kernel is recompiled occasionally when system changes require it.

**Kernel patch**. To create a new binary file for the core Linux operating system.

## L

**Log on/log off**. Connect to or disconnect from a network, such as the Internet or a corporate intranet. Also, to access a specified user account in the Linux system. Logging on requires a username and a password.

## M

**Man pages**. Information pages contained in Linux that contain documentation for the system commands, resources, configuration files, and other utilities.

**Master Boot Record**. The file used to boot your computer's operating system and configure it for all of your peripherals and utilities.

**Minimize**. To clear a window from the desktop and cause it to become an icon on the taskbar. To display the window, click on its icon on the taskbar.

**Mount**. A task that is performed before a device—for example a floppy disk drive or CD-ROM drive—can be accessed by the Linux file system.

## O

**Operating system**. Software that shares a computer system's resources, such as the processor, memory, and disk space, between users and the application programs that run.

## P

**Partition**. A physical portion of a disk. Disks are divided into partitions that are assigned to hold various file systems. The root file system is usually on the first partition and the user file system is on a different partition. The use of partitions provides flexibility and control of disk usage, but it is restricting in that it denies unlimited use of all the available space on a given disk for a given file.

**Password**. Your personal secret key that you use to log on to the Internet, access your network account, or work with files that are protected from general view.

**Pathname**. A filename given as a sequence of directories that leads to a particular file.

## R

**Root directory**. The base directory from which all subdirectories stem.

## S

**Static IP address.** An unchanging IP address, usually for those that are permanently connected to the Internet.

**Superuser account**. The root or administrator's account which has the ability to access the entire Linux system and any user accounts that have been set up. The Linux system manager uses the superuser account to install software, fix problems, and perform backup routines.

**Swap space**. A place on the computer hard disk drive that is set aside so that it can be used as virtual memory (extra RAM). Linux uses this swap space to store programs that may be running. This swap space is dedicated to virtual memory and cannot be accessed to store files for directories.

## U

**Unmount.** To remove a file system that has been previously mounted. Only the user or superuser that mounted the file system can unmount it.

**User**. A person who uses the Linux system and has been assigned a user account.

## V

**Virtual memory**. To use part of the hard disk to extend the amount of RAM the computer can use. When the computer has used the available RAM, it takes the contents of memory that are not needed to process current tasks and places that information on the hard drive.

# W

**Window.** A rectangular area that is visible when an application runs on the screen. Many windows can display on the screen at any time. You can move, resize, close, minimize, and open windows with the click of the mouse.

**Window manager.** The software that controls the way windows look, their functionality, and where they are placed in the KDE interface—the KDE interface that is installed with Caldera OpenLinux 2.2.

# X

**X Window.** The graphical system used by every Linux and UNIX operating system that provides an interface to your video hardware, manages windows and other objects on your screen, and controls the desktop (such as KDE).

# Index

# NOTES

# NOTES

# NOTES

# NOTES

# NOTES

# NOTES

# NOTES

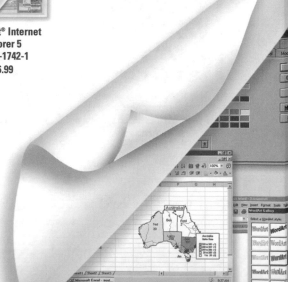